CHRISTIAN ENCOUNTERS

1. Lithograph illustration, reprinted from William Booth, *In Darkest England and the Way Out* (London: Salvation Army, 1890).

Christian Encounters with the Other

Edited by

John C. Hawley
Associate Professor of English Literature
Santa Clara University

NEW YORK UNIVERSITY PRESS
Washington Square, New York

First published in the U.S.A. in 1998 by
NEW YORK UNIVERSITY PRESS
Washington Square
New York, N.Y. 10003

This book is printed on paper suitable for recycling and
made from fully managed and sustained forest sources.

Library of Congress Cataloging-in-Publication Data
Christian encounters with the other / edited by John C. Hawley.
p.   cm.
Includes bibliographical references and index.
ISBN 0–8147–3568–1 (clothbound). — ISBN 0–8147–3569–X
(paperbound)
1. Missions—Sociological aspects—History.   2. Christianity and
other religions—History.   3. Missions in literature.
4. Christianity and other religions in literature.   I. Hawley, John
C. (John Charles), 1947–   .
BV2070.C4 1997
266—dc21   97–25273
                                                                CIP

Printed in Great Britain

For Mitoko Hirabayashi, Desmond Day, and Richard Perl, S.J.

Contents

Preface

After many years in the scholastic wilderness, Christian missions throughout the world are finally getting another look from scholars in various disciplines. They are reexamining the missionary enterprise as an important case study not just in religious domination, but also cultural contact. Increasingly, as our world has become smaller and we witness the homogenization of culture, scholars have become interested in the forms in which cultural contact has taken place. Historically for the West, Christian missions have played a very important role in this endeavor. In this sense, missions have warranted a reexamination. Moreover, missions are liminal places, where two cultures meet and where often a hybrid emerges that owes much to both its native and European origins. This is a new perspective, for a previous concentration on the heroic deeds of the missionaries left largely unexamined the actual effects of the missions on the people they presumed to convert. What scholars have found is that conversion as well as cultural assimilation are not the unproblematic concepts they were previously assumed to be. The complexities of these issues are fascinating and, as in many liminal situations, more clearly highlight the characteristics of both European and, at times, native cultures.

The analysis of literature dealing with the missions helps us figure out some of these issues and thus this volume is a welcome addition to the field. Whether examining the discourse of the missionaries themselves, literary accounts of mission experiences, or the expressions of the converted, the discipline of literary studies offers a sensitivity to words and to multiple meanings found only perhaps among cultural anthropologists. Analyzing these words helps establish motivations and insights into relationships between the missionaries and missionized difficult to achieve in any other way.

Establishing motivations is very important, for the nature of missionary Christianity until very recently has made it difficult to fathom the reasons for the actions we can document. After all, Christianity is, with Islam, a monotheistic faith that presumes its natural superiority to the exclusion of all other possible religions. This has meant that Christian missionaries have tried to convert with the absolute certainty that their way of thinking is the only correct one. The motivations of the Other (and even that of the missionary) have not merited consideration, since the teaching of the Gospel, it was assumed, was all that the potential convert needed; his or her previous knowledge was to be discarded.

Many of the best missionaries, especially for the Latin American case that I know best, have realized that one must first know the Other's belief system to be able to truly convert. How else could one know what approach might work best for conversion? How else could one know whether the Indians had truly converted? For this reason we have Fray Bernardino de Sahagún write the most complete description of central Mexican civilization in the sixteenth century, or Fr. Diego de Landa writing one of the best sources on Maya culture.

Interestingly enough, many of these missionaries, out in the field for many years, subtly changed their thinking as well, absorbing some concepts of the people they were trying to convert. Striking in this regard was for example the reaction of Fr. Doroteo Giannecchini, a Franciscan from Italy who became one of the most important missionaries of the Chiriguano people on the southeastern frontiers of nineteenth-century Bolivia and an accomplished linguist in Guaraní, the native language. When confronted by the traditional enemy of the Chiriguanos, the Tobas and Matacos, he cursed them in Guaraní by claiming that they were dirty and untrustworthy. The friar sounded just like the Chiriguanos to whom he had attempted to teach European ways and attitudes!

While becoming interpreters of native cultures and even adopting partially a native mindset, missionaries ironically also judge their own neophytes more harshly than those who already are Christians. Diego de Landa, for example, executed various Maya Indians whom he thought had diverged from the path of true orthodoxy. This harsh judgment also manifests itself in other ways. Until very recently, very few individuals raised on a mission had the possibility of becoming a priest or pastor themselves. They were seen as inferior in some spiritual way and even their best behavior could not get the missionaries to conceive that these people might be equals in faith. The lack of even eventual equality is corroborated by the fact that many of the missions were conceived of as part and parcel of a colonial enterprise. This was as much the case with the sixteenth-century Latin America missions as with those in nineteenth-century Africa. The contradictions between the role of the missionaries in the political schemes of the European powers and their assertions of saving souls for the spiritual good of the natives, while unproblematic in the sixteenth century, has bedeviled the missionary enterprise in the twentieth. After all, there are political consequences to the missionary enterprise, which include the spiritual (and, by implication political) immaturity of its inhabitants.

In the end, the missions often create Christians who are either completely culturally deracinated from both their original and from European societies (remember, the native usually is not accepted as an equal in a colonial setting, the most common place for missions), or who have creatively meshed Christianity with their indigenous culture where Christianity is often a veneer and indigenous culture provides the profound meaning. Is this what the missionary experience is supposed to bring about? I think not. Nevertheless, this is what many of the new studies on the missions have shown us.

—Erick D. Langer

Contributors

Troy Boone teaches in the Literature Board at the University of California at Santa Cruz. His articles have appeared in *Studies in the Novel, The Eighteenth Century: Theory and Interpretation,* and *Nineteenth-Century Contexts: An Interdisciplinary Journal.* His curent research focuses on urban spectatorship, the working class, and the British Empire.

Dolores Clavero is Assistant Professor of Spanish Literature at Simon Fraser University. Her book is *Romances viejos de temas épicos nacionales: Relaciones con gestas y crónicas* (Madrid: Ediciones del Orto, 1994).

Eileen Razzari Elrod is Assistant Professor of English at Santa Clara University. Her articles have appeared in *Journal of the American Academy of Religion, Legacy: A Journal of American Women Writers,* and *Studies in Puritan American Spirituality.*

Andrew Fleck is completing his dissertation in English literature at the Claremont Graduate School.

John C. Hawley is Associate Professor of English at Santa Clara University. He has edited *Reform and Counterreform* (Mouton de Gruyter, 1994), *Writing the Nation* (Rodopi, 1996), *Cross-Addressing: Resistance Literature and Cultural Borders* (SUNY, 1996), and *Through A Glass Darkly* (Fordham, 1996). He is past Chair of the Modern Language Association's executive committee on religious approaches to literature.

Syrine Hout is Assistant Professor of English at the University of Maine at Fort Kent. She has published articles on travel writers in the *Dictionary of Literary Biography.* Her book is *Viewing Europe from the Outside: Cultural Encounters and Critiques in the Eighteenth-Century Pseudo-Oriental Travelogue and the Nineteenth-Century 'Voyage en Orient'* (Peter Lang, 1997).

Teresa J. Kirschner is Professor in the Humanities Program at Simon Fraser University. She is past President of the Canadian Association of Hispanists and currently a member of the Executive Committee of the

Canadian Commission for UNESCO. Her book is *El protagonista colectivo en 'Fuenteovejuna' de Lope de Vega.*

Erick D. Langer is Associate Professor of History at Carnegie Mellon University. He is co-author, with Robert H. Jackson, of *The New Latin American Mission History* (U of Nebraska P, 1995) and the author of numerous articles on mission history in Latin America. He is presently finishing a book project on the Franciscan missions among the Chiriguano Indians of southeastern Bolivia in the nineteenth and twentieth centuries.

David Leigh, S.J. is Chair of the Department of English at Seattle University. His articles have appeared in *Modern Philology, Studies in Philology, Philosophy and Literature, Christianity and Literature,* and *Renascence.*

Edwin J. McAllister is teaching at the University of Oregon while completing a dissertation. He has published on Faulkner, and on American missionaries in the American West. He studied for two and a half years in mainland China.

Susan F. McAllister has extensive background in journalism, and lived for two and a half years in mainland China. She is completing a dissertation at the University of Oregon, where she also teaches.

John T. Netland is Associate Professor of English at Calvin College. Many of his articles focus on major poets of the Romantic and Victorian eras. He serves on the Board of Directors of the Conference on Christianity and Literature.

Andrea Remi Solomon received her doctorate in English Literature from the University of California at Berkeley. She has published in *Renaissance Quarterly.*

Laura Scavuzzo Wheeler teaches at the University of Southern California while finishing her dissertation on travel and women's fashions in the English Renaissance.

Making Disciples of All Nations

John C. Hawley

> The whole problem is this: how to utter God in a practice of faith where I must decide what I wish to do with the woman or man I find in my path—make of him or her a human being with a right to life or a slave for life.—Jean-Marc Ela (139)

> Perhaps there is such a thing as seduction. Conversion. Perhaps cultures absorb one another. If it is true that the Franciscan *padre* forced the Eucharist down the Indian's throat, maybe she forgot to close her mouth. Maybe she swallowed the Franciscan priest. After all, the churches of Latin America are crowded with Indians today. It is Europe that has lost its faith.—Richard Rodriguez (Crowley 9)

With this remarkable image Richard Rodriguez makes a point similar to one recently discussed at length by Kwame Anthony Appiah, to the effect that "the experience of the vast majority of [the] citizens of Europe's African colonies was one of an essentially shallow penetration by the colonizer" (Appiah 7). The notion assumes a variety of shapes in contemporary writing reaching the West from the missionary's target populations. In *The Poor Christ of Bomba* (1956), for example, a novel that reads like a manifesto for the liberation of the imaginations of his fellow Cameroonians, Mongo Beti offers a bitterly ironic salvation to the French Fr. Drumont, a 20-year veteran missionary. Only by rejecting the work that had given meaning to his adult life—only by accepting a dark epiphany that calls into question his zealotry and sends him home to France—does Drumont emerge with his integrity intact. In his bitter parting conversation with Monsieur Vidal, the smug colonial District Administrator who demanded the Church play a pacifying role, Drumont explains his decision:

"These people worshipped God without our help. What matter if they worshipped after their own fashion—by eating one another, or by dancing in the moonlight, or by wearing bark charms around their necks? Why do we insist on imposing our customs upon them?"

Vidal's mouth fell open and he flushed slowly as he gazed at the Father, who turned as he spoke and watched the courtyard slowly emptying.

"I've never asked myself this before. Why don't the Chinese devote themselves to converting all Paris to Confucianism or Buddhism or whatever? Oh, I'm not saying that I've solved the problem. Perhaps I'll never solve it, except by the Grace of God. But all the same, I'm certain that it's a serious question." (150–51)

It is not simply that some metaphorical version of Mr. Kurtz has now died in Drumont's eyes; nor, clearly, that the priest's God is dead. Rather, Drumont discerns that all of those who might find their own reflection in a Mr. Kurtz and in the idealized colonizing impulse that drives him (and them) into ever-new jungles, is death itself—the awesome, transmogrified into the horrible. And as Drumont remarks, this history raises a serious question: why does Christianity, vying with Islam for preeminence in this regard, feel the need to impose its "customs" on the rest of the world? The history of those encounters raises another question: why has an impulse at least partially driven by sincere concern for the "salvation" of others so often played into the hands of secular administrators who happily preempt Drumont's "Grace of God" that has had a vivifying effect in individual lives?

Of course, for many Christians the question has been seen from two sides. There are those who were once "pagans," for example, and who now self-identify as Christian; conversely, there are also pagans (or Muslims, Jews, etc.) who were once Christians. In both cases conversion involves not only the acceptance of a new faith, but also the rejection of another. "In one sense," John D. Barbour writes in his suggestive study of "deconversion," "the 'turning from' and 'turning to' are alternative perspectives on the same process of personal metamorphosis, stressing either the rejected past of the old self or the present convictions of the reborn self" (3). Janet Jacobs offers interesting insights into a similar, though extreme, process that sometimes occurs when one leaves a new age cult. In both conversion narratives and deconversion narratives, there is an element of self-consciousness with regard to choice that is generally absent in the lives of those who have simply wandered out of a doctrinal faith through a barely perceived process of secularization, and absent, as well, in the lives of those who keep the faith while avoiding confrontation with the metaphysical claims of their inherited belief system. Those who write about their new understanding of reality generally envision their movement as a journey away from a former, and less reflective, self. As Barbour notes, "a conscientious and responsible account of one's life may need to explain not only adherence to new convictions but also shifts, erosions, and losses of belief" (4).

There are also those who were baptized very young and who later, upon reflection and prayer, are "born again" into a genuine personal commitment and "conversion" to the faith that had, before, been imposed as a cultural template for social functioning. Significantly, in many of these cases the "new" man (or woman) shores up that conversion by distancing the old man, the former unconverted self, from the new, and by giving public testimony to the ontological change that has marvelously transpired. In a sense, the new convert divides him- or herself in half, now defining the regenerated self almost totally in contradistinction to that "other" self—the one that had been benighted but is now happily abandoned.

It comes as no surprise, therefore, that individuals whose self-definition depends upon their maintenance of the break with past customs would sometimes look with suspicion upon fellow converts—whose sincerity would be frequently tested. Broader social motives have also played a role in policing the community. Benzion Netanyahu's study of the Inquisition records the attack on Spain's so-called *conversos*, the Christian descendants of the Jews who had been forced to convert during the anti-Semitic riots that swept across Spain at the end of the fourteenth century. It was believed by many then (and now) that these converts were secretly still Jews. Netanyahu disagrees: his studies suggest that it was to remove the *conversos* from their high public offices and to prevent their intermarriage with the Spanish people that they were accused of being secret Judaizers and members of a "corrupt" race that would "pollute" the Spanish blood. "This was," he writes, "the first time that extreme anti-Semitism was wedded to a theory of race" (Netanyahu 1076). In his view,

The Spanish Inquisition was not created by 'believers in Christ' in order to 'perpetuate their belief,' but by Christians who wished to deny other Christians their rightful share in Spain's Christian society. It was an institution based mostly on false pretenses, sham pretexts, and invented accusations. For its purpose was not the exaltation of religion, but the suppression of a people that could not be reduced save by pinning on it the charge of heresy. (1076)

The issue, while couched in a zeal for religious purity, rooted itself in far less transcendent aims: money, land, power. For more than three and a half centuries the Inquisition extended its reach, supposedly in a holy crusade against insincerity. But, in Netanyahu's words,

What moved the Inquisitors (with a few exceptions, of course) to apply their dreadful techniques . . . was not devotion to this or that principle, but the desire to extend their controls and powers and demonstrate that extension in fact. They were certainly not enthusiastic at the prospect of making [a] Unity of Faith come true . . . ; for the ruthless persecution they launched . . . was not calculated to bring [others] closer to Christianity but to keep them as far from it as possible. (1080)

For a variety of reasons, therefore—a conviction of the truth of one's faith and a consequent generosity in sharing it, or fear of backsliding, or obsession with group identification—the impulse to display the *sincerity* of one's belief by becoming an enthusiastic apostle of the new faith typifies the Christian conversion experience. This begins most notably with Saul of Tarsus, whose name became Paul as a nominal vaccination against the disease of his former self. Among the various studies of the ramifications of this evangelical urge, that of Michael Ragussis on the role of Jewish conversion in Protestant England from the 1790s through the 1870s is one of the most thorough. For Ragussis, "the Jewish question" played a pivotal role during this period in defining not just the individual believer but the national identity of England, as well. This was principally because it represented, on a "local" scale, the mission that Christian England saw as the compelling moral justification for the extension of its economic and political empire. That mission was

the Evangelical crusade to reform England through a national conversion at home and the dissemination of the Gospel to "the heathen" abroad, a crusade that swept through every corner of England and every class of English society and whose effects were felt around the world, especially in India and Africa. (Ragussis 2)

Nonetheless, as with the Inquisition, there yet remained the suspicion that the convert in England itself just might not be Christian *enough*—as in the case of Disraeli, whose political foes described him as representative of "'the secret Jew' who invades England through the passport of conversion in order to undermine English culture" (13). To be English meant to be Christian, and there were gradations of "Englishness" correlative to one's branch of Christianity and one's obvious degree of religious conviction. The absurdity of these demarcations was brought home with vigor by a "ritualist" Anglo-Catholic at the time who had been accused by less "Roman" Christians of being "un-English." R.F. Littledale responded that

> Christianity itself is eminently unEnglish. It was cradled in Palestine, amidst Aramaic-speaking Jews; it was published in the East by Greek-speaking Hellenists; it was brought to our shores by Latin-speaking Italians. The most solemn of its rites cannot be celebrated without a liquor which England does not produce. Druidism may, perhaps, have been indigenous to Britain in some particulars, but Christianity in none. (Shipley 68, qtd in Reed 235)

Defenses such as Littledale's usually have little impact since, with personal and even national identity in the balance, the strongest attacks are metaphysical. As Elaine Pagels observes of the early Christians, they saw themselves "not as philosophers but as combatants in a cosmic struggle, God's warriors against Satan" (Pagels 116). One's role in the world gains a significance, even a grandeur, in one's embrace of a mission to make straight the way of the Lord. Personal *metanoia* leads, then, to important questions regarding one's changing role in society:

> All converts understood, of course, that baptism washes away sins and expels evil spirits, and conveys to the recipient the spirit of God, the spirit that transforms a sinner into an ally of Christ and his angels. But then what? What does a Christian

have to do to stand 'on the side of the angels' in this world? What precisely is required if, for example, the baptized Christian is married to a pagan, or is a soldier, who has sworn allegiance to the emperor, or is a slave?" (Pagels 149)

The answer is that one becomes, in turn, a missionary, at least in spirit— one makes the other a bit more like oneself. A need to paint a backdrop against which one's own defining characteristics come into sharper focus is, understandably, at the heart of this rigid binarism. Where it is combined with tolerance and even valorization of "the other" (in the Chinese rites controversy, for example, or the Jesuit reductions in Paraguay) the history of religions grows less scandalous, less repulsive. As Peter Mason notes, however, all too often strong psychological needs quickly come into play to overwhelm an ethics of common decency: "The question of alterity," he writes, "poses the question of the border: where is the rupture between self and other to be situated?" (Mason 1). This border begins with one's body, quickly extends to one's community, and soon becomes quite literally a *geography* of difference—us *here* and you *over there*:

> As for liminality, in the European imagination the monstrous human races can be located in a variety of places as long as their location is *elsewhere*, over the border . . . . In medieval epic or romance they may be situated in the forest or in the desert, both of which are places on the extreme margin. In ethnography and cartography it is the uninhabited areas of the globe which are their favourite haunts. Their steady relegation further out to the edge is in correlation to the relentless thrust of European expansion which is constantly extending its borders. (Mason 161)

But in the history of missiology there emerges an interesting bifurcation in response to this instinct for "othering" the rest of humanity. As Nicholas Thomas records, perhaps the majority of missionaries developed their methologies based upon "an 'incorporative' ideology and a religious framework [that] characterized Renaissance colonialism: others were represented as pagans rather than as savages or members of inferior races, and their conversion served at least to legitimize expansion, even when it was not systematically pursued" (Thomas 125). In this view, the "other" was seen as one's natural brother and sister; despite perceived unfortunate differences in customs they were considered capable of receiving the grace of God and of entering more fully into the benefits of Christendom. At its heart, this approach was egalitarian—even if dismissive of other cultures and, often enough, other values. Non-westerners were human, all right, but they were still children who needed a firm guiding hand.

Missionaries, however, needed transportation to the heart of darkness, and with the ships came the competing philosophy:

> At a general level this view of difference and history could be seen to be displaced by a secular ideology, which understood human variation in natural rather than religious terms, and which tended to postulate fixed hierarchies rather than mutable categories. The premise of stable racial difference underpinned not only slavery and apartheid, but also apparently more benevolent segregationist policies. (Thomas 125)

In other words, not only were these strange men and women pagans but they were actually not quite human, at all—or, more kindly, they were less fully human than the colonizer. Those rules of social exchange that had been so painfully legislated in Europe over the centuries need not be extended to these hominids. Very likely, their brutish minds would welcome the sense of purpose that the Westerner could happily provide them. Over the centuries these vying philosophies competed for dominance in the colonial territories, and variations evolved that sought to wed elements of both. If carried to its logical conclusion the secular ideology actually worked against the intentions of the missionaries, as Fr. Drumont learned: the differences between "us" and "them" are seen to be as natural and sustainable as those thought to divide man and woman:

> If one kind takes on the attributes or environment of the other, if a process of conversion is initiated, the result can only be repugnant or dangerous, as in the parody of the native who is a "bad imitation" of a European, manifestly threatening the British segregationist project . . . The notion that types are essentially stable in their differences, and that any admixture, hybridization or conversion can lead to no good is manifested in

many specific ways: for instance in the notion that ill-health and depopulation arise partly from the natives' inability to make sensible or correct use of European clothes. (Thomas 132–33)

Happily, such "hybridization" has frequently been attempted by missionaries to notable effect. Tzvetan Todorov discusses the Dominican friar Diego Duran, who had lived in Mexico since the age of six and who wrote, between 1576 and 1581 his *Historia de las Indias de Nueva Espana de la Tierra Firme*. As a Roman Catholic priest he called in the Inquisition to root out religious syncretism among the Indians, yet wrote in detail (for a European audience) of how their native rites paralleled the Christian. He concluded that St. Thomas (but now known to the Mexicans, it seems, as Topiltzin) must have preached to them, and he speaks of them as a lost tribe of Israel. Interestingly, Todorov, who calls Duran "the most accomplished cultural hybrid of the sixteenth century" (Todorov 210), speculates that the priest most likely came from a family of *conversos*. "We may see this," writes Todorov, "as the reason for the zeal with which he attaches himself to resemblances while neglecting differences: he must have already, and more or less consciously, performed an activity of this sort in an effort to reconcile the two religions, Jewish and Christian. Perhaps he was already predisposed toward cultural hybridization" (210). In any case, Duran apparently interpreted his missionary role as Janus-faced, turning to the Indian his rigid demands of orthodoxy, and to Europeans his desire that Indians be seen not as subhumans but as potential members of the body of Christ. As with similarly-minded missionaries, then and now, his scorn for the secular *conquistadores* is severe, and inconsequential. In any case, exponents of this hybridization are comparatively rare. Far more typical are rationales for depicting the alterity of the unrecognizable.

A similar embrace of alterity may shape the response of those "targets" of missionaries who choose to cope with the onslaught by insincerely succumbing while maintaining interior distance. Their response is various, sometimes respectful, often defensive. As Mason points out,

> In the work of assimilation, the relationship is never one of equivalence. On the one hand, the knowledge and power of the Whites may be recognized as a transformation and concentration of the shamanic power and knowledge which were once the prerogative of the Indians . . . . [In any case,] various strat-

egies may be adopted to cope with the White hegemony. One
is a form of resistance by encapsulation: the Whites are allowed
to enter native thought and life, but only in certain restricted
and circumscribed areas . . . . Another strategy is to devalue the
alleged superiority of the Whites. (Mason 164)

Devalued or not, however, the military superiority frequently enough
has carried the day and the tactics of the "target population" have proved
futile. A level of comfort is gradually achieved by the homogenization
of the foreign. "As a structure of alterity," Mason observes, "assimilation is a process by which the otherness of the other is eliminated and
the other is reduced to self. Assimilation works in both directions, for it
implies that, whether Indian is assimilated to European or European to
Indian, it is possible in either case to reduce the other to the familiar, to
self" (163).

Viewed from a psychological point of view, what seems to be de-
sired is the elimination of disturbance to one's hermeneutic framework.
As Elaine Pagels reports, some of the earliest Christian theorists felt the
need for univocity, a desire that appears, paradoxically, to have intensi-
fied within the many sects that later emerged from the Reformation. In
a church that frequently found itself (and still often finds itself) under
attack by civil authorities, it is not surprising that a circling of wagons
would be the order of the day. More perplexing, however, is the preva-
lence of paranoia in ages when civil and church authorities seemed to
speak with one voice. In 1199, for example, Pope Innocent III "equated
heresy with treason for the first time and threatened the perpetual disin-
heritance of the heirs of heretics" (Richards 54).

Pagels notes that both Irenaeus and Tertullian, around the year 180,
insist that what characterizes the true church is

unanimity—agreement in doctrine, morals, and leadership.
Christians, Tertullian says, quoting Paul, should 'all speak and
think the very same things.' Whoever deviates from the consensus is, by definition, a heretic; for, as Tertullian points out,
the Greek word translated 'heresy' (*hairesis*) literally means
'choice'; thus a 'heretic' is 'one who makes a choice.' (Pagels
163)

It is difficult to say for whom Tertullian speaks when he advises that

> [t]o stamp out heresy, . . . church leaders must not allow people
> to ask questions, for it is 'questions that make people heretics'—
> above all, questions like these: Whence comes evil? Why is it
> permitted? And what is the origin of human beings? Tertullian
> wants to stop such questions and impose upon all believers the
> same *regula fidei*, 'rule of faith,' or creed . . . . [for] 'Where
> will the end of seeking be? The point of seeking is to find; the
> purpose in finding, to believe.' Now that the church can pro-
> vide a direct and simple answer to all questions in its rule of
> faith, Tertullian says, the only excuse for continuing to seek is
> sheer obstinacy: 'Away with the one who is always seeking,
> for he never finds anything; for he is seeking where nothing
> can be found. Away with the one who is always knocking, for
> he knocks where there is no one to open; away with the one
> who is always asking, for he asks of one who does not hear.'
> (Pagels 163–64)

Though such authoritarian advice seems to fly in the face of the Biblical injunction to be persistent in one's besieging of heaven, it set the
stage for the demonization of a broad range of "others" who would not
stop knocking. Frequently enough, the attacks have been framed not
only as crusades against doctrinal impurity, but against sexual license,
as well. In his study of minority groups in the Middle Ages, among
whom he includes Jews, witches, heretics, homosexuals, prostitutes,
and lepers, Jeffrey Richards concludes that they were portrayed as having one failing in common: a perceived sexual deviancy (Richards 21,
58). Demands for conformity are not soon sated.

In sharp contrast to such intolerance is the contemporary approach to
missiology, which aligns itself in many ways with the sort of hybridization encouraged by Diego Duran. Morris Inch describes the approach
as "ethnotheology" (7), an attempt to conceive and express a commonly-
held faith in various cultural settings. Aylward Shorter similarly notes
an impressive development of inculturation theology since Vatican
Council II, but also notes a reluctance to put the theory into practice
(Shorter 241). But Jean-Marc Ela, the Cameroonian liberation theologian with whom this chapter opened, notes ominously that

> The church will have to be destroyed as a structure of
> Christendom in order to rediscover a creativity adequate to the
> problems posed by the shock of the gospel in an African cli-

mate . . . . All false universality, perforce, ends in institutional
and canonical rubble, for it is conceived without taking account
of the relationship with the Spirit that a church should live in
its relationship with a culture . . . . It is not necessarily true that
the Judaeo-Mediterranean culture that carried Christianity to
our shores is essential to the universality of that Christianity.
(108–12)

Tertullian might not recognize Ela's Catholicism. Yet even today there
are those who seek a purity that would seem proudly to embrace intolerance. Apparently arising from a dismay over the corruption of spiritual aims by secular demands for power, Jacques Ellul can sound, ironically, quite fascistic. In his view, "[w]e need keep the word *Christianity* only for the ideological and sociological movement which is its per-
version" (Ellul 11). Many practicing Christians no doubt share Ellul's
disgust over the "subversion" of their faith by the institutions that have
accreted over the centuries and that seem both self-perpetuating and
decaying. But whereas someone like Aylward Shorter may see signs of
hope in a theology that seeks to adapt to the culture in which it finds a
new home, Ellul despairs because

Christianity imbibes cultures like a sponge. Dominated by
Greco-Roman culture, it became territorial and feudal (ben-
efices) in the feudal world with all the beliefs . . . that back it. It
then became bourgeois, urban, and argentigerous with the capitalist system. It is now becoming socialist with the diffusion of
socialism . . . . Today it is letting itself be permeated by the
values of African, Oriental, and American Indian cultures . . . .
Tomorrow we might have adjustment to Islam as today we have
adjustment to Marxism. We now have a rationalist or liberal
Christianity as we used to have an Aristotelian or Platonic Christianity in a mockery of being 'all things to all men.' (18)

As high-minded and crusading as this criticism intends to sound, what
is its aim? Does it imagine any faith can be timeless, bodiless, and
purely interior? Should it withdraw from "the world" and serve, not as
a leaven, but as a fortress? In a nutshell, Ellul's approach is clear: "Syncretism is a triumph of the prince of lies" (48). The appeal of this pro-
saic defense against "subversion" has always been strong in human his-

tory, and its overlay of righteousness and personal asceticism has provided impetus to a type of personal conversion. "With the grace of God," it seems implicitly to say, "I will not be like the rest of men"— not, for example, like that poor publican in the back of the synagogue. Not like that "other" over there.

Taking much the same data, though, R.A. Markus demonstrates that in the first three centuries Christianity constantly reworked its notion of mission; not surprisingly, as culture became increasingly "christianized" conversion also had to take on ever new meanings. Similarly, today's optimists like Shorter can offer far more confident programs for future incursions of the "grace of God" that seem both less fearful (and fearsome) than Ellul's, and less dependent on human perfectibility:

> To take a monocultural view of the universal patrimony of the Church is patently false . . . . It is, for example, Greek and Slav, Coptic and Syrian. Its theological tradition is not merely Western, let alone Scholastic . . . . Among these precedents we must surely count former projects of inculturation which were not accepted at the time but which won the Church's recognition afterwards. (256)

But "afterwards" follows a painful path. If the history of conversion, Christian and otherwise, teaches nothing else, it surely suggests the need for a cautious response whenever anyone declares with confidence that he or she has discerned in someone "foreign" the activity of the devil. In fact, surveying the contemporary religious scene observers as diverse as Shorter and Richard Rodriguez can find the true source of spiritual power in the least familiar of "our" brothers and sisters. Rodriguez, for example, offers this provocative commentary on modern missionary efforts:

> Today's Indian convert to evangelical Protestantism could turn out to be an ecumenical pioneer. By casting so wide a net over the Catholic South, after all, Protestant missionaries may be harvesting more than they want. The accretions of the souls they reap may be a cultural Catholicism. Some ancient Catholic sensibility is finding its way into low-church Protestantism. (Crowley 11)

But a "cultural" Christianity, Catholic or Protestant, seems to be what disturbs critics like Ellul. Could not a purer doctrine, after all, stand outside culture as a prophetic voice of witness—as a call, like that of Jeremiah, to repentance and a renewed turning toward God? Human history suggests that the answer to that question is no. The central doctrine of Christianity, the Incarnation, likewise suggests that God himself does not stand outside culture, but enters in to it. But enter at what point? Veteran missionaries like Shorter, far from rejecting the enterprise as did Mongo Beti's disillusioned Frenchman, finds the true impetus for conversion coming these days from the voices of the *powerless*—those who, in ways that might placate Ellul, are perhaps most like the earliest Christians. "At the present time of writing, the vocation of the small Christian communities is to be the keeper of the Church's conscience for inculturation" (270). A *conscience for inculturation*: no longer anathema, but a command from *below*.

In the chapters that follow we offer a comparative historical survey of Christianity's encounters with the non-Christian, with the hope that readers may begin to answer Fr. Drumont's compelling question: why do Christians do this? We believe the sites of conversion that we have chosen to discuss are representative, fascinating and comprehensive in type, though this is a bold assertion in the face of the essential individuality of confessional documents. And, as with Karl F. Morrison in his study of Augustine, we are struck with the paradox that "there has been unusual consistency among a host of witnesses to this point: that the experience of conversion is beyond thought or words. Equally, there has been no lack of efforts to express the inconceivable and ineffable" (vii): the process of conversion generates, among other things, a plethora of texts. Reflection on such a powerful human experience has also produced a plethora of studies. David B. Barrett's, for example, provides a statistical accounting of the past, present, and future plans for Christian missiology. Among the most thoughtful recent studies is Lewis R. Rambo's, which demonstrates that

> for some people the consequence is a radically transformed life. Their patterns of beliefs and actions are significantly different from what they were before. Others gain a sense of mission and purpose, and yet others acquire a very quiet sense of security and peace. The conversion process can also have a destructive effect. . . . In any case, conversion is precarious. (170)

As in Barbour's study of deconversion, we are also interested in noting how the various individuals under discussion seek to find "metaphors and rhetorical strategies adequate to explain how the workings of conscience required the rejection of a former faith" (6)—and the acceptance of an Other. These studies reflect the fact that conversions, whether joyously embraced or cruelly imposed, upset human ecologies. They suggest that "true" conversion bubbles up from below, as Richard Rodriguez has suggested. "The agents of change and growth in the church," he writes, "are always the people in the pews, not the cardinals in their silks. The shepherd is moved by the sheep, even by the sinner within the flock. Isn't that the point of the Guadalupe story? The Spanish bishop is the last one to see" (Crowley 11). A similar sense of egalitarian availability to influence—which may appear to many as syncretism, senility or psychosis—closes Brian Friel's *Dancing at Lughnasa*. In that play's interesting mix of nostalgia, manic alienation, and hope, Mongo Beti's Drumont might find a kindred soul in Father Jack, an old man returning home to Ireland after twenty-five years of missionary work in Africa. To the dismay of his sisters he now calls Africa "home," and conducts a ritual as a fitting metaphor for the cross-cultural exchange at the heart of true gift-giving (and, some would add, of true missiology):

> Jack: Now, if I were at home, what we do when we swap or barter is this. I place my possession on the ground— (*He and Gerry enact this ritual.*) Go ahead. (*Of hat*) Put it on the grass— anywhere—just at your feet. Now take three steps away from it—yes?—a symbolic distancing of yourself from what you once possessed. Good. Now turn round once—like this—yes, a complete circle—and that's the formal rejection of what you once had—you no longer lay claim to it. Now I cross over to where you stand—right? And you come over to the position I have left. So. Excellent. The exchange is now formally and irrevocably complete. This is my straw hat. And that is your tricorn hat. Put it on. Splendid! And it suits you! (Act 2)

Fascinating examples of similar cultural exchanges in missionary work are available in studies by James Axtell and John V. Taylor, among others. Yet, the reactions of Fr. Jack's kind Christian kin to his unwelcome conversion remind theatergoers that the "invasion" of one religious culture by another is disturbing, generally casting the convert, for his former community, as one of the stricken.

If one recalls the skepticism greeting early converts in the New Testament when they returned to share their stories of wonder, it should be no surprise to imagine the scene from the eyes of any faith community today: here was one of "us," now corrupted and led astray by something which threatens to make him or her into someone we no longer recognize. But the shape of that apparent loss always carries marks of its origin (Barbour 211), as a seed reflects its soil. One's movement from one system of meaning to another is never pure and is always syncretic, and remains "precarious" no matter how binary and final the convert may appear to envision the rebirth ("I was blind, and now I see"). Who knows where such changes lead an individual, a religion, or a society? As Richard Rodriguez pointed out, "missionaries may be harvesting more than they want" (Crowley 11): willy nilly they ironically enact the Biblical injunction to bring in the weeds along with the wheat—even if some enemy hath done the sowing.

Works Cited

Appiah, Kwame Anthony. *In My Father's House: Africa in the Philosophy of Culture*. New York and Oxford: Oxford UP, 1992.

Axtell, James. *The Invasion Within: The Contest of Cultures in Colonial North America*. New York: Oxford UP, 1985.

Barbour, John D. *Versions of Deconversion: Autobiography and the Loss of Faith*. Charlottesville and London: UP of Virginia, 1994.

Barrett, David B. and James W. Reapsome. *Seven Hundred Plans to World-Class Cities and World Evangelization*. Birmingham, Alabama: New Hope, 1986.

Beti, Mongo. *The Poor Christ of Bomba*. Trans. by Gerald Moore. Oxford: Heinemann, 1971. [*Le Pauvre Christ de Bomba*, 1956].

Crowley, S.J., Paul. "An Ancient Catholic: An Interview with Richard Rodriguez." *America* (23 Sept. 1995): 8–11.

Donovan, Vincent J. *Christianity Rediscovered: An Epistle from the Masai*. Maryknoll, NY: Orbis, 1978.

Ela, Jean-Marc. *African Cry*. Trans. Robert Barr. Maryknoll, NY: Orbis, 1986.

Ellul, Jacques. *The Subversion of Christianity*. Grand Rapids: Eerdmans, 1986.

Friel, Brian. *Dancing at Lughnasa*. London: Faber and Faber, 1990.

Inch, Morris A. *Doing Theology Across Cultures*. Grand Rapids: Baker, 1982.

Jacobs, Janet Liebman. *Divine Disenchantment: Deconverting from New Religions*. Bloomington: Indiana UP, 1989.

Markus, R.A. *The End of Ancient Christianity*. Cambridge: Cambridge UP, 1990.

Mason, Peter. *Deconstructing America: Representations of the Other.* London and New York: Routledge, 1990.

Morrison, Karl F. *Conversion and Text: The Cases of Augustine of Hippo, Herman-Judah, and Constantine Tsatsos.* Charlottesville: UP of Virginia, 1992.

Netanyahu, Benzion. *The Origins of the Inquisition in Fifteenth-Century Spain.* New York: Random House, 1995.

Pagels, Elaine. *The Origin of Satan.* New York: Random House, 1995.

Ragussis, Michael. *Figures of Conversion: "The Jewish Question" and English National Identity.* Durham and London: Duke UP, 1995.

Rambo, Lewis R. *Understanding Religious Conversion.* New Haven and London: Yale UP, 1993.

Reed, John Shelton. *Glorious Battle: The Cultural Politics of Victorian Anglo-Catholicism.* Nashville: Vanderbilt UP, 1996.

Richards, Jeffrey. *Sex, Dissidence and Damnation: Minority Groups in the Middle Ages.* London and New York: Routledge, 1991.

Shipley, Orby, ed. *The Church and the World: Essays on Questions of the Day in 1868.* London: Longmans, Green, Reader, and Dyer, 1868.

Shorter, Aylward. *Toward a Theology of Inculturation.* Maryknoll, NY: Orbis, 1988.

Taylor, John V. *The Primal Vision: Christian Presence amid African Religion.* London: SCM, 1963.

Thomas, Nicholas. *Colonialism's Culture: Anthropology, Travel and Government.* Princeton, NJ: Princeton UP, 1994.

Todorov, Tzvetan. *The Conquest of America: The Question of the Other.* New York: Harper and Row, [1982] 1984.

"A Wild Shambles of Strange Gods":[1] The Conversion of Quisara in Fletcher's *The Island Princess*

Andrea Remi Solomon

Pocahontas occupies a strange place in the American imagination. She first appears in our childhoods, as part of the fairy tale of early white American history. Although the actual (historical) Native American princess performed a valuable function as adviser to and liaison between her people and the English colonists, the most exciting and famous parts of her story, the spectacles in song and in the Disney movie, are apocryphal. Her diplomatic skill and bravery in her encounter with the Other are less remembered than the fact that she had some sort of romantic relationship with John Smith, and known by far fewer, that she was converted to Christianity and married a different Englishman, John Rolfe.

Captain John Smith wrote "A True Relation of. . .Virginia" in 1607, describing his experiences in the new colony of Jamestown. Smith, a professional soldier, had already met the Virginian Chief Powhatan, and his daughter, Pocahontas, whom he called a "nonpareil," a woman of peerless beauty. She was about thirteen at the time. In the following years Pocahontas frequently visited the English colony at Jamestown, and became a familiar, even beloved face. Although historians disagree exactly how the events transpired, many agree that the Princess intervened one day and prevented her father from killing John Smith. The romanticized scenario is that she threw herself in between the prostrate Smith and a rock or warclub Powhatan held, poised to bash his head. Or as Peggy Lee sang in "Fever," "Captain Smith and Pocahontas had a very mad affair. When her daddy tried to kill him, she said, 'daddy now don't you dare. He gives me fever.'" The Englishman's life was spared, presumably out of respect for Pocahontas' feelings. Naturally, the Indian Princess and the English Captain were even closer friends after this episode. It seemed there was a special romantic connection between these two, and that an alliance might be forged with their marriage.

But what really happened is that Smith had no intention of marrying a heathen, no matter how grateful or enamored he might have been. Jeffrey Knapp believed Smith trifled with the possibility of "erotic disgrace" for diplomatic advantage (11–12), appearing to be a "colonist so enmired in settlement that he not only labors for his bread but. . .loves a savage princess" (188–89). Later Smith had to defend himself against having been "so debased as to want to live not just like a savage, but *with* one" (210). Yet no official union occurred. In 1609, John Smith, badly burned when a pipe spark ignited his gunpowder, sailed back to England for medical help. The inaccurate rumor reached America that Smith had died on the journey, and the grieving Pocahontas left her village and went to live in another.

In 1611 (some say 1613), when Pocahontas was sixteen or eighteen years old, she was lured onto a new English ship, kidnapped by the English Captain Samuel Argall, and brought to Jamestown as a captive. There she attended Bible classes, was converted to Christianity, and baptized "Lady Rebecca." In April of 1614 she married John Rolfe, and this union brought peace between the Native Americans and the English for several years, until after Powhatan's death in 1618. Such an interracial marriage was without precedent, and was not repeated for decades to follow.

This newcomer, the tobacco farmer Rolfe, did not figure largely in Pocahontas's pre-Christian life, and, at least in print, hardly seemed in love with her after her conversion. Rolfe described his wife as one "whose education hath been rude, her manners barbarous, her generation accursed," and rationalized his marriage only as a gesture of diplomacy and of charity, the saving of Pocahontas's "unregenerate" soul (Knapp 238); he claimed to marry her mostly for the good of the plantation and for the love of God. The next year, their son Thomas was born. In the spring of 1616, the Rolfes (Lady Rebecca, John, and their son Thomas) set sail for Rolfe's homeland, visited the English court, and were for the most part well received, the former heathen treated as a Princess. King James was even startled that a white man of no rank had married an Indian Princess. The next year, after much socializing, reknown, and court spectacle, the Rolfes prepared to return to America. But Pocahontas's voyage home was not to be; she contracted tuberculosis and died on board the docked ship; she was mourned and buried at St. George's Church in Gravesend, in 1617. Powhatan, upon learning the news of his favorite child's death, gave up his throne and went to live among the Potomacs, dying in 1618. He bequeathed land to his grandson Thomas, who sailed to America for the first time in 1635 to claim his land and expand colonization in the New World.

In the years following Pocahontas's visit, John Fletcher wrote a play called *The Island Princess*. Although he based the story on the 1609 play *Conquista de las Islas Moluccas*, written by the Spaniard Bartolome Leonardo de Argensola,[2] Fletcher made some key thematic changes which, I think, show his interest in religious current events, especially the issues sparked by the possibility of conversion and interracial marriage in the New World.[3] Argensola's islanders, like the actual Moluccans, were Muslim, but Fletcher makes their religious practices ambiguous, with only the vaguest of moorish overtones; these islanders are heathen, polytheistic, possibly cannibalistic—in short, more like Americans. The native princess Quisara, like Pocahontas, has her name linked romantically to two men, the first suitor of higher rank and longer acquaintance than his shotgun successor. Fletcher also created a double-edged potential of religious conversion. Armusia, the Christian hero, and Quisara, the pagan Princess, are each given a chance to convert to the other's alien religion, as John Smith and Pocahontas were each kidnapped and at the mercy of the opposite camp. Last, by simply calling the play *The Island Princess,* Fletcher shifts the focus from a vanquished land, the Moluccas, to a single victim, the future monarch Quisara, who in many respects replicates the predicament of the historical Pocahontas : as a woman, a heathen, and a Moluccan, she is an emblem of all that is alien. As marriageable royalty, she represents the fate of her nation.

The Island Princess was a very popular play in its time. It was first performed in 1621, entered in the Stationer's Register in 1646, seen several times by Samuel Pepys in 1699, and performed as far from London as Newcastle, both as a play and as an opera, in the first two decades of the eighteenth century (Wallis 244–45). Especially considering the play's popularity, and its historical, topical importance, curiously little has been written about the dense issues of colonialism, enslavement, interracial marriage, or religious conversion. In this chapter I hope to reinterpret Quisara's conversion, showing that it is more a function of Europe's complicated colonial rationalization, manifested through Fletcher's mouthpiece Armusia, than it is a sign of an individual character's ignorance, or her experience of grace.

The issue of religious difference is the crux of the encounter between the Portuguese sailors and the Moluccan royalty. Armusia, as a sort of spokesperson for Portuguese interests, acknowledges cultural variations such as race, customs, and political power structures, but those elements of the "new world" don't alienate him, or deter him in his love interest. Indeed, the Europeans in general have established themselves in the community and seem to be thriving. They also have shown no interest in, or the accoutrement of, being on a religious mission; they brought no clergymen, and don't speak of converting the islanders to Catholicism. But the ambiguous religion of the native population becomes a problem when two of the Portuguese sailors become romantically interested in the princess, and their desire for marriage is apparent.

But which "side" is to convert? One would expect an English author incorporating a Spanish source and American details to support conversion to Christianity, without even needing to dissect the reasons for religious superiority—there are souls to be saved. Yet Fletcher does in a way break ground with the route through which he reaches the major scene of religious conversion. He allows the possibility that a smitten European might, against all odds or sense of propriety, give up Christianity in favor of an alien religion. Armusia, like John Smith, has that option. Nevertheless, relinquishing the Catholic faith never occurs, and through a form of debate, Christianity is shown to be preferable. By intellectual discussion as well as by a leap of faith, the European colonists have chosen rightly, and receive their spiritual reward in heaven, their imperial reward on earth.

Anthony Pagden has written that "the word 'Indies'. . .became a term to describe any environment in which men lived in ignorance of the Christian faith. . . [the term Indian] extended to all men, regardless of their race, who deviated from orthodox faith" (97–98). In the minds of the Jacobean theatergoing public, exploiting such an expansive definition of the Indies enhanced cultural confusion about the Americas. At times foreign lands were so exoticized in English literature that distinctions among Others were obscured, and accuracy was irrelevant. Fletcher, however, in his improvisations on Argensola's work, added several characters, two of whom enhance the detail of the region: the King of Sidore [sic], and the Governor of Terna. In reality, Tidore and Ternate are islands, and the latter was an established island trading center of the geographical Moluccas. However, realistic detail is blurred again with the chosen setting of Fletcher's play: "The Scene: India." George W. Williams expressed confusion at the chosen locale, but did not resolve the issue. He notes, "the 'island', Ternata, of which the heroine is Princess, is one of the Moluccas, an archipelago south of the Philippine Islands, not near to India where the second Folio locates the scene, unless we take 'India' in the meaning of the 'Indies'" (Bowers 543). I propose we do, and must, to make a coherent reading of the play.

The Indies were regions inspiring to the imagination of both the Spanish and the English in the seventeenth century. The specific phrase,

"The Indies," was resonant of New World exploration and colonization, often used interchangeably with "America" and "the sea of India";
in *The Island Princess* there are themes which are most relevant when
seen through the lens of a European explorer of the New World. Of a
more tangible nature, there is a reference to native-grown potatoes (158),[4]
an example which shows the readiness to meld the Moluccas with the
Indies, or America. I feel the best way to make sense of Fletcher's play
is to set it in the ambiguous yet fertile region of the English imagination
about the New World. Only in this setting do the various themes and
observations of paradise, enslavement, religious conversion, colonialism, natives, and conquest cohere.

Charles Squier wrote that "Armusia's 'we are arrived among the
blessed Islands/ where every wind that rises blows perfumes' (99) is an
attempt to evoke the setting, but the islands are always hazy and finally
any foreign place might do as well" (81). The rest of Armusia's first
speech, uncited by Squier, does not support the idea that *any* alien locale would suffice. The Portuguese newcomer revels in the island's
trees, fruit, spices, rivers, gems. His description of Paradise sounds
much like that in the *Letter* of Columbus, of his first viewing of the
new found land. "All these islands are very beautiful. . .full of a great
diversity of trees touching the stars, which I believe are never bare of
leaves. . .some blossoming, some bearing fruit. . .the nightingale chat-
tered. . .all the rest of the trees, herbs and fruits easily excel ours. .
.various birds, a kind of honey, and various metals. . .spices, with gold
and with metals" (Campbell 174). And a remark by a Portuguese clinches
the parallel: ". . .*new worlds disclose their riches*/ Their beauties, and
their prides to our embraces,/ And we the first of Nations find these
wonders" (my italics). This is no idle musing; it is a call to action,
banking on knowledge of travel literature, a reminder of what a new
world discovery can mean. The speaker, like other Europeans, thinks
nothing of displacing the native society; they are not a "Nation."

Appreciation of *The Island Princess* hinges, I think, on the character
of Quisara, who in the past has mistakenly been written off as a stock
character of tragicomedy. Although for much of the play she is far
more than just a fickle female, some attention to the genre is appropriate. Tragicomedy is uniquely equipped to explicate and bolster English conscience about the New World; there are tragic elements, but,
unless you count the decimation of culture and character, there is no
death. I would like to take a fresh look at John Fletcher's play about the
responsibilities of invasion, and challenge the perception that Quisara,
cipher for the New World, is religiously fickle and politically uncom-

mitted. Philip Finkelpearl wrote "religion is the vehicle onto which she can now attach her idealistic ardor . . . clearly she has no idea what Christianity is, but she likes how it sounds" (295). Squier has written that Quisara's "conversion is . . . not of thematic importance" (84). This dismissal of Quisara's religiosity is, I believe, a misperception whose critical orthodoxy has sprung from the political and narrative authority of the Christian invaders who have a moral investment in proving that Quisara and her people deserve colonization and conversion. I find it interesting to note that these critics remember the Princess's "idealistic ardor," but fail to compare her to the colonizing hero Armusia, who reaches a pitch of evangelical hysteria in the fourth act. Finally, critics should consider Quisara's fate in the historical context of John Rolfe's shocking marriage with the native Pocahontas, the potential and problems of interracial union.

As the play opens the Portuguese have landed on the Spice Islands, and have ingratiated themselves with the Moluccans, especially with the lovely Princess Quisara, the heir to the throne now occupied by her brother the King. One foreigner, the Captain Ruy Dias, is favored by the princess; the rest of the Portuguese admirers are left to speak of Quisara's wondrous beauty. Piniero, the Captain's cynical nephew, holds no illusions about the underlying politics; he refuses to allow her a special status dissociated from her rank: "She is a Princess, and she must be fair/ That's the prerogative of being royal" (93). This comment holds a double valence. Quisara lives a life of leisure and can afford to avoid the sun. More biting, however, is Piniero's observation that the princess's rank automatically makes her beautiful to those in her dominion. Throughout the play, Piniero is the dissenting voice, unable to gloss over Quisara's difference. The other soldiers, however, outnumber him, saying, "The very Sun, I think, affects her sweetness/And dares not, as he does to all else, dye it/Into his livery" (93). She is a nonpareil, set apart from her darker compatriots. By imagining Quisara as unique and lightskinned, the Europeans can quell their anxieties about her racial otherness. Unlike John Smith, they can imagine her as more than an object of lust: she is potential mate, and she can make one of them a royal match.

Quisara's brother the King has been kidnapped by the Governor of a neighboring island in the Moluccas, a rejected suitor, and an "ill man" according to the dramatis personae. The Princess, knowing she has legions of men at her disposal, offers herself as the reward for he who rescues the King. Secretly she encourages her favored suitor Ruy Dias, who deliberates; apparently love and revenge are not enough inspiration. A Portuguese newcomer, Armusia, burning with love and a sense of justice, rescues the King by the beginning of Act II.[5] Quisara is enormously disappointed in her lover Ruy Dias, and frightened by the prospect of commitment to a complete stranger. In this liminal moment of Quisara's doubt, she grows reflective, and her character deepens. Her behavior in later acts becomes unpredictable and unruly, which is the manifestation, I think, of Fletcher's need to eventually destroy her credibility. The playwright sets her up to knock her down, reducing her to a figurehead which is all she deserves.

The latent cultural doublestandard is manifested when Ruy Dias plots to kill his successful foe Armusia. Quisara believes murder would prove something positive about her previously weak-willed lover; she is interested in any show of action and courage. For this tentative endorsement, she is condemned in an aside, a cunning and bloody woman. But the creative genius behind the murder plot, Ruy Dias, is not similarly reviled. Perhaps because he is a relative, a man, or a European, Piniero doesn't hold him to such high standards.

Armusia, meanwhile, wishes to see Quisara and quell her fears at his strangeness. At night he approaches her in her chambers. Through lovely speeches he convinces her of his good intentions.

> Look on me, and believe me; is this violence?
> Is it to fall thus prostrate to your beauty
> A ruffians boldness? is humility a rudeness?
> The griefs and sorrows that grow here an impudence?
> . . . .
> Alas dear Lady of my life, I came not
> With any purpose, rough or desperate,
> With any thought that was not smooth and gentle . (138)

Armusia's gentleness serves as a perfect foil for Ruy Dias, who bursts in on this scene, violent and impudent. Quisara is disgusted: "Sure I was blind when I first lov'd this fellow. . .how he blusters!" (140). Armusia leaves, and Ruy Dias repeatedly berates her, impugning her chastity and fidelity. Quietly she warns: "be more temperate" and "you are too forward." Eventually she loses her patience, and invokes her rank:

> "Do ye know what I am Sir, and my prerogative?
> Though you be a thing I have call'd by th'name of friend
> I never taught you to dispose my liberty;

. . . .
Thou poor unworthy thing, how have I grac'd thee!
. . . .
Was't not enough I saw thou were a Coward,
And shaddowed thee? . . .
Daily provok'd thee, and still found thee coward?
Rais'd noble causes for thee, strangers started at;
Yet still, still, still a Coward, ever Coward.
And with those taints, dost thou upbraid my virtues? (140)

This outburst seems long overdue: an army captain has no right to chas-
tise a princess, especially considering his own lack of nerve in romance
and adventure. Based on both her rank, and her innocence, Quisara
seems reasonable in her anger. Yet, her disenchantment with Ruy Dias
and her pulling rank is partly responsible for Quisara's low esteem with
modern critics, who view her with suspicion as a stock character of the
"unreliable woman" (Finkelpearl n11), one of unstable temperament
and aimless zeal.

Unsurprisingly, following such romantic renunciation, Quisara falls
in love with gentle Armusia. Although Romeo is allowed his Rosalind,
Quisara's change of heart is credited to behavior typical of her gender.
"She turns for millions . . . for a tun of Crowns she turns: she is a woman/
And much I fear, a worse than I expected" (131). Far more threatening
a rival than Ruy Dias is Armusia, a fearsome man of action. The
Governor's desire to bring destruction upon the heads of his fellow
Moluccans inspires him to dress up as a "moor-priest" and set into mo-
tion the major conflict in the play, the problem of theological differ-
ence. Religious strife, however, was inevitable, as foreshadowed in an
early scene when Ruy Dias admits that, even at great danger to his life,
he wished Quisara were a "sweet sould Christian" (97). Although
Quisara changed the subject, it resurfaces when more is at stake.

The disguised Governor, out for personal vengeance, says (in an aside)
to his island society, "I'll make ye curse religion e'er I leave ye" (141).
He is the Moluccan equivalent of the cynical Piniero; he too refuses to
pretend there is a perfect symbiosis between the natives and the new-
comers. The Governor is the one realist in a land of the happily in-
vaded. He knows that to undermine the religion of a society is to destroy it, and that his own culture is on the brink of domination by the
Christian Portuguese, the "smooth-fac'd strangers" (142).

Most importantly, the Governor knows he can capitalize on royal
naivete to catalyze the demolition. He first confronts the King, who

says the Portuguese have always seemed "gentle, faithful, valiant." The moor-priest reminds the simple King that "the future aims of men. . .above their present actions, and their glory/ Are to be looked at" (142). He accurately recounts the story of invasion: " these men came hither. . .weather-beaten, almost lost, starv'd, feebled/ Their vessels like themselves, most miserable. . . they landed, and to th'rate/ Grew rich and powerful, suckt the fat, and freedom/ Of this most blessed Isle, taught her to tremble/ Witness the Castle here, the Citadel" (142). This fictional invasion reads like the real histories of the Europeans in the Americas: Spanish conquistadors and English colonists arrived in the promised land sick, starving, and outnumbered. They too grew powerful and taught the natives to tremble. By the time *The Island Princess* was performed for the English public (and Argensola's *Conquista* for the Spanish), this scenario of imperial David overpowering native Goliath was already familiar. But the fictional Moluccans, save the Governor and possibly Quisara, are unaware of their fate. And the Governor, remarkably, is alone in his protest.

The Portuguese already have superior strength in arms. By marrying Quisara, the heir to the kingdom, Armusia and his countrymen stand to gain a more lasting strategic foothold in the area; thus they could change the local religion through evangelism, and force the natives to be traitors to their gods. The moor-priest suggests he would only trust Armusia if the foreigner were "season'd in the Faith we are/ In our Devotions learn'd" (143). What exactly their nonChristian faith is, (part Islam, part pagan), remains unclear. Regardless, the impressionable King agrees, and sends the moor-priest on to Quisara, to plan for Armusia's religious conversion.

Because in later scenes Fletcher clearly capitalizes on the formless and changeable traits of the Moluccan religion, it is interesting to note here the contemporary historical misconceptions about Indian religions. Armusia for instance likens the Moluccan religion to that of the Aztecs ("he that you offer human blood and life to/ And make sacrifice . . ." [155]), a reputation incongruous at least with perceptions of Islam by 1620. One critic who explored the frequent confusion with Islam recalls that Cortes called Aztec temples "mosques," and his contemporaries noted that both cultures, the Aztec and the Moorish, included the practice of polygamy and the grandiose architecture of palaces and extensive gardens. "In this way the conquest of Mexico was readily absorbed into the late medieval view of the world" (Honour 21). In other words, the new American "other" could be more easily understood if differences were glossed, and the new seemed more like the old.

Tzvetan Todorov notes that several sixteenth century commentators made analogies between Aztec and Roman gods (230), and it was commonly agreed that Mexicans were pagan. Fletcher has Armusia attack the local gods on the grounds that they are too human: "you make 'em sick, as we are, peevish, mad,/Subject to age; and how can they cure us/ That are not able to refine themselves" (154). Such a description resonates with belief in GrecoRoman gods and goddesses, immortals who acted on petty human emotions: jealousy, anger, vanity. In this way, Fletcher, through Armusia, conflates a range of suspicious religions—the classical, laughable gods, the familiar but untrustworthy Islam, and the vaguely understood but horrifying pagan Americans.

Further clouding the minds of the Jacobean audience, Fletcher has the Governor employ Christian imagery. The moor-priest tells Quisara that "the Portugals, like sharp thorns . . . stick in our sides, . . . wound Religion,/ Draw deep, they wound, till the Life-bloud follows, / Our gods they spurn at" (148) and that she alone can save the Moluccan gods. In an instant, Quisara's role as representative of her land and people expands to include religion as well—as the bargaining chip, she can manipulate her Christian suitor and bring about his religious conversion. Certainly this is a complicated and unique moment in literature of this time. Even though John Fletcher ultimately casts his lot with the Europeans, he allows a glimpse into the minds of the natives. The moor-priest's pronouncements are poignant, because they are true. The invaders have grown strong, they do have designs on the island nations, and they bear no respect for the native religion. This is the last point in the play when Quisara has any distance from, and therefore power over, her European lover. Fletcher's potential sympathy turns to, at best, ironic fatalism by the end. When she, ever wiser than her simpleton brother, falls, so goes her country.

The showdown occurs in the fourth act, when Armusia wishes to prove his courage and his love. The Princess boldly states her deepest wish: "change your Religion/ And be of one belief with me" (153). Quisara's tone here is remarkable, as if she is parodying the words of the conquistadors and missionaries who expected religious conversion to be virtually instantaneous. "Worship our Gods, renounce that faith ye are bred in;/ 'Tis easily done, I'll teach ye suddenly;/ And humbly on your knees" (154). Armusia's response to his lover's request: "I'll be hanged first." Until this point, the Portuguese nobleman could keep his image of Quisara separate from her nation's odd, nebulous religion, and she was a viable love object. But the machinations of the disguised Governor forced the issue of religious difference, and Armusia is cornered. He reevaluates his love, calls it lust, and abjures Quisara utterly.

This is the speech in which Armusia likens Moluccans to Aztecs and Romans, and he expands on his understanding of their religion, although as a new arrival he hasn't witnessed any of this firsthand. Moluccans, whose beauty and lust disguise true faith, have puppet gods, and offer to the devil, dogs, cats, worms, the sun and the moon. Armusia had expected the Princess to say "make me a Christian," to repent and be baptized, to destroy her country's "false Temples" (155). He calls Quisara his enemy, saying he'd rather love a disease. Quisara, reasonable as always, finds the powers and uses of her gods comparable with those of a Christian god. Armusia remains inflexible, accusing her of offering human sacrifice, and wishes she had instead sacrificed her own god. She thinks he has gone "too far." Perhaps too far is his inaccuracy regarding a bloodthirsty deity, or she protests that she needn't sacrifice and humiliate her own god even if she were to convert. Perhaps if her religion were more clearly delineated, this wouldn't be ambiguous. But as I posited earlier, the ambiguity serves Fletcher well. The moor-priest refers to "our" religion, as if he as a Muslim represented his people, but Armusia's discussion with Quisara illuminates contradictory elements: a multitude of whimsical gods, animism, planet worship, maybe even sacrifice and cannibalism. Ultimately, what is most important, in American history as well as in Fletcher's play, is the European *perception* of the native religion, because that is what will determine the choice to convert or exterminate. Unlike the Portuguese nobleman, Quisara is not a Christian. She now "looks ugly . . . like death itself," a "painted sister . . . [with] devilish Arts," and Armusia vows above all to destroy her "Mahumet gods . . . [her] shambles of wild worships" (156). Quisara's passive adherence to her native religion has transformed her, through European eyes, into a hideous witch, more distorted and alien than ever.

Despite the King's pleas, Armusia continues on his trajectory of threats and insults, and is finally arrested. As Armusia is taken away, Quisara utters a startling line: "Oh how I love this man, how truly honor him" She exits, the act over. How could an audience be anything but baffled at this unlikely response? I can't imagine how this line is carried off. As a simpering capitulation, or ironically? From a hypnotized zombie, arms stiffly leading her offstage? I think the complexity of the play collapses after this point, because Quisara 's character is flattened— through an unmotivated capitulation the Princess suddenly becomes a wavering subject in need of a decisive Christian leader. Surely love is a good reason to change one's mind, but the lover here is hateful and unrepentant. This scenario is an ill-planned solution grafted onto an unlikely defeat, where characterization is subverted to the time constraints of plot. The Europeans must be justified in their victory, and there is only one act left.

While Armusia is held captive, on a sort of death row, the Portuguese reconsider their feelings towards their hosts, now "barbarians" and "slaves." Led by Captains Ruy Dias and Piniero, the Portuguese vow to run amuck, to make use of the fort and burn the city. Meanwhile, the King regrets having imprisoned Armusia, his rescuer, but the Governor, still disguised, reminds the King that the honor of the gods is at stake, not just mere personal insult. In a moment of uncanny insight into the ravages of colonialism, the moorpriest warns that the "demolition of . . . Arms and Worship" strikes at the heart of a civilization. The King listens unconvinced, still feeling perverse tenderness and regret. The Governor is disgusted with his lack of vision.[6]

Quisara enters looking wild and distracted, her hands bound, so distraught over Armusia's fate that she is a danger to herself. This instant transformation is wrought when a loving heathen is shown the error of her ways by a vituperative, uncharitable Christian. Quisara turns on her own people. She calls her brother low, base, swarthy with ingratitude, and tells the moorpriest his severity has "made the gods hard too/ Against their sweet and patient natures, cruel" (161). So the gods are blamed rather than the transgressing humans. Armusia is brought in again for a chance to repent, reminded of the reward, honor, and glory due him, should he embrace their religion and marry Quisara (162). Predictably, the Christian hero (like John Smith) steadily refuses, placing his precious soul above love or diplomacy.

> Let the gods glut themselves with Christian bloud
> . . . .
> Your gods of gold shall melt and sink before it;
> Your Altars and your Temples shake to nothing;
> And you false worshipers, blind fools of ceremony,
> Shall seek for holes to hide your heads and fears in. (162)

Yet, he is not claiming he wants to be martyred. He states that his death will only hasten the defeat of the Moluccan gods, and worshipers will be driven underground. Armusia is a warrior, not a zealot in a colonial congregation. The natives have dared assert their own religion, and he will make them pay for their arrogance. The Governor, an Inquisitor at heart, responds by ordering the Christian's torture, and the changed

Quisara makes her bizarre speech.

Because she has tested Armusia in many ways and found him to be "perfect", she infers that "Your Faith, and your Religion must be like ye . . . I do embrace your faith." Among the qualities she admires are his temperance, and that he's not ruled by rage. Critics say Quisara doesn't understand Christianity, but it seems her grasp of human behavior is faulty as well. Ironically, in this new irrational mode, she resembles a Christian martyr, and to assist Armusia, she vows that her "affection . . . will rise to flames of glory" (163). Turning to her brother, she swears by her new faith that Armusia mustn't die. The Governor condemns them both to death instead, or else "they will corrupt all " with this fever for conversion. While the King ponders this, word comes at this critical point that in his kingdom, "the Castle plays and thunders/ The Town Rocks" (164). The insurrection of the invading Portuguese finally reaches royal ears.

At the climactic moment of battle, the Moluccans tell the Portuguese to cease their cannonfire, or else Armusia will die. The captive himself tells his countrymen to fight the good fight, burn the Moluccan palace and temples to the ground, and "on their scorn'd gods, erect my monument" (169). Quisara adds, "I must follow . . . one life, one death." Vengeance, it seems, surpasses the goal of mass conversion to Christianity. At this impasse, a miracle occurs. Piniero enters, having abducted the false moorpriest. In front of the whole company , Piniero meddles with the priest, and, as the stage direction reads, "pulls his beard and hair off," revealing the evil but ordinary Governor. The King reacts quite efficiently to the discovery: "We are abus'd/ Oh my dear Armusia—/Off with his chains. And now my noble Sister/ Rejoyce with me, I know ye are pleas'd as I am" (169–70). He repossesses the Governor's island, and joyfully turns over the "Town and Castle" to Piniero, the rest of the command to the Portuguese. This redistribution happens so quickly as to appear suspicious, rehearsed even, as if Fletcher had to subdue any hint that a native society could or should maintain autonomy—instead, he has the King himself parcel out the spoils of war. Like Powhatan, he has given land away to the progeny of European colonists, some of whom may very well be his sister's children.

Certainly I understand that the Governor is anathema as the kidnapper of the King. But it seems peculiar that the hokey trick of removing a false beard (thus discovering a false identity) would be enough to turn the tide in favor of the Portuguese. The enemy Governor could certainly be punished without the King of Sidore forfeiting his nation's autonomy. In the guise of a moorpriest, the Governor made warnings about that which was valid, crucial to Moluccan survival. His dire predictions about the Portuguese's ulterior motives came true; Armusia was willing to forsake and humiliate the unconverted Quisara, and his army was willing to destroy the country. The Portuguese struck at Moluccan arms and worship, and emerged victorious.

Perhaps this ending is supremely unsatisfying because of what seems to be Fletcher caving in to the justification and adulation of colonialism. But the unfortunate destiny of the Moluccas is overshadowed by the odd fate of Quisara, the island princess. After the moorpriest is disrobed and the relieved King frees Armusia, the former captive makes what he thinks is a rational explanation. It is interesting to remember that it is Quisara who has the reputation as flighty. Armusia says, "Good Sir, forget my rashness/ And noble Princess, for I was once angry,/ And out of that, might utter some distemper,/ Think not 'tis my nature" (170). Quisara's reaction? There is none. Fletcher did not give her any lines after "one life, one death." Apparently all is forgiven, because Armusia thanks Ruy Dias for his life, his *wife*, and his honor. But what are we to make of Quisara, and her conversion?

Quisara, like Ralegh's Guiana, hath yet her maydenhead. *The Island Princess* propagates the Christian European fantasy of the benefits of conquest; like the imagined Amazons and the actual Americans, Quisara is envisioned as a sexualized heathen, as terrain to be dominated. Because she is a woman, she is thought to be manipulative and unstable. Because she is not Christian, she is untrustworthy, a pagan, a cannibal. And because she is alien, a Moluccan, she is a disposable pawn in a political game. However improbably, though, these initial liabilities have to be reconfigured, because a diplomatic alliance and a new Christian soul are at stake. A smooth transition from Other to willing convert could encourage, even justify, the colonial project.

Quisara is therefore made acceptable to the Europeans by subverting and making common her looks, her politics, her power, her religion— in short, her otherness. She is considered beautiful by Portuguese standards, "tawny," not dark like her compatriots. As native monarch, her fears of "strangers" are projected onto another; the "evil" governor of Ternate publicly articulates Quisara's private worries that her country is being overrun by ungrateful thieves, and it is he, in the costume of a "moor-priest," who is pilloried by the Portuguese. Her political power is stripped when her brother is reinstated as King, and again when he gives away his nation's future. And most importantly, in a perplexing about-face, the pagan princess acquiesces to conversion in a moment of great romantic and political strife. Thus defanged, she is allowed to marry the Portuguese nobleman. Pocahontas, too, had her otherness quashed. Her beauty as a "nonpareil" set her apart from her fellow Americans. Her father Powhatan siphoned off the political power associated with an alliance through marriage. And crucially, Pocahontas's identity was officially changed when she was converted to Christianity, baptized Rebecca, and married off to an Englishman.

Quisara's transformation, I think, speaks to the European colonial projects in the New World, which claimed the religious mandate of saving Christian souls in order to clear the way for colonization. The Virginia Company, embarrassed by Spain's record of conversions numbering in the millions, declared, on paper at least, evangelism its highest priority. In one grand gesture, John Rolfe got to save Pocahontas's unregenerate soul and guarantee peace in Jamestown. As mentioned above, critics have called Quisara religiously and politically uncommitted, and her conversion, irrelevant. I don't posit that her conversion is actually a shrewd political move, an act of desperation in the face of imminent conquest, or a manifestation of a broken will. I don't think Fletcher was concerned with Quisara's agency at all. She is, after all, silenced, evacuated by her literary creator. It is the King who abandons his people by leaving them no national inheritance. Quisara's conversion is the final nail in the coffin of Moluccan self-determination. The island will, praise God, be peopled with Christians.

Notes

1. A phrase I borrowed from Blau. "Armusia sees any other worship as a wild shambles of strange gods and will have his devotion unpolluted if the plague should rage about him and the whole State storms" (548).
2. It is even possible that Argensola was influenced by the story of Pocahontas, because Smith's *Proceedings*, although published in 1612, had been back in England in 1609, and "manuscripts of the work or rumors about Pocahontas could easily have been circulated earlier" (Knapp 337 n38).
3. For a brief exploration of Fletcher's deviations from and variations on the Spanish source, see Edward Lewis.
4. I used the Cambridge Classics edition (ed. Waller), which is only broken down into acts and scenes. All references are to the *page* on which the quotation appears.
5. The prompt rescue is quite baffling to the reader, although it might have appeared less so on stage. Philip Edwards believes that "the seventeenth century audience . . . were not deterred by the conventions of improbability,

or by lack of depth in the playwright's views" (177) and that they would have responded to Armusia's refusal to renounce Christianity as a typical scenario of a conflict of wills, rather than one of topical importance. Still, I believe audience plot expectation of a conflict between suitors would be confounded, until the more compelling issues of cultural conflict and religious conversion emerged.

6. The connection among marriage, conversion, fertility and imperialism is foreshadowed when Piniero, prescient as usual, suggests to Quisara's waiting woman, "I'll get thee with Christian,/ The best way to convert thee" (166).

Works Cited

Blau, Herbert. "The Absolved Riddle: Sovereign Pleasures and the Baroque Subject in the Tragicomedies of John Fletcher." *New Literary History: A Journal of Theory and Interpretation* 17.3 (1986 Spring): 539–54.

Campbell, Mary B. *The Witness and the Other World: Exotic European Travel Writing, 400–1600.* Ithaca: Cornell UP, 1988.

Edwards, Philip. "The danger not the death." *Stratford-Upon-Avon Studies*, Vol.1. Eds. John Brown, B. Harris. London: Edward Arnold, 1960. 1577.

Finkelpearl, Philip. "John Fletcher as Spenserian Playwright: The Faithful Shepherdess and the Island Princess." *Studies in English Literature, 1500–1900.* 27.2 (1987 Spring): 285–302.

Fletcher, John. *The Island Princess. The Works of Francis Beaumont and John Fletcher.* Ed. A.R. Waller. Vol. 8. Cambridge: Cambridge UP, 1910.

Honour, Hugh. *The New Golden Land: European Images of America from the Discoveries to the Present Time.* New York: Pantheon, 1975.

Knapp, Jeffrey. *An Empire Nowhere: England, America, and Literature from Utopia to The Tempest.* Berkeley: U of California P, 1992.

Lee, Peggy. "Fever." By Johnny Davenport and Eddie Cooley. *Bewitching-Lee.* New York, 1958.

Lewis, Edward Danby. "John Fletcher: his distinctive structural and stylistic contribution to English drama." Diss. Yale U, 1941.

Pagden, Anthony. *The Fall of Natural Man: The American Indian and the Origins of Comparative Ethnology.* Cambridge: Cambridge UP, 1982.

Smith, John. *Complete Works.* Ed. Philip L. Barbour. 3 vols. Chapel Hill: U of California P, 1986.

Squier, Charles. *John Fletcher.* Boston: Twayne, 1986.

Todorov, Tzevtan. *The Conquest of America: The Question of the Other.* Trans. Richard Howard. New York: Harper & Row, 1984.

Wallis, Lawrence. *Fletcher, Beaumont and Company.* New York: Kings Crown, 1947.

Williams, George Walton. Introduction. *The Island Princess.* By John Fletcher. *Beaumont and Fletcher : Dramatic Works.* Ed. Fredson Bowers. Vol. V. Cambridge: Cambridge UP, 1982.

• 3 •

Encounter and Assimilation of the Other in *Arauco domado* and *La Araucana* by Lope de Vega

Teresa J. Kirschner

The Seventeenth Century Spanish playwright, Lope de Vega, in his so-called American plays,[1] tried to represent the arcane wonders of the New World—a world where the sacred and the secular were differentiated by a cosmology which was grossly misunderstood, if not altogether ignored by most of his contemporaries. As Edmundo O'Gorman has already explained in *The Invention of America*, the Europeans had great difficulty in accepting the existence of an inhabited Fourth Continent, and in incorporating the newly discovered landscapes and civilizations in their Old World collective consciousness (O'Gorman 138–39). Furthermore, Stephen Gilman, in his incisive essay on Lope's American plays, explained the implicit difficulty that lay in the dramatization of materials which had neither been poeticall*y* processed, nor previously included in a literary tradition (Gilman 107). Lope was, thus, a true pioneer in being the first Spanish playwright, and one of the earlier (if not the earliest) European dramatists, who dared to stage and give a material entity to the Americas. In order to do so, he created a purely imaginative dramatic space in which he tried to convey the compelling mystery and beauty of the Otherness of the New World. This invention was necessary not only because he had never set foot on American soil, but because he placed on stage and gave life to a new character, native to this Other Continent, the American Indian.

In this study, and by means of the analysis of two plays connected with the conquest of Chile by the Spaniards—the three act *Arauco domado*[2] *(Tamed Arauco)* and the one act religious piece, called *La Araucana*[3] *(The Araucana)*,—I will examine how Lope integrates the Indian figure in his dramaturgy, within what parameters, what values, and with what strategies.

Arauco domado

In *Arauco domado*, the Indian figure is neither portrayed as a solitary and monstrous Caliban, nor a metaphysical abstraction of the Noble or Bad Savage. He belongs to the category of characters (such as the Peasant) that Lope idealizes (Ruiz Ramón 1989: 230) in order to rescue them from a subservient or antagonistic position. I do not plan to discuss here the historic, geographic or ethnographic exactitude (or rather inexactitude) of the Araucan world view as portrayed by Lope. These topics have already been examined by the critics (see in particular Corominas, Dixon: 1992, Lee, Shannon). As is known, when Lope writes a historical play, he draws from all the materials he is acquainted with, oral and written alike, and then he proceeds to extract from the multiple sources those elements or features which best suit the particular structure of his own creative work. What I find interesting in *Arauco domado* is that in spite of his own obvious eurocentrism and that of his public, Lope tries to portray the indigenous world with an ontological cohesiveness intended to reflect the native cosmogony.

Too often the literary study of dramatic texts has been reduced to the analysis of dialogue. However, a proportion of the verbal element will remain obscure without an imaginative reconstruction of the performance that the text was designed to evoke. I will therefore pay particular attention to this imprint by studying the presence of Spaniards and Indians, as well as the enactment of their rituals in the play. Since talking about something or someone is not the same as staging this very something or someone, I will examine the dramatic processes through which the otherness of the native world is conveyed. Due to the critics' interest in the figure of Don García Hurtado de Mendoza and in the exposition of the hegemonic discourse (Dixon 1993, Kirschner, Lauer), very little attention has been paid to the weight of the physical presence on the Indian characters in this *comedia*. However, as we shall see, their role is extremely important.

To begin with, the aristocratic Spanish hero, Don García, has his counterpart in the leading Amerindian hero, the godlike King Caupolicán (I, vv. 215 and 538). Lope presents the Spaniard in the paradigmatic function of the Christian warrior who is at the sole service of God, King and Country. He has neither a private nor a sentimental life. In spite of his youth, Don García lacks both the impetuousness and the amorous inclination expected of his age. The Indian characters, on the other hand, have a rich emotional life: Tucapel is enamored of Gualeva, and

Talguén of Quidora (Lee 129); Caupolicán is married to the tempestuous Fresia and has a son, Mengol, old enough to confront him. Later, after the torture and death of his father, Mengol will vow to continue the Arauco's fight against the Spanish invaders.

As to the individualization of characters, it is worth noting that the Indian contingent is larger than the Spanish one, and that the list of "figures of the tragicomedy" is headed by the Indians, although the action begins in the Spanish camp. The seven Spanish characters with a given name (Don García de Mendoza, Don Felipe de Mendoza, Don Alonso de Ercilla, Captain Viedma, Captain Alarcón, Rebolledo, and Avendaño) are overpowered by the 16 Araucans (Tipalco, Pillardo, Talguano, Caupolicán, Tucapel, Rengo, Orompello, Talguén, Quidora, Fresia, Gualeva, Millaura, Pillalonco, Engol, Galbarino, and Puquelco), and the two native supernatural beings (Lautaro who appears dead in the form of a shadow [48], and the devil Pillán [64]).

The very structure of this battle play also contributes to heighten the role of the indigenous peoples since all the action takes place in Chile and is presented by means of a scenic division which alternates between the Spanish and the Araucan camps. This contrastive structure is even duplicated in the acts' closures: the first act ends with Don García's challenge, "¡Chile, yo he de sujetarte, / o tú quitarme la vida!" (I, vv.1018–19) (Chile, I will subdue you, or you will claim my life!); the second one with Caupolicán's answer, "¡Al arma, Araucanos fuertes! / ¡Muera España, viva Chile!" (II, vv.1966–67) (To arms, strong Araucans! Death to Spain, long live Chile!); and the third act finishes with the triumphant and supposedly conciliatory cheer from Don García, "¡Viva el invicto Felipe, /Rey Español, Rey Indiano!" (Long live the invincible Philip, Spanish King, American King) and from his soldiers when they all shout in unison, "¡Viva el Rey Felipe!" (III, vv. 1045–47) (Long live King Philip!).

Although the Indian characters are on stage intermittently, they have, nonetheless, a great impact on the audience because of the complexity and variety of this group, and because of the length of the scenes in which they participate. The numerical force and the unanimous will of the indigenous collectivity is shown in the creation of the character "All," whose voice in unison thunders in the spectators' ears. This collective character of the American Indian is shown on stage on two occasions. The first occurs during Act I, when the Araucan warriors join their voices in a bellicose song, just before their attack on Penco, a Spanish held fort. The rhythmic repetition (every 3 and 7 verses) of the refrain "Caupolicán" (I, vv. 587–630) serves as a war cry which stirs up the

psyches of both the spectators and the attackers. The second appearance happens during Act III when, after the deliberations of the war
council and Galvarino's arrival at the Araucan camp with his hands cut
off, the whole community makes the decision to renew the attack. Their
solemnly unanimous oath is expressed with the words "!Sí juramos!"
(Yes, we swear!) and "!Viva!" (Hurrah!) (III, vv. 437 and 458).

According to Victor Turner, a society can be viewed as a process
punctuated by performances of various kinds so that ritual, ceremony,
festival, spectacle, and parade form, "on various levels and in various
verbal and nonverbal codes, a set of intersecting metalanguages" (Turner
100–01). Luis Millones in his introductory study to the ceremonial
ethos conveys the same idea when he says that an ideology, cosmogony
or type of behavior can be expressed by means of a festival, parade or
masquerade (Millones 9). Accordingly, Lope, besides showing us the
collective will and physical presence of the two contesting homoge-
neous groups, also shows us the differences in mentality through the
representation of their separate festivities, habits, and sacred rituals.

Arauco domado opens with the celebration of a Christian religious
ceremony (I, vv.1–62). The ritual of the procession and display of the
tabernacle by the Spaniards is contiguous to and synchronic with the
purifying ritualistic bath before sexual intercourse of Caupolicán and
his wife Fresia (I, vv. 177–275; 416–515). Thus, while Don García and
his troops, separated from their families and communities, are observ-
ing a festivity (Lauer 99) and a sacred rite of the Old World, the
unsubmissive Indians (rebellious, according to the Spaniards) carry on
with their own lives in their own world with their own traditions of a
more open sexuality and a shared communal life more equal among
sexes, whether in war and in peace. The animistic communion with
nature and the couple's ecstasy create a privileged environment in which
sexual activity becomes holy. This scene clearly establishes the relationship between the sexuality of the native male hero (Caupolicán)
and the tantalizing appeal of his wife (Fresia) who has conquered him
as Diane, the pagan huntress Goddess.

The contrasting alternacy of Christian and Aboriginal rituals in the
first act is duplicated in the two following ones. While the Spaniards
are commemorating Saint Andrew's day (II, vv. 636–75) with the observance of mass, the singing of a religious hymn with a repeated refrain (Umpierre 77), the playing of a military band, and the displaying
of horsemanship, we watch the silent assault of the Indians on the Spanish camp (II, vv. 771–99). They creep on stage without their feathers so
that the enemy may not hear them, and that they may not be easily

spotted (II, v.770; v.772 and v.815). We thus watch the staging of a war stratagem which, in time, will become emblematic of Indian warfare. (Think of all the Hollywood cowboy-and-Indian B movies). If during the second act the Indians interrupted the Spanish festivities, in the third act the situation reverses itself and it is the Spaniards who, in turn, interrupt the Araucan's celebration of a "solemn areito"[4] (III, vv. 582–662).

All the male and female Indians are present on stage for this great scene of the final act (III, 180). The rhythmic dance, the entrancing repetition of certain sounds in the wording of their song (*Piraguamonte, piragua, piragua, Xevizarizagua, bío bío*) (III, vv. 582–665), the structure of their psalmodic chant which requires that the whole congregation repeat the refrain in unison, the exhilaration with the drinking[5] of fermented liquids and the libation of the enemy's blood in Valdivia's gilded skull (III, vv. 650–55) which transfers to them the strength and valor of the enemy (Lee 145), form part of the rituals that the Araucan warriors (male and female alike) partake in order to ready themselves for combat. Other customs are also portrayed or alluded to in the play, such as the ritualistic cannibalism from which Rebolledo manages to escape (II, vv.198–244); the participation of the Araucan women in the war effort (I, vv. 628–765); or the ceremonial sitting which determines the participants status with Caupolicán as head in the center and the nearby seats reserved for the elite of his retinue ("los principales") (II, vv. 298–99).

In addition to vividly depicting habits and ceremonies which reveal the different socio-political structures of the American and the European collectivities, Lope represents the conflict in their beliefs and religions. The Araucan's reliance on auguries[6] is portrayed since the first act (I, vv 288–352). In mid stage, the "priest" Pillalonco conjures the Araucan God Pillán, with a hank of wool and a small tree branch (I, 63). The conjuration's effect is immediate. A radiant and beautiful Pillán (I, 64) appears, dressed in a costume that connects him both with the Indigenous Solar Divinity and with the gold of the Indies, the mineral coveted by the Europeans (Ruiz Ramón 1993: 40). But this "divine Pillán," as Pillalonco calls him, enters the stage through the floor trap, so that, according to the synecdochic relationship within the scenic space, he appears from below. Therefore, while the Araucans perceive Pillán as their God, the spectators view Him automatically as the Devil, the infernal deity. But Pillán is powerful enough to scold Caupolicán in his bath and to auger correctly that the people of Arauco will be defeated by Don García's forces, and that His power will be overturned by the Christian faith. In the second act, the anguish of the female warriors to find out if their mates have survived the battle is heightened by the occurrence of bad omens (II, vv. 874–76). Later, Lautaro's supernatural appearance from inside a tree (II, 149) forces Caupolicán to acknowledge the long tradition of the Arauco fight—Lautaro having been an Indian house servant of Valdivia, who, after escaping from the Spanish camp, became one of the most effective leaders of the Arauco forces (Crow 114).

Finally, in the third act, the religious, political, and ideological conflict of one culture against the other comes to a head with Caupolicán's capture, incarceration, scoffing (by his own people), conversion, torture, public impalement, and death. The ceremony of his baptism and conversion, which is the rite of initiation into the Christian community, is only alluded to and dispatched literally in four verses (III, vv. 900–04). On the other hand, his torture and death is staged in the recess of the discovery space. A double door opens exposing Caupolicán impaled "on a stick" (III, 201), a living scene that brings to the spectator's mind the iconographic depiction of the crucified Christ. Thus Caupolicán is integrated in the mythical aura of sacrifice and regeneration (Beane and Doty: Vol. I, 213 and 215). His farewell sonnet is supposedly directed to the Christian God which he addresses as "Señor" (Lord). However, it is ambivalent enough to be permeated by a religious syncretism which allows the convergence of Christian and Indigenous ancestral values. "O sol, autor del Sol, pues luz me distes, / con esa misma vuestro rayo adoro! (Oh sun, author of the Sun, since you gave me light, with the very same I adore your ray! (III, vv. 977–78). In Joseph Campbell's own words: "The God idea is always culturally conditioned, always. And even when a missionary brings what he thinks is God, his God, that God is transformed in terms of what people are able to think as a divinity" (Campbell 101).

The living tableau of Caupolican's impalement is immediately followed by another one which reveals the effigy of young Philip II under a flowering arch (III, 204). Given the ongoing debate which was taking place in Spain about the exploitation of the Indians, the rightness of forced conversions, and, in general, the moral and ethical considerations raised by the Spanish presence in the Indies, the impact of the parallelism of these two discoveries, that of the impaled Indian king and that of the ruling Christian king, undermines the apparently triumphant ending of the play. The superimposition of images in the same location of the stage, a location that, because of its recess and its being concealed by a curtain is often used to bring forth the element of surprise, points out and emphasizes that the true perpetrator of savagery is the Spanish Crown and, by delegation of power, its representatives in the Indies.

Although Lope includes in *Arauco domado* the arguments in favor of the Conquest, and shows the brutal process of the encounter of two peoples, when he sets himself to depict the collective will of the American Indian and to represent his customs, rituals and beliefs, he becomes enamored of his character. He becomes so enamored of the bravery with which the Araucans fought for their freedom that, as we shall see, he will rewrite this play as a religious Christian allegory with solely Indian characters.

La Araucana

In this *auto,* Lope combines the discourse about the Indian with that of the Christian hegemonic religion so that, in a clear case of metanoia, the redemption of the Araucan Nation becomes the redemption of Humanity. Lope changes in this polyphonic composition the name and ethnic makeup of Biblical characters: the Indian Colocolo looks like St. John the Baptist (139) and embodies his persona announcing the arrival of the Redemptor; Christ, dressed magnificently as an Indian, descends from up above "in the figure of Caupolicán" (151); and the infernal Rengo (vv. 440 and 602), also dressed in the stereotyped Indian getup with feathers, darts and a mantle (135), is the impersonation of Satan as the Fallen Angel.

The fusion between the Native and the Christian codes is such that the ancestral Araucan custom of the "contest of the log" (v. 519) is linked to the carrying of the Holy Cross by Christ (v. 574). The Araucans would choose as their new leader the man who could carry a big piece of timber for the longer period of time. Caupolicán wins over his contestants, including Rengo, to become the Indian cacique, defendant of the Araucan people against the invading foreign forces who rob them of their liberty and their material treasures (vv. 5–16). At the same time, as Christ, and by embracing the cross and carrying it for three days, Caupolicán gains the Kingdom of Heaven and defeats the diabolical force impersonated by Rengo who keeps on tantalizing and tempting him on three different occasions. Later on, the Indian Christ crucified will ascend (169) to the top of the stage. This visual image brings forth again the memory of the impaled historical Caupolicán and reinforces the connection between Caupolicán's and Christ's role as leaders of persecuted flocks. His ascent to Heaven connects the plight of the indigenous people, defenders of the Araucan cause, with that of Christ's own fight against the persecutors of his followers.

The link between the two plays *Arauco domado* and *La Araucana* goes beyond the recycling of names of characters such as Caupolicán, Rengo, Teucapel (Tucapel in *Arauco*), the displaying of exotic dress and setting, and the establishment of a parallel between one story told as a historic elaboration of an event and another one told as a religious quest or saga. It also includes the appropriation of words, motifs, songs and situations which acquire a different meaning in the new spiritual context, a context propitiated by the very genre of the *auto* which centers around the poetic rendering of myths and parables.

As we have seen, *Arauco domado,* includes an important number of songs and dances. The lyric aspect of the *comedia*, however, will be greatly increased in this particular *auto,* to the point that it will become its most salient formal characteristic. The exact title of the text of *La Araucana,* as it has reached us, is that of *Famoso canto de la Araucana (Famous song of the Araucana).* The play indeed has numerous affinities with a work such as the biblical *Song of Songs* because of the metaphorical use of language and the multi-leveled dialogue. But, it better relates to the genre of the cantata or recitative because of the very great number of songs included in it. Indeed, *La Araucana* opens and closes with a choral song and, out of the 862 verses which constitute the whole spoken text, 218 verses (a little less than a fourth) are sung. Furthermore, these melodies greatly alter the very substance of the Araucan community as we had seen it in the previous play, by transforming it into a passive, peaceful, serene and harmonious collectivity and by erasing all traces of its previous bellicosity. The form of the songs themselves greatly follow the pattern of the most famous and diaphanous one to be found in *Arauco domado* to the point of even repeating the pseudo Amerindian vocabulary that Lope compiled and/or invented on his own. "Piraguamonte, Piragua, /Piragua, Xevizarizagua" (*Arauco* III, vv. 582–83) says the refrain in *Arauco domado,* while the text of *La Araucana* echoes: "Piraguamonte, piragua, /genicaris agua, /rrunfale" (*Araucana* vv. 472–74). But while the song in *Arauco domado* develops the topic of amorous sensuality, that of the *auto* refers to failure, silence, and death—ominous foreshadowing of Christ-Caupolitán's death.

The play ends with the staging of the apocalyptic "cosmic war" which, according to Elaine Pagels, "has pervaded the imagination of millions of people for two thousand years" (Pagels 182) and involves "a split society, divided between 'sons of light,' allied with angels, and 'sons of darkness,' in league with the power of evil" (Pagels 179). This split is represented in the *auto* with two clouds: one blue and white, and the other black. They both burst open at the same time and reveal Caupolicán in the first, holding a chalice in his hand, and Rengo in the second, with a plate of snakes (173). The perennial association of good with lightness and bad with darkness persists. Caupolicán, the Prince of Light, is surrounded with the bright pure colors (blue and white), his enemy, Rengo, the Prince of Dankness, is in a black cloud.

The exaltation of the Indian ethos is such that even the cannibalistic tendencies (which Lope attributed to the Araucans in *Arauco domado* and which represented their most negative trait) are revindicated here as a positive attribute when linked with the mystery of the transubstantiation of bread and wine into Christ's flesh and blood in the sacrament of the Eucharist:

> y por ver que sois amigos
> de carne umana, oy os ago
> plato de mi carne misma,
> ¡mirad si es sabroso el plato!
> Comed mi carne y bebed
> mi sangre; que regalaros
> con aquello mismo quiero
> de que todos gustáis tanto. (vv. 746–54)

("and since I see that you like/ human flesh, today I am preparing for you/ a dish of my very own flesh,/ see if it is a tasty dish!/ Eat my flesh and drink/ my blood; for I want to treat you/ with the very thing/ which you all so much love").

The last contest between Caupolitán and Renco is over how to win over their followers. It comes down to a clear choice between those who want to eat "pan de bida (sic)" ("bread of life") (v. 829) versus those who prefer to eat "pan de muerte" ("bread of death") (v. 845). The bread of life is simply offered while the bread of death is served on a silver and gold platter. The Araucan indians choose en masse to eat the bread of life offered by Caupolicán while rejecting Rengo's bread of death. The discourse about the Indian has been totally mystified. The converted Indian is no longer the Other but Oneself. The process of assimilation and appropriation has been completed.

At present and centuries later, the encounter on the American Continent between Europeans and Natives is still being perceived as the shock produced by the violent imposition of the Christian point of view on the aboriginal population (Rodríguez Monegal 407). In *Arauco domado* Lope's vision represents and foretells a receptive overture to the "Other"; in *La Araucana* he equates the saga of the converted Indian Caupolicán to Christ's own suffering. In both plays he makes the spectators at all times pay attention to the humanity, heroism, and tragedy of the Native Peoples of the New World.

Notes

1. Consisting in : three full-length three-act plays or *comedias* (*Arauco domado* [*Tamed Arauco*], *El Brasil restituido* [*Brazil restored*], and *El Nuevo Mundo descubierto por Cristóbal Colón* [*The New World Discovered by Christopher Columbus*]) together with one short one-act religious play or *auto* entitled *La Araucana*.
2. I follow Whalen's edition because the verses are numbered. This is not the case with Ruiz Ramón's version included in *America en el teatro clásico español* (75–140), nor with the text included in *Teatro indiano de los Siglos de Oro* (107–56).
3. I follow the numbered verse edition of John H. Hamilton in *Dos obras de Lope de Vega con tema americano* (134–78).
4. The *areito* is a communal celebration involving ritualistic dancing and inebriation. Both Fernández de Oviedo and López de Gómara described it at length in their chronicles. Fernández de Oviedo makes the distinction between an "areito" and a "solemn areito." The latter is reserved for significant events such as a wedding, a burial, a coronation of a new king, a battle, or a victory. The solemn *areito* involves drunkenness while the common one does not (*BAE*, vol. 117, 115b).
5. Before the *areito* scene, the drinking of chicha has already been mentioned (III, v. 125). See also López de Gómara (*BAE*, vol. 22, 207).
6. Oviedo speaks of the diviners who were revered as Christian priests (*BAE*, vol. 117, 112b).

Works Cited

Beane, Wendell C. and Doty, William G. eds. *Myths, Rites, Symbols. A Mircea Eliade Reader.* Vols. I and II. New York, Harper, 1976.
Campbell, Joseph with Moyers Bill. *The Power of Myth.* New York, Doubleday, 1988.
Corominas, Juan M. "Las fuentes literarias del 'Arauco domado' de Lope de Vega," *Lope de Vega y los orígenes del teatro español*, Madrid, ed. Criado de Val. Edi 6, 1981. 161–70.

Crow, John A. *The Epic of Latin America.* New York, Doubleday, 1946.

Dixon, Victor. "Lope de Vega and America: *The New World* and *Arauco tamed.*" *Renaissance Studies* 6.3–4 (1992) 249–69.

____. "Lope de Vega, Chile and a Propaganda Campaign," in *The Comedia in the Age of Calderón. Studies in Honour of Albert Sloman, Bulletin of Hispanic Studies* 70 (1993): 79–95.

Fernández de Oviedo, Gonzalo. *Historia general y natural de las Indias,* ed. Juan Pérez de Tudela Bueso, BAE Vols. 117–21. Madrid: Atlas, 1959.

Gilman, Stephen. "Lope de Vega and the 'Indias en su ingenio'", in *Spanische Literatur im Goldenen Zeitalter,* ed. Horst Baader and Erich Loos. Frankfurt: Vittorio Klostermann, 1973.

Hamilton, John H. *Dos obras de Lope de Vega con tema americano.* Auburn, Alabama: Auburn UP, 1968.

Kirschner, Teresa J. "Enmascaramiento y desenmascaramiento del discurso sobre el 'indio' en el teatro del 'Nuevo Mundo' de Lope de Vega," in *Relaciones literarias entre España y América en los siglos XVI y XVII.* U Autónoma de Ciudad Juárez P. 1992: I, 47–64.

Lauer, A. Robert. "La conquista de Chile en el teatro español del Siglo de Oro," in *El escritor y la escena II,* ed. Ysla Campbell. Ciudad Juárez, Universidad Autónoma de Ciudad Juárez, 1994, 95–103.

Lee, Mónica Lucía. *De la crónica a la escena: Arauco en el teatro del Siglo de Oro.* Doctoral Thesis, Vancouver, Canada, U of British Columbia, 1993.

López de Gómara, Francisco. *Historia General de las Indias,* in *Historiadores primitivos de Indias.* Enrique de Vedia ed., BAE Vol. 22. Madrid: Atlas, 1946.

Millones, Luis and Onuki, Yoshio eds. *El mundo ceremonial andino. Senri Ethnological Studies* 37. Osaka: Museo Nacional de Etnología, 1993.

O'Gorman, Edmundo. *The Invention of America.* Bloomington, Indiana UP, 1961.

Pagels, Elaine. *The Origin of Satan.* New York: Random House, 1995.

Rodríguez Monegal, Emir. "Carnaval/antropofagia/parodia," *Revista iberoamericana* 45 (1979): 399–412.

Ruiz Ramón, Francisco. "El héroe americano en Lope y Tirso: de la guerra de los hombres a la guerra de los dioses," in *El mundo del teatro español en su Siglo de Oro. Ensayos dedicados a John E. Varey,* ed. J. M. Ruano de la Haza . Ottawa, 1989. 229–48.

____ ed. *América en el teatro clásico español. Estudio y textos.* Pamplona, Ediciones Universidad de Navarra, 1993.

Shannon, Robert M. *Visions of the New World in the Drama of Lope de Vega.* New York, Peter Lang, 1989.

Teatro indiano de los Siglos de Oro. Introducción de Arturo Souto Alabarce. Mexico: Editorial Trillas, 1988.

Turner, Victor. *From Ritual to Theatre. The Human Seriousness of Play.* New York City, Performing Arts Journal Publications, 1982.

Umpierre, Gustavo. *Songs in the Plays of Lope de Vega. A Study of their Dramatic Function.* London, Tamesis, 1975.

Whalen, Edna Sofía. *Edición crítica del Arauco Domado de Lope de Vega.* Doctoral Thesis, University of Iowa, 1973.

The Discourse of the Newly-Converted Christian in the Work of the Andean Chronicler Guaman Poma de Ayala

Dolores Clavero

One of the oldest driving forces of Christianity, the desire to preach the gospel to all nations of the earth, acquired a particular urgency in medieval Spain due to specific historical circumstances. By the year 1200 the Christians in the Iberian Peninsula had reconquered more than half of the land from the Moslems, and it was at this time that the ideal of the peaceful conversion of the conquered infidels by means of rational argument took root in Christian Spain. The Reconquest had left the Moslems and Jews who were previously living in Moslem territory subject to Castillian and Aragonese rule, and the existence of these communities provided a strong incentive to missionaries to preach or dispute with them on religious matters (Daniel 7).

The efforts dedicated to the conversion of these non-Christian groups coincided with the foundation of two orders of friars highly imbued with the spirit of mission: the Dominicans and the Franciscans. Although they were contemporary, and in many respects similar, the first aimed at saving souls by preaching and disputation, while the second were admonished to convert by example. In other words, the purpose of the Dominicans was mainly theological, while the Franciscans chose to emphasize ethical behaviour (Daniel 38). At the time of their foundation, a powerful ingredient came to be incorporated into both monastic orders' sense of mission: the millenarist expectations of the end of history and of the renewal of the Church which had been fostered by the Joachite tradition of apocalyptic conversion.[1] Although this eschatological element was more prevalent among the Franciscans, some Dominicans also believed that history was moving towards its culmination and would climax with the miraculous conversion of non-Christians and the final age of universal peace (Reeves 172).

When in 1492 the last Moslem bastion in Spain, the kingdom of Granada, fell to Ferdinand of Aragon and Isabella of Castille, these so-called Catholic monarchs forged with strong determination the modern Spanish state along lines which they hoped would leave behind for ever the turbulent feudal past. Their goal was to end secular pluralism by instituting a politics of religious coalescence directed to the elimination of any opposition. Such a strong alliance of the secular and the religious, found strong support among those elements within the Church attached to the idea of Christianity as an order which should infiltrate and control all aspects of life. However, it also coincided with the climax in Europe of a dissatisfied stream of thought already present at least since the Middle Ages among ascetic monks and other critics of the Church's growing worldly orientation. This critical position understood Christianity in terms of the strict observance of an edifying lifestyle as well as in terms of the doctrine of poverty associated with the primitive Apostolic Church, ideals lying also, as we have seen, at the very core of the Franciscan order. In Spain, this postulated renewal of the evangelic spirit was undertaken with great vigor by no other than the confessor of Queen Isabella, Cardinal Jiménez de Cisneros, Archbishop of Toledo and Provincial of the Franciscans in Castile. Cisneros was determined to call to order the unruly and lax secular clergy, and to rigorously observe personally, from his own archiepiscopal throne, the rules of Franciscan poverty. This project found strong opposition among certain sectors of the Church, and even the Pope had to call Cisneros to the "decent observance" of his position (Bataillon 4).

Such was the historical climate when Castille, having just triumphed in its secular struggle against the internal "Other," the Moslems and Jews, had to confront now not only the challenge presented by the Jews who, having been forced to convert to Christianity were being accused of cryptojudaism, but also the external "Other," the Indians, recently introduced to the national consciousness by the conquest of America. The intention of this chapter is to focus specifically on some of the problems which conversion to Christianity brought to two very different and distinct ethnic groups: the Jews in the Peninsula, and the Indians of the old nobility of Peru. I consider the case of the Spanish Jews paradigmatic, since the upheaval created by the pogroms of 1391 and the subsequent conversions on a grand scale took place earlier than the conversion of the native Americans.[2] Baptism granted those Jews who chose to convert rather than to go into exile a plenitude of rights which permitted them to expand their opportunities beyond their traditional professions, even allowing them to reach high ecclesiastical positions. The *converso* (or Jew newly-converted to Christianity) achieved, in general terms, higher social, administrative and economic status than many "Old Christians," a fact that provoked the latters' resentment. Their reaction was to accuse the New Christians of false conversion. To have a Jewish ancestry now became highly suspicious, and this accounts for the Old Christians' delirious concept of nobility based on the racist idea that purity of blood, untainted by Judaism, was the best guarantee of genuine Christian religiosity (Castro 28–40; Domínguez 56–58). On their part, the *conversos* reacted against the forces which attempted their social exclusion by creating for themselves a space at the very heart of the religious discourse. They would claim a higher type of spiritual commitment than the mechanical practice of Old Christians.

In adopting this position, the *conversos* were vindicating the stream of thought already alluded to, which emphasized asceticism and a strict observance of the Christian code of ethics. The link with this line of thought was established through the mendicant orders, particularly Dominicans and Franciscans, under whose arduous proselytizing many Jews had undergone conversion. The same ideal of a return to the simplicity of the primitive Church resurfaced in the Spanish colonies of America. It was disseminated also by members of the religious orders, and in some cases it fostered thoughts of rebellion among those Indians who were dissatisfied with colonial rule. This is the reason why I have chosen to call this common discursive framework "the discourse of the newly-converted Christian."

I depart from a concept of narrative discourse understood as an intersubjective communicative process which, coded in language, calls upon shared values; that is, it presupposes an interaction with institutional dimensions (Foucault 215–38). The dominant or official discourse of a society participates in the political, economic and cultural powers which determine who can speak and how. Because of their social marginalization, converted Jews and literate Indians accused of doubtful conversion tried to achieve a more central position and to make themselves heard by using the official religious discourse to show its contradictions. By advocating and practicing a purer form of Christianity they were able to place themselves to their advantage in the gap created by the disparity existing between doctrine and the actual religious practice of the Old Christians.

It is difficult, if not impossible, to determine to what an extent the accusations of false conversion made against the *conversos* had a real basis. Most likely there would have been a wide spectrum ranging from those who had genuinely undergone a religious change, to those who, under false protestations of sincerity, continued practicing their old faith at great personal risk. But even in the case of genuine conversion it is logical to assume that the spiritual upheaval provoked by such a drastic inner transformation must have required a thorough catharsis leading, beyond the routine practice of Christianity, to paths of spiritual renewal verging, in some cases, on the heterodox. Theirs was a purified and decanted faith not without ambiguities, contaminations, ambivalences and attempts at syncretism, all of which were highly suspicious in the eyes of their enemies.

To come down from the level of generality to the specific, I will mention a case which illustrates the tendency of the *converso* to live the tenets of Christianity to the letter. At the beginning of the 16th century, the activities of a certain Fray Melchor were brought to the attention of the Spanish ecclesiastical authorities because of his suspicious reformist and prophetic fervor. He belonged to a family of *conversos* from the mercantile aristocracy of Burgos, in northern Spain, but his religious vocation had led him to take the frock not in one, but in a number of monastic orders, since he felt that in all of them most of their members did nor serve God but their "stomachs and their passions." He claimed that the monasteries of minor friars, which initially attracted him because of their supposed closeness to a more genuine type of Christianity, were in fact abodes of the devil. Considering himself chosen by God, and with full permission from the General of the Franciscan Order, he went from monastery to monastery fulfilling his prophetic mission by predicting a triumphant renewal of the Church, now in the hands of rapacious and cruel Inquisitors. This was a dangerous message but one which was apparently most welcome among *conversos*. However, not even his critics attacked Fray Melchor or presented him as a madman or as an impostor. On the contrary, he was said to be a devout and holy man who subjected himself to very strict penitence and continuous prayers, being rewarded for his virtue with the achievement of ecstasy (Bataillon 62–71).

It was his practice of a sublimely Christian way of life which allowed Fray Melchor to speak with such moral authority against the evils of the religious establishment, and which gave weight to his petitions for Church renewal, both at the individual and the institutional levels. He did not leave any written records, and we do not know the extent of the influence he exercised in the course of his pilgrimages. We do know that he travelled throughout Spain and that he seems to have disappeared without trace, probably into France. But he left behind him a significant contribution to pre-reformist expectations among *conversos*: it is well established that, since its inception, the Spanish Erasmian movement counted with an important *converso* presence, and equally

well established is the inclination of many *conversos* towards the ecclesiastical state and to a deeply felt religious life-style that in many cases
reached mystical heights.[3] Again, this was perceived as dangerous excess. Complaints against *conversos*, particularly in enclosed systems
like those of the religious orders, mention with remarkable consistency
the following features: critical spirit, dissatisfaction, contempt for the
accepted norm, and a permanent search for a more meaningful religious
life.[4]

   In spite of these problems it could be said that, at least in theory,
national unification in the Peninsula at both the political and the religious levels had been achieved, seemingly bringing to an end the conversion of the infidel. However, the universalist claims of the Christian
Church were greatly fostered with the discovery of the New World
making real the possibility of bringing the gospel to all peoples and all
races. In the case of Peru, the military conquest of 1533 went hand in
hand with the "spiritual conquest," and systematic proselytizing began
early with the mendicant orders taking the lead. Unlike the case of
Mexico, there is a lack of documentary material regarding Church activity in 16th Century Peru, although the role of the Dominicans is well
known, since they accompanied Pizarro in his campaigns of conquest.
It is more difficult to find documentary proof of the Franciscans' early
presence, but there do seem to have been some friars of this Order who,
as early as 1531, accompanied Sebastián de Benalcázar in his trip of
exploration from Nicaragua to Peru (Tibesar 8). The Indians, unlike
their Jewish counterparts in the Peninsula, were to be won to Christianity by preaching and example rather than by coercion and, logically,
expulsion of those who refused baptism was not an option in this case.
However, suspicions of false conversions were common, since many
priests believed that Indians showed great cunning at concealing their
traditional practices under Christian guise. At the social level this brought
difficulties for the Indians to achieve ecclesiastical positions when competing with Spaniards (Zapata 13) and, as a consequence, some of the
ethnic lords who were sufficiently acculturated took the pen and wrote
chronicle texts with the intention of vindicating the sincerity of the Indians' Catholic practice. The chronicles, or historical narratives of the
time, became thus the arena in which important practical and philo-
sophical problems created by the conquest and colonization of America
were fought. As in the case of the Jews, the religious discourse used by
these Indians incorporated a somewhat heterodox trend along the lines
of the ideal of poverty, simplicity and disinterest in material goods which
the Franciscans wanted to implement among Indian communities by

separating them from the Europeans and putting them under their exclusive guidance. It was precisely the radicalism of this project which brought the missionaries into a confrontation with the secular clergy, as well as with the Crown and with the ruling criollo elite (Florescano 89). Not surprisingly the Crown started to combat this dangerous tendency, and in 1577, Philip II issued a notorious decree banning the publication of works on indigenous traditions prepared by missionaries (Brading 120). This decision resulted in the weakening of the power of the monastic orders while strengthening that of the secular priests. But the ban was also extended to chronicles produced in the capitals of the viceroyalties, and henceforth, an author who wanted to see a work published had to take the precaution of dedicating it to the monarch himself or to a notable person close to him (Florescano, 98).

It is in this context that I would like to examine briefly the life and work of the Indian chronicler Guaman Poma de Ayala, whose attempts at integration into the colonial society of early 17th century Peru were combined with an appeal to tradition in order to recapture, as far as possible, the order existing prior to the conquest. However, this initial attempt ended up in profound disillusion, leading him to write a conflictive and contradictory work, the *Nueva crónica y buen gobierno*, designed to give advice to the Spanish authorities on appropriate ways to govern colonial society. This work was finished in approximately 1613 following thirty years of intense travelling to compile first hand evidence. Addressed to king Philip III of Spain, it combined a written text of about 1200 pages with 400 pictures drawn by the author.[5]

It is difficult to find a coherent structure in this manuscript, since it encompasses a great diversity of aspects dealing with colonial life, but it does attempt to follow the linear, chronological and teleological structure of the European historiography of the time, showing in this respect a cultural dependency also visible in the need for self-justification vis-à-vis the conqueror's religion. However, from this position, which implies a difficulty on the part of the colonized to escape the gaze of the colonizer, Guaman Poma turns the language and the conceptual apparatus of the colonizer against itself. I will show how, by using the discourse of the *converso*, he does this with regard to the accusations brought against the Indians of false conversion or defective Christian practice.

First of all, he states at the beginning of his work that he intends it for the preservation of the "blessed Catholic faith," and assumes a lofty position in matters of religiosity which combines the functions of judge and teacher. In the "Prologue to the Christian reader" (9) he proclaims that his book will be of great benefit to those Christians who need correcting in their sinful and mistaken ways. It will also be of help to priests, so that they learn how to prepare the Indians for the salvation of their souls. Since this position of authority in which Guaman Poma appoints himself does not quite fit his much humbler reality as an obnoxious Indian litigant involved in bitter land claims, he resorts with great cunning to using his own converted family and, particularly, the figure of his half-brother, the priest Martín de Ayala, as living examples of authentic Christian behaviour. He starts by telling the intended reader, the king, and also to the implied Christian European reader, that it was his father's example which inspired his older mestizo brother, the son of his mother and a Spanish captain, to enter into God's service (12), and this brother, in his turn, had had a decisive Christian influence on his entire family. This "holy man," as he calls him, did not aspire to any important clerical position. On the contrary, in his capacity as chaplain of the church at Guamanga hospital, he dedicated thirty years of his life to the poor. His life-style could not be more simple and ascetic: a rooster was the clock which would wake him up in time for prayers and for the visits he dedicated to the poor and the ill. He did a great deal of penance, sleeping little and on a humble mattress filled with straw, disciplined his flesh, and permanently wore a punitive hair shirt. He never blasphemed or had hard words for men, women, or indeed for any living creature, since he also had a great respect for animals. This last point in particular seems to have been inspired by the most bucolic aspects of Saint Francis Assisi's life, since Guaman Poma observes that birds used to come to sing for his brother. Even mice remained transfixed in respect while he was dedicated to his devotions. The author also has special care to show how Martín de Ayala lived a chaste life as a celibate priest, to the point that when he spoke to women he would draw his eyes to the ground to avoid the slightest temptation. As to his generosity, it is beyond reproach: in spite of his own lack of economic resources, he always gave alms to the poor. So much virtue in one single individual had been most pleasing in the eyes of God, something made manifest in the fact that the angels from heaven would appear regularly to Martín (14–16). After such an exemplary life, this holy man died in Guamanga leaving his few possessions to the hospital to be further used among the poor of the town who, all of them, lamented his death (18). This was, no doubt, a well-deserved tribute to a life well lived.

The missionaries sent to America were permanently afraid that the often unchristian behaviour of the Spanish laymen might make the new religion appear as a mockery to the natives (Phelan 98). Guaman Poma goes even further: his strongest attacks are directed not at the layman, but at the unethical deportment of the clergy, particularly the secular. He favorably compares Indian life under the Incas to life under the Spaniards on the grounds that the latter exhibit negative traits that encourage misbehavior. In his view, New Christians have a clear advantage over Old Christians, and they would continue to have it if only they were well instructed and presented with positive moral examples by the clergy (1024).

It is not surprising, then, that after having learned at the beginning of the chronicle about the paragon of perfect Christianity presented by Martín de Ayala, we should later encounter examples far less edifying among the Spanish clergy. Guaman Poma opens the section dedicated to the Christian priests in "the kingdom of Peru," by focusing on the social role of the Church, its ministers and its teachings. What he presents here stands in stark contrast to what the reader remembers about the life of his dead brother. Charging against the "pestilence of bad Christians," Guaman Poma enumerates in this section (594–658) a veritable catalogue of unchristian behaviour on the part of priests (*padres de las doctrinas*)[6] who abandon themselves to the possession of silver, rich clothes, "things of this world" and sins of the flesh. This, he writes, is not the type of example that Spaniards need, let alone the new Christians, namely, the Indians and Blacks. How can a priest like this thunder against fornication, wonders Guaman Poma, when he himself has a dozen children? How can he confess or absolve sinners when he himself has sinned mortally? But still more serious is the fact that the priests betray their role as converters of infidels through their satanic pride and choleric temper, and that they interfere with the wills of dying Indians, endangering the intention that the lands and houses of the dead pass to the family or the community. It is in fact a recurrent complaint of Guaman Poma that secular priests take justice in their own hands, without proper recourse to the authorities appointed by the Crown. This was obviously a sensitive question about which he felt deeply. In sum, these priests act more like feudal lords than like patient and loving teachers, owning slaves and mistreating the Indians, who fear them and end up escaping to the mountains.

If, as stated above, the official position regarding conversion of the Indians was to win them for Christianity through example and not coercion, Guaman Poma leaves the reader in no doubt as to who had better accomplish this task: certainly not the Spanish priests, alienating native people with their behaviour, but the humble "mestizo" who had set a living example for the entire community.

However, it is significant that not all the Peruvian clergy comes under the hammer of Guaman Poma's systematic attacks. After page 658, he starts his positive presentation of Christian practice among men dedicated to God's service, and although, at the very beginning of his book, he had granted a privileged and paradigmatic position to his own brother, he now generously extends his appreciation to Franciscans and Jesuits.[7] Of the first, he praises their saintliness and Christianity, their obedience and humble charity, their love of their neighbor and, particularly, of the poor. No complaints have ever been heard against them regarding the mismanagement of justice, and to confess with them, unlike confession with the secular priests of the *doctrinas*, is a pleasure. The love that humble people feel for them is clearly visible in that when the friars come to the Indian villages, everybody rushes to kiss their hands. The priests of the Society of Jesus, are also full of love and charity. Like the Franciscans, they do not get involved in litigious matters, nor do they covet other people's property. On the contrary, they freely give of what is theirs. They are so fully dedicated to their task that they never leave their house without their superior's permission. They are erudite and great preachers, addressing not only to Spaniards and criollos, but also to Indians. After their Order came to the kingdom of Peru, one could say that God himself had arrived in this land (682). Secular priests should imitate the reverend fathers of the Society of Jesus, Franciscans and hermits and regard them with the utmost consideration, since they attract Christians with their love and charity. They observe a retired and exemplary life in their monasteries or communities, and that is what good priests should also do. They should humiliate themselves under God and leave the riches and vanities of the world, casting off the flesh and the devil and winning souls to be presented to "the eyes of the Holy Trinity." It was for this that Christ made himself into a man and became an apostle (640).

It is obvious where Guaman Poma stands with regards to the controversy in the American Church between the regular and the secular clergy. Monastic or cloistered life was for him of the essence when it came to men dedicated to God's service. Life in the world as practiced by the secular clergy predisposes to lust, a lack of humility, and the desire to increase their revenues and the prerogatives of their office. Although he admits the well-deserved reputation of the Dominicans as learned men and good preachers who have converted many people in the whole world to the true faith, he criticizes them on the basis of their arrogance and propensity to cruel punishment in their *doctrinas*. His advice is that they should restrict themselves to life in their monasteries, as their founder Saint Dominic had done and had intended them to do (692).

So far, research on Guaman Poma has focused mostly on those aspects of his work which emphasize the indigenous social resistance to the colonial system, and has tended to consider that he uses religious language in order to better assert his own claims and those of his people. There is no doubt that the diatribe against bad Christians, which occupies such a prominent place in Guaman Poma's chronicle, is linked to a more general denunciation of the colonial social structure, but there is also a sense of moral outrage in his accusations which rings a true note, and which make the author sound like the proverbial prophet wailing in the desert. This was a man who thought that Christianity was nothing if not a lived experience, and who could have made Christ's words his own: "By their fruits ye shall know them" (St. Matthew 7:20).

In the same way, in the Peninsula, the charges of slack practice by the New Christians against the Old, were part of a wider denunciation, in this case against the inquisitorial apparatus and the systematic persecution of the Jews made under pretext of their false conversion. However, my interest in this chapter has been to isolate from the larger context a particular discourse that, in the name of what is considered to be most genuinely Christian, sought to legitimize the human value and social worth of two ethnic groups, the Peninsular Jews and the Amerindians, accused and marginalized, paradoxically, in the name of Christianity. Skillfully turning the table against the accuser, both Jew and Indian engaged in an emotional and rhetorical contest which, at least in the eyes of History and at the textual level, won for them the authority and dignity refused to them by their contemporaries.

Notes

1. Joachim of Fiore (c. 1135–1202) was a Calabrian mystical prophet who divided human history into three great epochs: The age of God the Father, from Adam to Christ; the age of God the Son, from Christ to 1260; and a prophesied age of the Holy Ghost which would begin in 1260. This third age, Joachim's version of the millennial kingdom of the Apocalypse, would bring, after a period of great troubles, a resurrection of the Spiritual Church leading to contemplative life and the practice of apostolic poverty. The preparation for this period would be carried out by a new order of monks who would preach the new gospel throughout the world (Phelan 14–15).

2. In June 1391 the populace of Seville undertook the assault and destruction

of the Jewish quarters. This terrible event, the reasons for which are still insufficiently understood by historians, brought death or expedient baptism to the majority of its inhabitants, and was swiftly followed by similar pogroms in other towns of Andalucía and of the Mediterranean coast. But it was not until the decree of expulsion of March 31, 1492 that the Jews were forced to choose between baptism or exile.

3. At the beginning of the 16th Century, Cardinal Juan Martínez Silíceo promulgated in his archiepiscopal see of Toledo a Statute of Blood Purity which prevented *conversos* from acceding to any positions in the chapter of the cathedral. His decision was based on the fact that an enormous proportion of the clergy in the diocese was of Jewish origin (Domínguez 81).

4. I will mention here two typical examples of complaints about the *conversos'* restlessness: In 1532, Abbot Edme de Saulieu, visiting numerous Cistercian monasteries in the Peninsula, was disturbed to encounter in them an abundance of a type of neophyte whose psychological disposition he considered "dangerous." Some years earlier, in 1525, the Grand Inquisitor Valdés had complained to Pope Julius III that among the Observant Franciscans the New Christians scorned and verbally abused Old Christians. He even insinuated that the former were plotting the total control of the Order to return "en masse" to Judaism (Domínguez 99).

5. The manuscript, however, never reached the king's hands. For whatever the reason, it got lost in the Crown's bureaucratic machinery, and it ended up in the Royal Library of Denmark, in Copenhagen, where it was "discovered" by the German bibliophile Richard A. Pietschman in 1908.

6. The *doctrinas* were Indian parishes in which the local youth of both sexes were instructed in the Christian faith. It became customary for the viceroy to establish the spheres of religious activity between the mendicant orders and the parochial, or diocesan clergy. While the parish priest lived in the immediate vicinity, administering his parish and tending to the daily needs of his people, the friar worked wherever the opportunity presented itself or his superiors commanded. The reluctance of the latter to restrict their movements by involving themselves in the *doctrinas* is shown in that it was only in 1557 that the Franciscans in Peru began to accept parishes of Indians. Even until much later, the friars newly arrived from Spain to Peru kept a prejudice against the *frailes doctrineros*, whom they considered as "friars on the road to ruin" (Tibesar 37–38). No doubt Guaman Poma shared this prejudice, as it is clear in his lashing against those priests who publicly sinned with the unmarried women gathered under their charge in the *doctrina*.

7. The Jesuit presence in Peru is attested to date from at least 1571, when Father José de Acosta (a descendant of Jews, incidentally), was requested by the General of the Order, Father Francisco de Borja, to organize the first Andean *prioridades*. In 1576, Acosta called the First Provincial Peruvian Congregation of the Society of Jesus. He remained in Peru, actively involved in the creation of schools, until May 1586, when he left the country to establish his residence in Mexico (O'Gorman 174–75).

Works Cited

Bataillon, Marcel. *Erasmo y España.* Madrid, Fondo de Cultura Económica, 1991.

Brading, D.A. *The First America. The Spanish Monarchy, Creole Patriots, and the Liberal State. 1492–1867.* Cambridge UP, 1991.

Castro, Américo. *De la edad conflictiva.* Madrid, Taurus, 1972.

Daniel, E. Randolph. *The Franciscan Concept of Mission in the High Middle Ages.* Lexington: UP of Kentucky, 1975.

Domínguez Ortiz, Antonio. *Los judeoconversos en España y América.* Madrid, Istmo, 1988.

Florescano, Enrique. *Memory, Myth and Time in Mexico. From the Aztecs to Independence.* Austin: U of Texas P, 1994.

Foucault, Michel. "The discourse on language", in *The Archaeology of Knowledge.* New York: Harper & Row, 1972. 215–38.

Guaman Poma de Ayala, Felipe. *Nueva crónica y buen gobierno.* Eds. John V. Murra, Rolena Adorno, Jorge L. Urioste. Madrid, Historia 16, 1987.

O'Gorman, Edmundo. *Cuatro historiadores de Indias.* México, D.F.: Alianza Editorial Mexicana, 1989.

Phelan, John Leddy. *The Millennial Kingdom of the Franciscans in the New World.* Berkeley and Los Angeles: U of California P, 1970.

Reeves, Marjorie. *The Influence of Prophecy in the Later Middle Ages. A Study in Joachimism.* Oxford: Clarendon P, 1969.

Tibesar, Antonine. *Franciscan Beginnings in Colonial Peru.* Washington, D.C.: Academy of American Franciscan History, 1953.

Zapata, Roger A. *Guaman Poma, indigenismo y estética de la dependencia en la cultura peruana.* Minneapolis: Institute for the Study of Ideologies and Literature, 1989.

• 5 •

The Development of an Englishman:
Thomas Nashe's *The Unfortunate Traveller*

Laura Scavuzzo Wheeler

Thomas Nashe's 1594 fictional account of an Englishman abroad, *The Unfortunate Traveller; or, the Life of Jack Wilton*, brings to the forefront many of the prejudices present in Elizabethan society. The hero of the work, the irreverent page Jack Wilton, encounters an array of foreign figures grotesque and comical in his travels through Europe, which culminate in Jack's confrontations with the dangers of a corrupt and degenerate Italy. *The Unfortunate Traveller* draws on many of the most popular genres of its time, as Nashe's character recounts for his English audience the adventures he undergoes while outside the boundaries of a safer England. Alternating between serious and flippant tones, Jack describes locales he encounters in the style of current travelogues and provides commentary on the wild events he depicts. Throughout, Jack proves a narrator hardly to be trusted, a quality which he constantly points out to his audience with sarcastic asides. Ann Rosalind Jones notes that Nashe "plunges, one by one, into the oral and written forms of his time: humanist oration, Anglican sermon, jest-book anecdotes, urban journalism, satire, aristocratic lyric, revenge tragedy," without committing to any one of these literary modes ("Inside the Outsider" 64). Although these various modes are held together by the forceful voice of Nashe's character Jack Wilton, the book's many elements have led to much critical argument over how the novel as a whole should be labeled.[1]

Although Nashe's novel resists easy categorization and challenges the genres of its age as it plays with literary convention, in its treatment of the Other the novel's ideas prove less innovative. Nashe draws on pejorative stereotypes in his portrayal of the foreigners who assault mischievous Jack on his travels. The French, Italians, and Dutch, Anabaptists, Saracens and Jews, among many other groups such as women and Catholics, appear as exaggerated types who pose many dangers to the unwary Englishman. The foreign, "naturally" grotesque, threatens Jack's life, character and religion—indeed, his national and personal identity—and therefore must be destroyed within the context of his *Life*. Despite the lighthearted tone in which these ideas are presented, Nashe's fictional treatment of outsiders corresponds quite closely to commonly-held attitudes toward women, travel, and the foreign in Elizabethan England. The Elizabethan could establish standards for his own identity through his engagement with such grotesque figures as Nashe presents, clearly delineating by contrast the profile of a proper English gentleman and his proper English state.

The figure of the English traveler provides a particularly interesting way for the modern critic to examine the anxieties which occupied those who remained in England. Once the traveler departs from the security of home, he becomes an outsider in a foreign land, at the mercy of uncertain circumstances and unfamiliar cultures. His reactions to such strangeness reveal many of his culture's assumptions and methods of thought. As G. K. Hunter remarks, "The impact of foreigners on a community or culture is affected, obviously enough, both by the opportunities for contact and knowledge that exist, and by the framework of assumptions within which information about foreign lands and customs is presented and received" (3). At home in England's self-proclaimed Protestant culture, the values of the Englishman's culture are transparent. Abroad, however, the Englishman is suddenly made aware of values which are not his own, and he is the outsider. Ironically, he responds to his marginalized condition by denouncing the dominant cultures which he encounters. Consistently we see that the English traveler carries his prejudices along with him; he knows what he will see, he projects his worldview onto the landscape he meets, and his descriptions of his travels for the English audience inevitably confirm its prejudices. Through the eyes of many English travelers, foreigners, even though they are at home, are the outsiders—inappropriate, corrupt, and grotesque.

Of course, the suspicion and fear which surround discussions of travel were grounded in real dangers which faced the Renaissance traveler. As Clare Howard points out in her study of English Renaissance travelers, during the war between England and Spain, any Englishman caught on Spanish territory was a lawful prisoner for ransom, and Spanish territory included Sicily, Naples and Milan, and to a certain degree Rome because of the papal alliance with Spain (76–77). In addition, agents of the Inquisition worked alongside the persuasive Jesuits to convert Protestants back to Catholicism, and the cases of English travelers who converted while far from home and subject to Catholic pressures prompted many Englishmen to discourage foreign travel because of the threats to their religion (77_89). Adventurous accounts of travelers' encounters with highwaymen, swindlers and "the subtelty of spies, the wonderful cunning of Inn-keepers and baudes" (Kirchnerus) indicate that other problems faced the Renaissance traveler as well. Henry Peacham's 1638 collection of essays *The Truth of Our Times* includes such pragmatic advice as how to conduct oneself carefully in foreign inns, how to protect one's money, and what to eat while traveling (217–22). Warnings against travel to Italy were especially strong, invoking the dangers of *bandettos*, jealous lovers, lewd women, and Catholic agents who attempt to take advantage of the incautious. The risks and discomforts of travel suggested by such accounts are also evident in the relation between the words *travel* and *travail,* which spring from the same root and which in Renaissance spelling, are often used interchangeably.

Not all of these fears can be located in physical dangers posed to the person of the traveler, however. In advice books, treatises on travel, travel accounts as well as fiction, the Englishman abroad is portrayed as a perpetually endangered figure who is threatened in mind as well as in spirit. Some of his troubles reside in the indignities of having to behave according to non-English rules. Jack Wilton frequently excuses his misfortunes abroad by claiming, "my fault was more pardonable in that I was a stranger altogether ignorant of their customs" (270). More bitter, Nashe's character of an exiled English Earl complains of his lack of authority in Italy, assigning animalistic traits to the disempowered traveler:

> He that is a traveller must have the back of an ass to bear all, a tongue like the tail of a dog to flatter all, the mouth of a hog to eat what is set before him, the ear of a merchant to hear all and say nothing; and if this be not the highest step of thralldom, there is no liberty or freedom. It is but a mild kind of subjection to be the servant of one master at once, but when thou hast a thousand thousand masters, as the veriest botcher, tinker, or cobbler freeborn will domineer over a foreigner, and think to be his better or master in company, then shalt thou find there's no such hell as to leave thy father's house (thy natural habitation) to live in the land of bondage. (283)[2]

The exiled Englishman is not pleased with his status as "Other" in Italy, a condition created by his lack of power in the face of foreign signs which he is not at liberty to interpret. The native tinker or cobbler has greater knowledge than does he, the unwilling foreigner, thus creating a balance of power disagreeable to the nobleman both in personal relations and in terms of class structure. Outside of his homeland, the class distinctions so important to the nobleman dissolve. The Earl advises Jack to avoid travel and its accompanying dangers altogether, and cautions that the Englishman is best at home in England: "Believe me, no air, no bread, no fire, no water agree with a man or doth him any good out of his own country. Cold fruits never prosper in a hot soil, nor hot in a cold" (287). His advice coincides with commonly articulated fears based on the theory of climatic influence, that inhabitants of cool northern regions such as England were not only uncomfortable in the hotter southern regions of the world, but because of their climate, possessed less subtlety than Mediterraneans. Thus in their hearty plainness, the English were at the mercy of the sneaky southerners in matters politic.[3] Hunter notes that the traditional opposition between Northern phlegm and Southern blood was "much invoked to contrast the grossness of the Teutons with the passionate conduct of the Latins" (15); the balance between extremes, of course, was held by the English. "He is not fit to travel," Nashe's gentleman warns, "that cannot . . . live on serpents, make nourishing food even of poison" (284).

Italy stood as the pinnacle of southern debauchery and spiritual corruption. In his 1570 educational treatise *The Scholemaster*, Roger Ascham articulates a common fear in early modern England of the fate of the English traveler in Italy:

> He, that by liuing, & traueling in *Italie*, bringeth home into England out of *Italie*, the Religion, the learning, the policie, the experience, the maners of *Italie*. That is to say, for Religion, Papistrie or worse: for learnyng, lesse commonly than they caried out with them: for pollicie, a factious hart, a discoursing head, a mynde to medle in all mens matters: for experience, plentie of new mischieues neuer knowne in England before: for maners, varietie of vanities, and chaunge of filthy lyuing. These be the inchantementes of *Circes*, brought out of *Italie*, to marre mens maners in England . . . . (229–30)

Ascham's fears of the Italian relate to deep-rooted religious and cultural prejudices which Elizabethans maintained against Italy as the center of Catholicism and as a place of corruption and frivolity. But while suspicion toward Italy was common in English writings, it was by no means universal. That Italy occupied conflicting positions in the minds of the English complicated the issue of foreign travel to Italy. As Ascham warns, Italy may have contained dangerous temptations for the traveling Englishman, but it was the inheritor of the glory of ancient Rome, and as the country in which numerous classical texts had been rediscovered and studied by early humanists, and as the culture in which Castiglione's esteemed *Il Cortegiano* originated, Italy promised to cultivate and polish a young Englishman for life at court.[4] Thus the English traveler to Italy trod a dangerous line: while he could gain sophistication and knowledge, he ran the risk of succumbing to Italian corruptions and subsequently, of occupying a doubtful space in English society on his return as a result of the undesirable Italian qualities he had acquired.

The threats which Englishmen saw in travel to Italy were numerous: while there, the infamous lasciviousness of Italians endangered the traveler's virtue, just as the Catholic Church would assault his Protestantism. Ascham admits to having traveled to Italy once, where he "sawe in that litle tyme, in one Citie, more libertie to sinne, than euer I hard tell of in our noble Citie of London in ix. yeare" (234). Such lewdness, he then cautions, will assault the Englishman from the moment he enters Italy, and will corrupt his morals to such a degree that when he returns to England, he will be among those "common contemners of mariage and readie persuaders of all other to the same" (235).[5] The fame of Italian, especially Venetian, courtesans contributed to the portrayal of Italy as a place of "vanitie and vice" (223), a characterization on which the travel writer Thomas Coryat capitalizes in his scurrilous *Coryat's Crudities* in 1611. Antony Munday represents Italy as menacing not only to the individual traveler's integrity, but also to England itself: in his 1582 *The English Romayne Lyfe*, he describes English Catholics in Rome as they torture the martyr Richard Atkins (who tried to convert the Pope) and train to overthrow Elizabeth's Protestant rule (5–17, 100).

In addition, the English traveler could affect Italian mannerisms and return fancified and effete. In anti-travel literature, the Italianate Englishman described as "un diabolo incarnato"[6] represents the ultimate degradation of an honorable Englishman as a result of foolish travel, and provides material for numerous parodies and ridicule. The traveler to Italy who has become too Italian is often depicted as both ridiculous and as an opponent to English values. Jack Wilton's gentlemanly advisor tells him of the metamorphosis Italy will enact on English plainness:

It makes [the Englishman] to kiss his hand like an ape, cringe his neck like a starveling . . . . From thence he brings atheism, the art of epicurizing, the art of whoring, the art of poisoning, the art of sodomitry. The only probable good thing they have to keep us from utterly condemning it is that it maketh a man an excellent courtier, a curious carpet knight—which is, by interpretation, a fine close lecher, a glorious hypocrite. (286)

Elsewhere Thomas Nashe describes Italianate Englishmen as "taffeta fools with their feathers" and mocks their literary pretensions:

Tut, says our English Italians, the finest wits our climate sends forth are but dry-brained dolts in comparison of other countries; whom if you interrupt with *redde rationem*, they will tell you of Petrarch, Tasso, Celiano, with an infinite number of others, to whom if I should oppose Chaucer, Lydgate, Gower, with such like that lived under the tyrrany of ignorance, I do think their best lovers would be much discontented with the collation of contraries if I should write over all their heads "Hail fellow, well met!" One thing I am sure of, that each of these three have vaunted their meters with as much admiration in English as ever the proudest Ariosto did his verse in Italian. (Preface to *Menaphon* 430)

Even the aspects of Italian travel which are most strongly defended—the opportunity to gain knowledge and to complete the education of a gentleman—become suspect when they threaten one's allegiance to English things.

From the first mention of Italy in *The Unfortunate Traveller* Nashe capitalizes on stereotypes of Italy. Jack Wilton, a page to the Earl of Surrey, after several episodes of mischief in the English camps meets up with his master, and the two set out for Italy, "that country which was such a curious moulder of wits" (248). Jack himself questions their destination, "musing what changeable humour had so suddenly seduced him [the Earl] from his native soil to seek out needless perils in these parts beyond sea . . . " (238). The ordinarily sober Earl has undertaken his travels, not for respectable, educational purposes, but for love of a Florentine beauty newly arrived in England. The besotted Earl describes Geraldine in exotic, decidedly foreign terms, evoking the wonders of the East:

> She it is that is come out of Italy to bewitch all the wise men of England . . . Her high exalted sunbeams have set the pheonix nest of my breast on fire, and I myself have brought Arabian spiceries of sweet passions and praises to furnish out the funeral flame of my folly. (238)

Despite the romantic vocabulary with which Jack and his master begin their voyage, the moment the two arrive in Venice an assortment of exaggerated Italian evils assaults them. Jack describes their reception:

> having scarce looked about us, a precious supernatural pander, apparelled in all points like a gentleman and having half a dozen languages in his purse, entertained us in our own tongue very paraphrastically and eloquently, and maugre all other pretended acquaintance would have us in a violent kind of courtesy to be the guests of his appointment. His name was Petro de Campo Frego, a notable practitioner in the policy of bawdry. The place whither he brought us was a pernicious courtesan's house named Tabitha the Temptress's, a wench that could set as civil a face on it as chastity's first martyr Lucretia. (248)

The fame of Venetian courtesans such as Tabitha symbolized to English eyes Italy's sexual lasciviousness and looseness. In *The Scholemaster* Roger Ascham mentions the thousands of courtesans with which Italy is teeming. Several years later, Thomas Coryat portrays his meeting with a courtesan as a central element of his 1611 travelogue *Coryat's Crudities*; as he explains, "I will . . . make relation of their Cortezans also, as being a thing incident and very proper to this discourse, especially because the name of a Courtezan of Venice is famoused ouer all Christendome" (261). He continues, "so infinite are the allurements of these amorous Calypsoes, that the fame of them hath drawn many to Venice from some of the remotest parts of Christendome, to contemplate their beauties, and enioy their pleasing dalliances" (265). Ann Rosalind Jones points out that Coryat links the erotic power of the courtesan to the splendor of her city, portraying Venice "as an insistently feminine landscape" which must, like a shameful woman, ultimately be rejected despite its great beauty ("Italians and

Others" 108).

Similarly, the courtesan Jack first meets turns out to be a "graceless fornicatress," a "whore, this quean, this courtesan, this common of ten thousand . . . !" (250). But before denouncing her, Jack leads his audience with fascination through the interior of the courtesan Tabitha's house. His descriptions, again calling to mind the even more foreign Orient, serve several purposes. In illustrating the extent of her ability to deceive, Jack's details link that deceiving ability to her Catholicism and emphasize the foreignness of the realm in which the two Englishmen are now immersed:

> What will you conceit to be in any saint's house that was there to seek? Books, pictures, beads, crucifixes—why there was a haberdasher's shop of them in every chamber. I warrant you should not see one set of her neckercher perverted or turned awry, not a piece of hair displaced. On her beds there was not a wrinkle of any wallowing to be found; her pillows bare out as smooth as a groaning wife's belly, and yet she was a Turk and an infidel, and had more doings than all her neighbours besides. Us for our money they used like emperors. (248)

Catholic elements of worship litter the courtesan's abode. In a diluted version of iconoclastic attacks on Rome, Jack points to what, in Protestant views, are signs of a dead theology based on empty show. And yet, despite the icons and crucifixes, the den of iniquity that Jack obviously expects in Tabitha's quarters, is instead a house which appears respectable, emphasizing how little Jack the Englishman can trust appearances in Italy. Like the panderer, who greets them eloquently and "like a gentleman," the courtesan seems to be a lady. The panderer, too, proves unworthy of his initial impression, and Jack rejects him in a violent diatribe, proclaiming that his body should reflect his inner evil:

> Detestable, detestable, that the flesh and the devil should deal by their factors! I'll stand to it, there is not a pander but hath vowed paganism. The devil himself is not such a devil as he, so be he perform his function aright. He must have the back of an ass, the snout of an elephant, the wit of a fox, and the teeth of a wolf; he must fawn like a spaniel, crouch like a Jew, leer like a sheepbiter. If he be half a puritan and have scripture

continually in his mouth he speeds the better . . . God be merciful to our pander . . . he was seen in all the seven liberal deadly sciences; not a sin but he was as absolute in as Satan himself. Satan could never have supplanted us so as he did. I may say to you he planted in us the first Italianate wit that we had. (252)

Thus the two figures Jack meets immediately upon entering Italy represent common stereotypes of the Italian, which Jack links to the demonic as soon as he catches sight of their "true" natures.

Margaret Scott has shown that many of the English ideas of deceitful Italians relate to Elizabethan perceptions of Machiavelli's political writings:

As the devil's henchman, or even the devil incarnate, Machiavelli became associated with every kind of sin . . . the Machiavel . . . who in the context of Elizabethan drama seeks to exploit religion for his own ends or to persuade others to accept his authority and his precepts, is necessarily the enemy of true religion, established order, and real virtue. (154, 163)

The Machiavel's refusal to recognize the higher authority of God, of course, explains much of the dread he inspired. Jack Wilton describes the Machiavel as worse than Satan in his trickery. But greater than the fear of his beliefs was the threat that the Machiavel can appear one way, and be another underneath: the Machiavel's deceit is not always apparent. The exiled Englishman warns Jack that Italians will deliberately deceive the honest Englishman, "the plainest dealing soul that ever God put life in . . . the Italians [have] no such sport as to see poor English asses how soberly they swallow Spanish [poisoned] figs; devour any hook baited for them" (284). When Jack arrives in Rome, he hears of the bandettos, who murder around Rome and Naples. An example of the general danger and savagery of Italy, the bandettos are additionally threatening because they do not declare themselves:

Disguised as they go, they are not known from strangers; sometimes they will shroud themselves under the habit of grave citizens. In this consideration, neither citizen nor stranger, gentleman, knight, marquis, or any other may wear any weapon endamageable upon pain of the strappado. (270)

Although the English traveler enters Italy armed with the knowledge of the Italians' dishonesty and lasciviousness, he could be led astray by seemingly innocuous signs. Jack and his master's experiences illustrate that the possibility of contradiction between outer appearance and inner self constantly confronts the traveler in Italy, where Machiavellian characters such as the "chaste" courtesan, the cunning pimp, and disguised *bandettos* populate every scene. The consistent ridicule of and distrust exhibited toward the Italianate Englishman, the "carpet knight" overly-trained in the manners of Italy, reveal Elizabethan culture's uncertainty over just how and why the "plain Englishman" can change while away from England. As Jack Wilton declares, the panderer's corruption "planted in us the first Italianate wit that we had" (252)—the beginnings of a transformation to Machiavellian deceitfulness. Elizabethans' defense against uncertainties over the transformative effects of travel often emphasize the differences between their culture and those of foreign countries, by exaggerating the identifying features of other nationalities. G. K. Hunter notes that "[t]he foreigner could only 'mean' something important, and so be effective as a literary figure, when the qualities observed in him were seen to involve a simple and significant relationship to real life at home" (13).

One of the easiest forms of ridicule focused on the excesses of fashion. Vitriolic attacks on the frivolities of dress spring from a long tradition, and benefit from the strength of a misogynistic discourse which traditionally rejected fashion as effeminate and foolish. An exaggeration of customs in dress visibly illustrates differences among nationalities. Throughout *The Unfortunate Traveller*, Nashe's narrator Jack consistently describes others, and himself, by their attire. Fashion offers the traveler a clue to the nature of the wearer, and the traveler is provided with a system, however inaccurate, for reading the others he meets. Nashe's use of clothing to delineate character resembles the approaches found in common misogynistic diatribes which demonize women in their foolish abuse of fashion. Stephen Gosson's 1595 tract addressed to English women, *Quippes for upstart newfangled gentlewomen* contains vehement invectives against the "fantastical forreigne toyes, daylie used in womens apparell."[7] The *Quippes* outlines in scurrilous detail the excesses in "garish pompe" which Englishwomen are displaying, and chastises the foolish women for their shameful public marketing of themselves. In addition to the sexual license which the fashions suggest, the tract identifies women's fashion as a highly visible site of national susceptibility to foreign infection. English women, Gosson emphasizes repeatedly, should never wear the "fashions fonde" of another nation. What we find later, as the English begin to establish themselves as a nation unique and separate from their European neighbors, is that fashions are used to delineate differences not only between the sexes, but also between England and her neighbors.

By focusing on the dress of his characters, Thomas Nashe can play with the identity of his narrator and with Jack's own view of himself while traveling. Early on in the narrative, the "ugly mechanicall Captain," persuaded by Jack that he is a "myraculous polititian," deserts the English army to the French, but caught in his own stupidity, he is flogged and sent back to the English, who in turn flog him again. Although Nashe presents this absurd Machiavellian character at the start of the novel and ridicules his attempts at pretense, he continues to explore the idea of disguise. For example, as Jonathan Crewe notes, Jack Wilton wears clothes which "allow him to proclaim himself" because they don't hide what is underneath; "forsaking naked innocence, the speaker paradoxically recovers it to a degree by being what he seems and hiding nothing, not even the artfulness of his self-exposure" (69). Confronting the idea of the disguised English traveler brought up earlier in the figure of the Captain, Jack opens himself to scrutiny. His outfit, it turns out, is an amalgamation of national fashions. Jack's apparel resembles just that which William Harrison, in his sketch of Elizabethan apparel for *Holinshed's Chronicles*, decries: the Englishman has no apparel of his own by which to declare himself; rather, he turns from one foreign fashion to the next. Jack has adopted the signs of other cultures, and he wears a hodgepodge of foreign nationalities on his body. The fears of the exiled Englishman are realized in the person of the traveler Jack Wilton, who once away from England abandons his society's values.

Yet, although Jack proves a rather amoral, opportunistic and irreverent Englishman, he nowhere approaches the grotesque extremes of behavior and appearance as do the foreigners he meets. Most of the women Jack meets are grotesque, sexually voracious and corrupt beneath their initially attractive appearances. The women in Nashe's *Unfortunate Traveller* are not, however, alone in their dissoluteness: nearly everyone Jack encounters on his adventures is grotesque. *The Unfortunate Traveller* is a novel about Jack's confrontation with multiple Others—foreigners and others excluded from Englishness—and the transformations wrought on Jack through those encounters. Through the irreverent character of Jack Wilton, Nashe explores the nature of the traveler who moves from one social class to another, among nationalities and from alliance to alliance. At the end, Jack marries "his rich courtesan," the recent widow of a wealthy Italian, and returns to the service of the English king. He is a traveler who assumes the negative traits of the nationalities he encounters, while at the same time constantly criticizing anything non-English. Each type Jack meets is made obvious by country, ethnicity, religion, or gender. The importance of outward appearance is established early on in the novel, as Jack and other pages in Henry VIII's court, concerned about how to identify a gentleman, outwardly mark the visitors' bodies:

> In which regard it was considered of by the common table of the cupbearers what a perilsome thing it was to let any stranger or out-dweller approach so near the precincts of the prince as the great chamber without examining what he was and giving him his pass. Whereupon we established the like order, but took no money of them as they did, only for a sign that he had not passed our hands unexamined we set a red mark on either of his ears, and so let him walk as authentical. (225)

Although labeling strangers does not always prove so easy, Jack's descriptions indicate that most others wear a "red mark" of some sort, usually in their dress. For instance, Jack witnesses John Leyden and the Anabaptists as they come forth onto the battlefield at Munster; their ridiculous, common attire for the battle illustrates for Jack the error of their ways (229). Part of the Anabaptists' error, it appears, is linked to their lower class; yet Jack goes on to link their problems to their foreignness when he remarks,

> So fares it up and down with our cynical, reformed foreign churches, they will digest no grapes of great bishoprics, forsooth, because they cannot tell how to come by them. They must shape their coats, good men, according to their cloth, and do as they may, not as they would, yet they must give us leave here in England that are their honest neighbors, if we have more cloth than they, to make our garment somewhat larger. (233–34)

Jack uses the metaphor of clothing to express his scornful attitude toward the Anabaptists.

This approach to description continues as he travels through Germany and mocks the scholastics and townspeople of Wittenberg. The language Jack hears there, and the people's appearance confirm stereotypes of Germans as boorish drunks.[8] Jack notes that the "distinguished liveries" of the burghers are "livery faces . . . for they were most of them hot-livered drunkards, and had all the coat colours of sanguine, purple, crimson, copper, carnation, that were to be had in their countenances. Filthy knaves . . ." (241). The grotesque Germans even come to resemble more distant, inhuman foreigners: one German orator "had a sulphurous big swollen large face like a Saracen, eyes like two Kentish oysters, a mouth that opened as wide every time he spake as one of those old knit trap doors, a beard as though it had been made of a bird's nest plucked in pieces, which consisteth of straw, hair, and dirt mixed together. He was apparelled in black leather new liquored . . . faced before and behind with a boisterous bear skin . . ." (241–42). The speech delivered by this fantastic foreigner ends up comparing the Munsterians to infidels, as the man puns on the etymology of his social class's title: "Mechanical men they call us, and not amiss, for most of us being *Maechi*, that is, cuckolds and whoremasters, fetch our antiquity from the temple of *Maecha*, where Mahomet is hung up" (243).

Despite the grotesque natures of the Germans and the exaggerated Italian stereotypes Jack meets, no characters are portrayed as viciously as the Jews Zadok and Zachary who betray Jack. "Of an ill tree I hope you are not so ill-sighted in grafting to expect good fruit," Jack warns the audience of the Jewish characters (293). Not just the Jews' clothing illustrates their corruption; their very bodies, grotesque in the extreme, reveal the error of their religious and social values. Jack, held captive by the carnivorous Doctor Zachary, observes the Jew's lifestyle with all the horror of the Englishman viewing the grotesque Other:

> Not the very crumbs that fall from his table but Zachary sweeps together and of them moulds up a manna. Of the ashy parings of his bread he would make conserve of chippings. Out of bones after the meat was eaten off he would alchemize an oil that he sold for a shilling a dram. His snot and spittle a hundred times he hath put over to his apothecary for snow-water. Any spider he would temper to perfect mithridate. His rheumatic eyes when he went in the wind, or rose early in a morning, dropped as cool alum water as you would request. He was Dame Niggardise's sole heir and executor . . . The liquor out of his shoes he would wring to make a sacred balsamum against barrenness. (290)

Nashe even places some of the stereotypes into the mouths of the Jewish characters themselves: for example, he has Zadok comment, "I know my breath stinks so already that it is within half a degree of poison" as the Jew plots the death of Juliana with the poison of his own body (295). Of course the Jews' actions follow the worst anti-Jewish propaganda and leave no doubt about their race's intrinsic evil: they sell Jack and his courtesan Diamante as chattel; Doctor Zachary plans to dissect Jack in his anatomical experiments; the lecher Zadok daily strips and scourges Diamante for his pleasure; later as revenge, Zadok threatens to poison the springs which supply the city of Rome, and plans to serve the children of the city as dinner to the Pope. Jack calls Zadok's death a triumph; he describes the torture and pain of the Jew without compassion, in lengthy and excruciating detail (298–99).

Although they are portrayed as some of the most disgusting characters, within the context of Nashe's narrative the Jews are incidental, little different from the Germans or Italians except perhaps in their repulsive physicality and inhuman nature. They are important for the plot, but otherwise are just another set of foreigners whom Jack meets and rejects as part of his return to England and English values. Perhaps the most shocking element of *The Unfortunate Traveller* for the modern reader is the extreme way the novel rejects these Others whom Jack meets in the course of his travels. The violent deaths and tortures suddenly intrude on Jack's flippant narrative, and illustrate that the Englishman must not only show his difference from the grotesque Others; he must, in addition, destroy them. Zadok's torture and agony, the "end of the whipping Jew," are presented as if for the pleasure of the viewer, with no mention of the suffering of a human being. While the "unpitied and well-performed slaughter" of the Anabaptists incites even Jack's compassion, it is the same compassion he would feel at seeing a bear, "the most cruellest of all beasts," killed by too many dogs in an unfair match (236). And Jack still describes the Anabaptists' deaths in gory detail, noting at the end of his account, "So ordinary at every footstep was the imbruement of iron in blood that one could hardly discern heads from bullets, or clotted hair from mangled flesh hung with gore" (236). He ends the episode by reminding his audience of the Anabaptists' heresy, and bemoans the effects the slaughter has had on *him:* "what with talking of cobblers and tinkers and ropemakers and botchers and dirt-daubers, the mark is clean gone out of my muse's mouth, and I am, as it were, more than duncified twixt divinity and poetry" (236). The end of the novel has Jack give up his "foreign" behavior, marry his courtesan, and return home to English culture. Jack's immoral behavior, while the source of amusement in the course of the novel, is best left abroad.

For all of Jack Wilton's irreverent attitude, his disobedience to the rules of English class structure and his disregard for decorum, Nashe's book serves to reinforce conservative views: Nashe's very playfulness with Jack's identity, his mutability while abroad, emphasize the need for the Englishman to establish his identity as solid and unchangeable, *different* from the untrustworthy foreigners who do not play according to English rules of behavior. Nashe's attention to the details of changing fashions in Jack Wilton's tale points to the English traveler's concern over disjunctions between appearance and reality. The stereotypes who frequent Jack's travels suggest a desire to avoid such complications and complexity as more balanced portrayals of the foreign might require. By placing his Englishman abroad, rather than focusing on Others at home in England, Nashe is able to recount the tale of Jack Wilton's realization of, and return to, his own Englishness. While other examples of foreign settings, such as the many Shakespeare plays set in Italy, use the exoticism and distance of the foreign site to play out native problems, Nashe's tale can utilize the 'real' genre of the travelogue in emphasizing the differences between foreign vice and English virtue. The construction of Otherness in Nashe's *Unfortunate Traveller* comes about through an examination of superficial detail as though it were an adequate measure of more essential difference.

Notes

1. In his introduction to *An Anthology of Elizabethan Prose Fiction* (Oxford: Oxford UP, 1987), Paul Salzman notes that "It was once fashionable to see [*The Unfortunate Traveller*] as a picaresque novel, but recent scholars have stressed more disjunctive characteristics, linking it to the grotesque mode, to Nashe's highly self-conscious engagement with language . . . This most linguistically self-conscious work eventually finds no secure resting place on the page or in the voice" (xx–xxi).
2. All references to Nashe's text refer to Salman's *Anthology of Elizabethan Prose Fiction*, 207–309.
3. This theory of climatic influence is explained by Zera S. Fink in Appendix A of *The Classical Republicans: An Essay in the Recovery of a Pattern of Thought in Seventeenth Century England* (Evanston: Northwestern UP, 1945), 191–92.
4. The popularity of Italian court culture during Elizabeth's reign is testified to by the ten editions of Castiglione's *Courtier* which were printed in England

during the sixteenth and early seventeenth centuries, exerting an "influence on Elizabethan taste and manners [that] can hardly be exaggerated," J. Buxton, *Sir Philip Sidney and the English Renaissance* (London: Macmillan, 1954), 19; qtd. in Kenneth R. Bartlett, 257. Other Italian manner-books, such as Stefano Guazzo's *La Civile Conversazione*, 1574, (with English translations in 1581 and 1586) and Giovanni della Casa's *Galateo of Manners and Behavior* in 1576 indicate that Italians were considerable authorities on the proper behavior of both courtiers and the middle classes in England; Queen Elizabeth herself was well-versed in Italian, and her court found it expedient to follow her lead (Lievsay 17).

5. This argument begins in the Protestant objection to celibate priests; celibacy in the priesthood becomes conflated with a general objection to marriage and the encouragement of vice.

6. In English "a devil incarnate." *Inglese italianato è un diabolo incarnato* was a familiar proverb, cited by Ascham.

7. Most scholars assume that Stephen Gosson authored the work, whose full title is *Quippes for upstart newfangled gentlewomen. Or, a glasse to view the pride of vainglorious women. Containiing. A pleasant invective against the fantastical forreigne toyes, daylie used in womens apparell*, although the writer's identity is not certain. Citations of the work are taken from E.J. Howard's edition.

8. The frontispiece to *Coryat's Crudities* depicts the three countries of Germany, France and Italy as women, dressed in the fashions of their nations, grouped around a portrait of Coryat. The German woman is shown vomiting onto Coryat's head. As John Davie's ecphrastic poem explains of the engraving, "A dainty Dame (not dainty of her vomit)/ Powres downe upon him (like a blazing commet)/ The streame of her abundance from her Gullet,/ And hits him on the Noddle, like a Bullet, . . . Which Damsell, with her free ebriety,/ Doth lie, or sit, or stand for Germany." Cited in Jones, "Italians" (107). Hunter cites from John Marston's *The Malcontent* an example of generalizations by country: "The Dutchman for a drunkard/ The Dane for golden locks,/ The Irishman for usquebaugh/ The Frenchman for the [pox]" (15). The English earl who lectures Jack on the evils of travel similarly (and in greater detail) provides a catalogue of each nation's problems. The Italian is violent, deceitful and wanton, especially the Neapolitan, who "carrieth the bloodiest wreakful mind" (284); the French effeminate in fashion and slovenly; the Danes and the Dutch are drunkards (284–87).

Works Cited

Ascham, Roger. *English Works: Toxophilus, Report of the Affaires and State of Germany, The Scholemaster*. Ed. William Aldis Wright. Cambridge: Cambridge UP, 1904.

72 Laura Scavuzzo Wheeler

72   *Laura Scavuzzo Wheeler*

Bartlett, Kenneth R. "The Courtyer of Count Baldasser Castilio: Italian Manners and the English Court in the Sixteenth Century," *Quaderni d'Italianistica: Official Journal of the Canadian Society for Italian Studies*, 6 (1985): 249–58.

Buxton, J. *Sir Philip Sidney and the English Renaissance*. London: Macmillan, 1954.

Coryate, Thomas. *Coryats Crudities Hastily gobled vp in fiue Moneths trauells in France, Sauoy, Italy, Rhetia comonly called the Grisons country, Heluetia aliàs Switzerland, some parts of high Germany, and the Netherlands; Newly digested in the hungry aire of Odcombe in the County of Somerset, & now dispersed to the nourishment of the trauelling Members of his Kingdome*. London, printed by W. S. 1611.

Crewe, Jonathan V. *Unredeemed Rhetoric: Thomas Nashe and the Scandal of Authorship*. Baltimore: The Johns Hopkins UP, 1982.

Fink, Zera S. *The Classical Republicans: An Essay in the Recovery of a Pattern of Thought in Seventeenth Century England*. Evanston: Northwestern UP, 1945.

Gosson, Stephen. *Quippes for upstart newfangled gentlewomen. Or, a glasse to view the pride of vainglorious women. Containing. A pleasant invective against the fantastical forreigne toyes, daylie used in womens apparell*. Ed. Edwin Johnston Howard. Oxford, Ohio: The Anchor, 1942.

Harrison, William. *A Description of Elizabethan England written for Holinshed's Chronicles, 1577. In Chronicle and Romance: Froissart, Malory, Holinshed*. New York: P. F. Collier & Son, 1910.

Howard, Clare. *English Travellers of the Renaissance*. London: John Lane, Bodley Head, 1914.

Hunter, G. K. *Dramatic Identities and Cultural Tradition: Studies in Shakespeare and His Contemporaries*. New York: Barnes & Noble, 1978.

Jones, Ann Rosalind. "Inside the Outsider: Nashe's Unfortunate Traveller and Bakhtin's Polyphonic Novel." *ELH* (1983) 50: 61–81.

Jones, Ann Rosalind. "Italians and Others: Venice and the Irish in Coryat's Crudities and The White Devil." *Renaissance Drama* 18 (1987): 101–19.

King James Bible.

Kirchnerus, Hermannus. *An Oration made by Hermannus Kirchnerus . . . concerning this subject; that young men ought to travell into forraine coutnryes, and all those that desire the praise of learning and atchieving worthy actions both at home and abroad*, in Coryat's *Crudities*, vol. i., 131.

Lievsay, John. *The Elizabethan Image of Italy*. Washington: Folger Shakespeare Library, 1979.

Munday, Anthony. *The English Romayne Lyfe. Discovering: The liues of the Englishmen at Roome: the orders of the English Seminarie: the dissention betweene the Englishmen and the Welshmen: the banishing of the Englishmen out of Roome: their Vautes vnder the grounde: their holy Pilgrimages: and a number of other matters, worthy to be read and regarded of euery one. There vnto is added, the cruell tiranny, vsed on an English man at Roome, his Christian suffering, and notable*

Martirdome, for the Gospell of Iesus Christe, in Anno. 1581. Written by A. M. sometime the Popes scholler in the Seminarie among them . . . Seene and allowed. Imprinted at London, by John Charlewoode, for Nicholas Ling: dwelling in Paules Churchyarde, at the signe of the Maremaide. 1582.

Nashe, Thomas.   Preface to Robert Greene's *Menaphon: Camillas alarum to slumbering Euphues, 1589.* In *Prose of the English Renaissance.* Eds. William J. Hebel et al. New York: Appleton-Century-Crofts, 1952.

Nashe, Thomas. *The Unfortunate Traveller; Or, the Life of Jack Wilton. Anthology of Elizabethan Prose Fiction.* Ed. Paul Salzman. Oxford: Oxford UP, 1987. 207–309.

Peacham, Henry. "Of Travel." *The Complete Gentleman, The Truth of Our Times, and The Art of Living in London.* Ed. Virgil B. Heltzel. Ithaca: Cornell UP, 1962. 217–22.

Salzman, Paul. Introduction. *An Anthology of Elizabethan Prose Fiction.* Oxford: Oxford UP, 1987. vii–xxiv.

Scott, Margaret. "Machiavelli and the Machiavel." *Renaissance Drama*, New series xv. Evanston: Northwestern UP, 1984. 147–74.

• 6 •

Crusoe's Shadow: Christianity, Colonization and the Other

Andrew Fleck

The rise of the British novel is inextricably linked to the growth of the European colonialist project. In fact, Edward Said has recently suggested that "[w]ithout empire . . . there is no European novel as we know it" (*Culture* 69). The fact that Daniel Defoe's great novel, *Robinson Crusoe* (1719), stands near the beginning of the rapid expansion of the novel as both a literary genre, and reflects the period's imperialist discourse,[1] prompted Martin Green to begin his study of the relationship between empire and the novel with the argument "that the adventure tales that formed the light reading of Englishmen for two hundred years and more after *Robinson Crusoe* were, in fact, the energizing myth of English imperialism" (3).[2] While many studies of Defoe's novel acknowledge this important link, very few adequately address Crusoe's encounter with Friday. Such treatments briefly note that this meeting is a significant part of the novel, but then move on to other issues without examining the complex dynamic of their relationship. The expanding body of postcolonial criticism necessitates a proper examination of *Robinson Crusoe*'s representation of the meeting between a "civilized" European and a "savage" inhabitant of the New World since, as Helen Tiffin argues, this novel "was a part of the process of 'fixing' relations between Europe and its 'others,' of establishing patterns of reading alterity at the same time as it inscribed the 'fixity' of that alterity" (98). In Crusoe's ambivalent attitude towards his enslaved native,[3] whose difference poses a temporary threat to Crusoe's sense of self, Christianity plays a crucial role in maintaining his sense of a stable identity. Friday's imperfect conversion to Christianity allows Crusoe to reassert his sense of a superior self, possessed of Christian knowledge and enlightenment, while subjugating Friday as the other who can approach but never attain the European standard of Christianity.[4]

Through the first half of the novel, Crusoe develops a stable sense of self through a process of negation. He relates to God, the island and to himself in terms of what these relationships are not. This process occurs most frequently after Crusoe's spiritual rebirth and his feelings that he should be thankful for God's deliverance. At one point, for example, he compares his "present condition with what [he] at first expected it should be; nay with what it would certainly have been, if the good providence of God had not ordered the ship to be cast up nearer the shore" an event which enabled Crusoe to salvage tools and weapons, without which he "should certainly have lived, if [he] had not perished, like a meer savage" (141). Because God had not left him stranded on the island without the implements of civilization, and because the island did not subdue him, but was instead mastered by him, Crusoe is able to live not like a "meer savage" and is instead able to establish a semblance of the civilization to which he is accustomed. He represents God's benevolence in terms of what worse possibilities God did *not* inflict on him. Crusoe is grateful that God left him on an island where at least he "found no ravenous beast, no furious wolves or tygers to threaten [his] life . . . no savages to murther and devour [him]" (143). As John Richetti suggests, "what Crusoe really learns to do in every way through his conversion is to experience by means of contradiction, to keep before himself (in his terms) what he might have been if God had indeed abandoned him" (49).[5] Crusoe understands his self in terms of civilized standards which God's providence has allowed him to maintain. When he kills an animal for food, he is not forced, like a barbarian, to "gnaw it with my teeth and pull it with my claws like a beast" (141). Crusoe repeats this process of understanding himself through negation in various scenes throughout the novel.

By the middle of the novel, Crusoe has firmly established his mechanisms for maintaining his sense of self. When a strong current pulls Crusoe and his new canoe out to sea, he gazes back at the island he had so detested and "reproached [him] self with [his] unthankful temper and how [he] had repined at [his] solitary condition . . . Thus we never see the true state of our condition till it is illustrated to us by its contraries" (149). Only a few pages after Crusoe considers the role of opposites in understanding one's true self, he discovers a footprint in the sand, a sign of one of his gravest fears. He notes the impact of this incident, which lies at the exact center of the novel,[6] on the rest of his narrative: "But now I come to a new scene in my life" (162). The mark leaves him "thunder-struck" and more importantly, "like a man perfectly confused and out of my self" (162). Crusoe's identity has been constructed on the basis of the absence of human others,[7] and this sudden signal of their presence threatens to destabilize his system of maintaining a sense of self. Through the rest of the novel, Crusoe is forced to

reconstruct a self which will account for this new presence on his island.

The knowledge that natives from the nearby mainland occasionally
visit the island provokes an ambivalent reaction in Crusoe. This response
is especially instructive in that, as one of the first British novels, written
as British imperial expansion was about to experience a period of ex-
plosive growth, *Robinson Crusoe* establishes a paradigm frequently repeated over the course of the next two centuries. Abdul R. JanMohamed's
exploration of this pattern usefully explains Crusoe's various reactions
to his other. JanMohamed writes that when "[f]aced with an incompre-
hensible and multifaceted alterity, the European theoretically has the
option of responding to the Other in terms of identity or difference"
(83). Over the course of the rest of the novel, Crusoe exhibits both of
these tendencies. At first, the natives are faceless beings whom he encounters only through absence. The footprint and the remnants of a cannibalistic feast indicate to Crusoe that they have been on the island, but
he does not encounter them in person until several years after the initial
signals of their presence. While the natives remain faceless, Crusoe
imagines them in terms of the second half of JanMohamed's model.
From Crusoe's perspective, they are radically different. His thoughts
about who made the footprint inspire "apprehensions of its being the
devil," whom Crusoe has already overcome in the dream which prompted
his conversion, but these thoughts are replaced by the conviction that
the person who made the footprint is something worse: "I presently
concluded then, that it must be some more dangerous creature, viz. That
it must be some of the savages of the main land over-against me" (163).[8]
This fear of an other more terrifying than Satan poses a real threat to
Crusoe's sense of self and leaves him with the fear that the "savages"
might return to the island "again in greater numbers and devour me"
(163).[9] This fear corrodes his relationship with God and his sense of
identity. His faith in God is ruined as "fear banished all [his] religious
hope; all that former confidence in God, which was founded upon such
wonderful experience as [he] had of His goodness, now vanished" while
his feelings about himself as industrious master of the island are replaced when he reproaches "[him] self with [his] easiness, that would
not sow any more corn one year than would just serve [him] till the next
season" (164). The absent presence of the evil other causes Crusoe to
live for two years with feelings of "discomposure" which prevent him
from making proper application to God. Crusoe's understanding of self
through negation finally begins to operate again when he discovers the
remains of a cannibalistic feast. He "gave God thanks that had cast [his]

first lot in a part of the world where [he] was distinguished from such dreadful creatures as these" (172). Once again, Crusoe experiences God and his self through contemplation of what he is not. He imagines a system in which the cannibals occupy a position of radical difference opposite the civilized European self.

Eventually, however, Crusoe's continued contemplation of the terrifying other evinces a certain ambivalence. While consumed by the desire to destroy this threat to himself, he allows for the possibility that his "bloody schemes for the destruction of innocent creatures . . . would have been no less a sin than that of wilful murther if [he] had committed it" (179). He practices a kind of cultural relativism in comparing programmatic Spanish brutality in the American colonies to the brutal practices of these "idolaters and barbarians . . . [who] were yet, to the Spaniards, very innocent people" (178). Later, he dreams of killing all but one of a group of natives in order to enslave a native who might be able to guide him off the island and back to European colonies, but "thoughts of shedding humane blood for [his] deliverance were very terrible to [him]" (203). These somewhat positive thoughts about the natives are ultimately fleeting, and he resolves to enslave a captive of the cannibals, "cost what it would" (203).[10] He ignores the possibility of the natives' innocence in order to subjugate them for his own purposes.

When Crusoe finally confronts the other in the person of Friday, he participates in the alternative possibility in JanMohamed's model by experiencing the other in terms of identification. Crusoe's feelings of similarity with the native he saves are perhaps strongest in his initial impression of him. After rescuing Friday, Crusoe makes several observations:

> He was a comely fellow, perfectly well made; with straight strong limbs, not too large; tall and well shaped, and, as I reckon, about twenty six years of age. He had a very good countenance, not a fierce and surly aspect; but seemed to have something very manly in his face, and yet *he had all the sweetness and softness of an European countenance too*, especially when he smiled. His hair was long and black, not curled like wool; his forehead very high and large, and a great vivacity and sparkling sharpness in his eyes. The color of his skin was not quite black, but very tawny; and yet not of an ugly yellow nauseous tawny, as the Brasilians, and Virginians, and other natives of America are; but of a bright kind of dun olive color, that had in

it *something very agreeable,* tho' not very easy to describe.
His face was round and plump; his nose small, not flat like the
negroes, a very good mouth, thin lips, and his teeth well set,
and white as ivory. (208–09, my emphasis).

This curious description indicates the difficulty of keeping the other
clearly distinct from the self. Friday's "agreeable" appearance and
vaguely "European countenance," bears out JanMohamed's claim that
the colonizer could respond to the other in terms of identity. In fact,
Crusoe's description reveals the kind of ambivalent "disavowal of difference" which Homi K. Bhabha identifies at the center of colonial stereotypes. The other is different, but somehow almost the same. Crusoe's
ambivalent response to Friday's body reveals a fetishistic desire to bring
the other into the self. Bhabha claims that the "fetish or stereotype gives
access to an 'identity' which is predicated as much on mastery and pleasure as it is on anxiety and defence, for it is a form of multiple and
contradictory belief in its recognition of difference and disavowal of it"
(75). While describing Friday's difference, especially with respect to
his facial features, Crusoe nearly erases the difference he sets out to
demonstrate.

Crusoe's initial observation of his new slave's manners and bearing
continues to obscure the distinction between categories of difference.
Friday seems to be properly submissive to Crusoe's authority, prompt-
ing Crusoe to note that Friday, and presumably others like him, have
"the *same* powers, the *same* reason, the *same* affections, the *same* sen-
timents of kindness and obligation, the *same* passions and resentments
of wrongs, the *same* sense of gratitude, sincerity, fidelity and all the
capacities of doing good and receiving good, that [God] has given to
us" (212; my emphasis). Several things happen at once in Crusoe's observation. First, he appropriates all of these qualities for his own self.
He compares Friday to a standard of virtue which has meaning to certain Europeans and which he, as the naturally-superior colonizer completely fulfills. Friday has many of the same good qualities as Crusoe,
but they are only good because they are valued by the speaker, a dominant European who passes judgment on what constitutes "the good."
This evaluation of Friday bears out JanMohamed's argument that when
the other is viewed in terms of similarity, the European "would tend to
ignore the significant divergences and to judge the Other according to
his own cultural values" (84). In the repetition of the word "same,"
Crusoe risks erasing the difference between the self and the other alto-

gether. It seems as if Friday would no longer be different if he were not dark-skinned. Crusoe even mentions that in some ways, this particular other might be better than some Europeans. He is "melancholly . . . in reflecting . . . how mean a use we make of these [powers]" (212). Because a member of an inferior people has made better use of its gifts than the supposedly superior Europeans have, the other threatens to supplant the self by more fully exemplifying the traits valued by that self.

Crusoe does not consistently identify with Friday, however. His ambivalent response includes several overt efforts to subjugate this inferior other. Throughout their initial meeting Crusoe seizes and interprets Friday's acts of communication for his own benefit. After being saved from the cannibals, Friday cautiously approaches Crusoe and his smoking gun and abases himself at his feet. Crusoe notes that Friday "kneeled down again, kissed the ground, and laid his head upon the ground, and taking me by the foot, set my foot upon his head; this *it seems* was in token of swearing to be my slave for ever" (207, my emphasis). Here Crusoe appropriates Friday's gestures for his own use.[11] Ian A. Bell understands these gestures in the same way Crusoe does: "Friday voluntarily offers himself into subjection, after Crusoe saved his life" (31). With his arsenal, however, Crusoe has absolute power in this situation and thus possesses the authority of interpretation which James H. Maddox, Jr. argues "is the ultimate form of power in Defoe's novel: the ability to tell one's own story, one's own interpretation of things, and have everyone else take a subsidiary role in it" (42).[12] Friday does not have this power, and so his initial communication is taken away from him and given the meaning which best serves Crusoe's ends. A similar situation occurs soon after the cannibals are vanquished, when Friday is introduced to "civilized" speech. Crusoe begins his linguistic lesson by giving his slave a new, English name, Friday. Whatever his name might once have been, the colonizer erases it and inscribes on the other a name of his own choosing. Friday then learns that he is to call Crusoe "Master" (209), giving Crusoe the title he has wished for.[13] Friday's voice is lost with his name, and he is forced to respond in the colonizer's terms. Thus, Gayatri Chakravorty Spivak's claim that "the subaltern cannot speak" (308) holds true in this case, especially since, as Hugh Ridley notes, Crusoe "sees Friday merely as a means to fulfill his own personality, never asking his actual name but blithely assuming that Friday exists and is worthy of a name only within his relationship to Crusoe" (6). Through these various means of negating and subjugating Friday, Crusoe can further strengthen his own sense of self.

JanMohamed contends that "[b]y thus subjugating the native, the European settler is able to compel the Other's recognition of him and, in the process, allow his own identity to become deeply dependent on his position as a master" (85). The inscription of Friday in an inferior position confirms and supports Crusoe's own conception of his superior place in the cosmos.

Finally, in Crusoe's litany of Friday's "sameness," where the difference threatens to collapse, Crusoe makes a distinction which is ultimately insurmountable and keeps categories of self and other clearly separated. After considering how alike he and Friday are, and the extent to which some natives surpass Europeans in virtuous characteristics, Crusoe determines that the only difference between Friday and Europeans is that "we have these powers enlightened by the great lamp of instruction, the spirit of God and the knowledge of His word" while American natives do not, even though to "judge by this poor *savage*, [they] would make much better use of it than we did" (212, my emphasis). After clearly outlining a kind of similarity, the sudden, jarring appearance of the word "savage" drives a wedge between himself and Friday which will ensure that the other will never be completely like the self. Crusoe lets Friday approach the ideal of the European self, but at the last minute he undercuts his ability to fulfill that ideal. This attraction and repulsion towards Friday enacts the ambivalent mimicry described by Bhabha who claims that the colonizer looks for imitation of his own ideals in the colonized, but designates that imitation as necessarily insufficient in order, finally, to maintain the boundaries of the relationship. Bhabha writes that "colonial mimicry is the desire for a reformed, recognizable Other, *as a subject of difference which is almost the same but not quite*" (86, his emphasis). Christian inspiration becomes the necessary trait in becoming a civilized human being. Whenever the lines between self and other are in danger of becoming blurred, Crusoe always has recourse to his version of Christianity in order to reassert difference.

As Crusoe is aware, however, the conversion of natives to Christianity is one of the principal justifications for imperial expansion like that he practices on the island.[14] Crusoe feels compelled to educate Friday in the ways of Western Christianity. He explains that while teaching Friday to understand English, he "was not wanting to lay a foundation of religious knowledge in his mind" (218). As a kind of Christian pedagogue, Crusoe resolves to erase Friday's existing religious "foundation" which includes a belief in Benamuckee, and to turn Friday into a kind of palimpsest on which he will inscribe knowledge of what he calls the "true" religion. His first task is to show Friday the inferiority of the native beliefs, which appear to have no element of worship. Friday's response, that "'All things do say O to [Benamuckee],'" and that he believes in an afterlife for everyone, catches Crusoe off guard and forces him to recognize that Friday's people have a more complex belief system than he imagined. Realizing that he cannot merely attack this system, Crusoe sets out to undercut the system and "instruct [Friday] in the knowledge of the true God" (218). He offers Friday a version of God which partially convinces him that since the Christian God is "able to hear us, even into heaven . . . He must needs be a greater god than their Benamuckee, who lived but a little way off, and yet could not hear till they went up to the great mountains where he dwelt to speak to him" (218–19).

Friday's initial acceptance of God's superiority does not satisfy Crusoe, who further degrades the value of Friday's belief system. Crusoe tries to free Friday from the "fraud" he believes holds together the natives' religion. He learns that Friday and his people have no direct access to their deity, but instead rely on mediators, "their *oowocakee*, that is . . . their religious, or clergy, and that they went to say O (so he called saying prayers) and then came back, and told them what Benamuckee said" (219). This account offends Crusoe's Christian sensibilities. His own experience of God is immediate; God acts or refrains from action directly in his life. His understanding of Christianity on the island is a simple, Reformed version. Friday's explanation of the native priesthood inspires revulsion in Crusoe who detects superstitious similarities between Friday's religious system and the corrupt Christianity of Spanish Catholics: "By this I observed that there is priestcraft even amongst the most blinded pagans in the world; and the policy of making a secret religion, in order to preserve the veneration of the people to the clergy, is not only to be found in the Roman, but perhaps among all religions in the world, even among the most brutish and barbarous savages" (219). Crusoe explains that any being with whom the *oowocakee* communicate must be an "evil spirit" and begins "a long discourse with [Friday] about the devil, the original of him, his rebellion against God, his enmity to man, the reason of it, his setting himself up in the dark parts of the world to be worship'd instead of God, and as God" (219). Friday's Benamuckee is turned into Crusoe's Satan. This interpretation of Friday's beliefs as a kind of evil religion, rather than a good one, deploys the kind of assimilation Edward Said describes. He suggests that out of the space between the new and the known, "a new category emerges, a category that allows one to see new things, things seen for the first time, as versions of a previously known thing. In essence, such a category is not so much a way of receiving new information as it is a method of controlling what seems to be a threat to some established view of things" (*Orientalism* 59). By claiming that Benamuckee is a manifestation of Satan, Crusoe contains the potential threat of Friday's religion which superficially resembles Christianity since both are monotheistic, condone a form of cannibalism, and posit an afterlife. This move, however, finally derails Friday's conversion.

Crusoe has great difficulties educating Friday about the nature of the devil. In nature he can find numerous examples of God's power and benevolence, but "there appeared nothing of all this in the notion of an evil spirit; of his original, his being, his nature and above all of his inclination to do evil, and to draw us in to do so too" (219). Perhaps Friday's resistance to this idea comes from the fact that Crusoe has appropriated and inverted his entire belief system. What Friday thought was good is now the ultimate evil. In an effort to understand this change, he asks a series of questions which Crusoe has real difficulty answering. First, Friday turns some of Crusoe's earlier conversion techniques against this new concept of the God-Satan/Benamuckee binary. He asks Crusoe if "'God is so strong, so great, is He not much strong, much might as the devil?'" to which Crusoe replies "'Yes, yes . . . Friday, God is stronger than the devil.'" Friday's related question, "'if God much strong, much might as the devil, why God no kill the devil, so make him no more do wicked,'" leaves Crusoe "strangely surprised" (220). Friday redirects Crusoe's previous logic, that God is more powerful and hence better than Benamuckee, and leaves Crusoe grasping for answers. In fact, the question so flusters Crusoe that he "pretended not to hear him," but Friday insists that Crusoe answer him. His first answer, "'God will at last punish [the devil] severely'" does not satisfy Friday who wonders why Satan was not punished "'great ago'" when he first offended. At last, Friday fastens on to Crusoe's remarks that humans are "'preserved to repent and be pardoned'" and concludes, "'so you, I, devil, all wicked, all preserve, repent, God pardon all'" (220). Crusoe does not know how to make Friday see the difference between sinners and Satan, so he gives up and leaves Friday with imperfect notions about Christianity.

Friday's difficult questions may, in fact, be "precisely the kinds of questions missionaries to the Indians were being asked" and demonstrate Defoe's concern to make "a strong case for the necessity of revelation" (Blackburn 373–74). On the other hand, they may serve as a way of maintaining difference. Crusoe is so exasperated by the difficulties he has in instructing Friday that he concludes that while a basic belief in God can be induced from examples in nature

> yet nothing but divine revelation can form the knowledge of Jesus Christ . . . nothing but a revelation from heaven can form these in the soul, and that therefore the gospel of our Lord and Saviour Jesus Christ, I mean the word of God, and the spirit of God promised for a guide and sanctifier of His people, are the *absolutely necessary* instructors of the souls of men in the saving knowledge of God and the means of salvation (221 my emphasis).

Crusoe makes divine revelation, which he supposes he possesses in full, function as the difference between savage and civilized humanity. He is himself the arbiter of who has this revelation and who does not, and ironically, becomes the mediator between Friday and direct religious experience, thus replacing the natives' *oowocakee*. Since Crusoe is the judge of who has this revelation and is thus a true Christian, he can withhold this trait from Friday and maintain the difference between self and other.[15] From the outset, Friday could never measure up to Crusoe's standards for conversion. As David Lloyd suggests, in a system where the pedagogue assumes a universal standard of truth, the student can never reach that ideal: "The necessary contingent inadequacy of the student to the ideal projected by pedagogy, a function so to speak, of lacking age, experience, erudition, or whatever, as well as of institutional positioning, is here no more than the expression of a systematic incapacity" (39). There is no way for Friday to pass the test; the system requires that he fail. In fact, in his imperfect conversion, Friday's failure further strengthens Crusoe's sense of self by deepening his own understanding of Christianity.[16] His attempts to answer Friday "really informed and instructed [Crusoe] in many things that either [he] did not know, or had not fully considered before, but which occurred naturally to [his] mind, upon [his] searching into them for the information of this poor savage" (221). Crusoe's further instructions become self-affirming so that Friday's spiritual state is no longer of consequence. That his interests are lost does not concern Crusoe, however, because in teaching Friday about Christianity, Crusoe more clearly defines his self and differentiates the not-fully-Christian other.[17]

Friday's failure not only strengthens Crusoe's sense of self, it also pushes Friday into a position of alterity from which he cannot escape.

Crusoe's attitude towards Friday immediately turns from benevolence
to a slightly more hostile feeling. Although Crusoe prays for God's guidance in further instructing Friday, he everywhere undercuts this philan-
thropic desire. He sends Friday on an errand so he can collect his
thoughts, then prays that God "would enable [him] to instruct savingly
this poor *savage*" (221 my emphasis). He considers himself "an instru-
ment under Providence to save the life, and, for ought [he] knew, the
soul of this poor savage, and bring him to the true religion, and of the
Christian doctrine" (222). It is important to notice that these are Crusoe's
thoughts *after* the failure of his pedagogical attempts with Friday, and
that the refrain, "this poor savage," is repeated five times in the two
pages of reflection following his frustration with Friday. This repeated
phrase looks back to his previous use of the term and serves to undo the
feelings of "sameness" which Crusoe had earlier observed. Even though
Friday outwardly conforms to the basic tenets of Christianity, enough
that Crusoe notes that the "savage was now a good Christian" (222), his
beliefs do not have the veracity Crusoe claims for himself. Friday's
Christianity is really only an advanced version of the imitative speech
of Crusoe's parrot, Poll, and he remains nothing more than an uncom-
prehending "savage."

Defoe's novel does not overtly display the mechanisms behind the
ambivalent, but ultimately final, anchoring of Friday's difference. J. A.
Downie argues that the fact that *Robinson Crusoe* and Defoe's other
novels "do not nakedly state a thesis in favor of empire is a mark of the
subtlety with which Defoe approaches a subject" (74). Even if the presence of these mechanisms is veiled, they still work to inscribe Friday in
a position of alterity. Friday's Christianity embodies the ambivalence
Bhabha identifies in colonial mimicry: "The success of colonial appropriation depends on a proliferation of inappropriate objects that ensure
its strategic failure, so that mimicry is at once resemblance and men-
ace" (86). Even though Friday approaches the standards imposed by
Crusoe, his conversion must ultimately fail and ensure his difference.
By using a trait whose access Crusoe controls to anchor Friday in a
position of inferiority, Crusoe and Defoe can justify the continuation of
the civilizing mission ostensibly motivating the colonizing drive.
JanMohamed concludes that colonialist literature like *Robinson Crusoe*
tries to "demonstrate that the barbarism of the native is irrevocable, or
at least very deeply ingrained . . . [so that] the European's attempt to
civilize him can continue indefinitely . . . and the European can persist
in enjoying a position of moral superiority" (81). As long as Crusoe and
the colonizers can claim that Friday and the natives have not received

the necessary revelation and become true Christians, imperial expansion can continue unimpeded.

Notes

1. In any discussion of the origin of this genre, it is important to remember that *Robinson Crusoe* was not the first English novel, since it was written more than thirty years after Aphra Behn's *Oroonoko*, which was first published in 1688. I have chosen to focus on *Robinson Crusoe* for the use it makes of Christianity in the service of empire. I would like to thank Marc Redfield and Constance Jordan at the Claremont Graduate School for their help in preparing the final version of this paper.

2. Edward Said draws a similar conclusion about *Robinson Crusoe*. He writes: "No less significantly, the novel is inaugurated in England by *Robinson Crusoe*, a work whose protagonist is the founder of a new world, which he rules and reclaims for Christianity and England" (*Culture* 70). For a contrasting opinion about this novel's place in the history of the genre, see Fiona J. Stafford's *The Last of the Race*, which argues that "Defoe's status as 'father of the novel' becomes rather less certain" in light of recent scholarhip (65).

3. I have chosen to use the term "native" as a less value-laden term than Crusoe's constant references to "savages," even though they are natives of the mainland Crusoe can see from the highest points on the island and in some sense are visitors to the island Crusoe has inhabited for fifteen years before the appearance of the footprint.

4. Myra Jehlen suggests that the use of the term "difference" is a more positive and open alternative to the idea of "otherness." She writes, "Describing oneself or one's kind as 'other,' one would not only represent the very meaning of alienation but be incapable of further self-definition and even speech; while to declare oneself 'different' leads logically to self-description" (2). While I hope to be as sensitive as possible to these connotations, Crusoe and Defoe are clearly representing the indigenous people of the New World in terms of otherness and are not concerned with leaving open the possibility of valuable difference. When I use the term "other" I am doing so with the intention of explaining the representational strategies at work in the novel.

5. Similarly, Daniel Cottom concludes: "Crusoe typically describes his experience of Providence by placing it in the context of imaginary situations in which he supposes Providence would be absent . . . it is only through negations that he can understand Providence in a positive way" (275).

6. Many critics note the narrative and thematic centrality of the lone footprint in the sand. J.R. Hammond, for example, writes that "Defoe places the discovery of the footprint in the sand at the exact mid-point of the narrative, as

if to emphasize its thematic importance" (73). The fears this mark inspires haunt Crusoe for the rest of the narrative and eventually are given corporeal form in his interaction with the people who visit his island.

7. Stafford argues that Crusoe eventually experiences a "movement from despair to resignation" in response to his isolation as a kind of last-of-the-race survivor" (73). Eric Jager notes the various non-human others in the novel who inhabit the island before Friday, including Poll, Crusoe's parrot, and his own "internal voice, or other self, [who] counteracts the imbalance of the psyche" (319). The footprint signals that Crusoe must now accept the possibility of a real, human other on his island, against which he will define his new self.

8. The equation of the natives with Satan further reinforces JanMohamed's view that the underlying basis of colonialist literature is a belief that Europeans and natives were engaged in a Manichean struggle between good (the colonists) and evil (the colonized).

9. Many studies of *Robinson Crusoe* focus on Crusoe's fear of cannibalism as it relates to the rapacious capitalism, a kind of social cannibalism, which he practices throughout the novel. For example, Dianne Armstrong argues that Crusoe, a kind of social cannibal, is most afraid "that his identity will be 'swallowed up' in some other corpus, father, god, savage" (218). See also Margaret Anne Carter, Spiritual Rebirth in *Robinson Crusoe*: The Western Religious Search and Its Effect upon Friday," diss., Claremont Graduate School, 1995, 178–80; Martin J. Gliserman, "*Robinson Crusoe*: The Vicissitudes of Greed—Cannibalism and Capitalism," *American Imago* 47 (1990): 197–231; and Neil Heims, "*Robinson Crusoe* and the Fear of Being Eaten," *Colby Library Quarterly* 19 (1983): 190–93. Equally important to the novel, however, is cannibalism's initial function as a sign of the "savage" as opposed to the "civilized," practiced by the other and not by the self.

10. Several critics have noted that Defoe seems to have approved of the English control of the slave trade. Paula R. Backscheider notes that Defoe's *Colonel Jack* is "an enthusiastic endorsement of the colonies and a carefully developed model for controlling slaves on a North American plantation" (49). J.A. Downie outlines Defoe's attitudes towards the colonial project while Laura Brown offers a feminist perspective on Defoe's imperialist attitudes. In addition, it is worth remembering that Crusoe was on a mission to buy slaves to sell in Brazil when his ship was caught in the storm which brought him to the island.

11. Fakrul Alam argues that in this moment, language is almost "dismissed as an obstacle in communication between peoples; as if the most rudimentary gestures were enough to claim or yield sovreignty" (120). Throughout the novel Crusoe offers to interpret Friday's gestures and broken English for the reader. Thus, his later remark that, frightened of his gun, Friday "said many things I did not understand; but I could easily see that the meaning was to pray me not to kill him" is emblematic of the fact that Friday's voice is consistently expropriated from him. As Gareth Griffiths has commented in a

slightly different context, "within colonial discourse . . . the possibilities of subaltern speech are contained by the discourse of the oppressor" (238).

12. Martin J. Gliserman, for example, argues that Friday is submissive not out of gratitude but out of fear after seeing the destructive power of Crusoe's gun: "[Friday] thinks there is a 'wonderful Fund of Death and Destruction' in it. Friday is utterly submissive to this fecal phallus and he puts Crusoe's foot upon his head to signify his position" (221).

13. As Alam suggests of Defoe's other novels, it becomes clear that "language instruction is the indispensable first step to be taken in setting the natives to work in any colonial venture" (121). When Crusoe's slave can understand his master's commands, he can more easily perform his duties.

14. JanMohamed distinguishes between the "covert" aspects of colonization (economic exploitation) and "the overt aim" which was to 'civilize' the savage" (81). Said notes that a "complex apparatus" for the promotion and protection of Christian interests in the colonies developed in the early part of the eighteenth century (*Orientalism* 100).

15. I would thus qualify Alam's assertion that "Friday, of course, is Crusoe's greatest triumph as a missionary and illustrates the connection between religious conversion and colonization" (118). Crusoe deems the conversion a partial failure because Friday has not received the necessary revelation, but, paradoxically, the inadequate conversion makes Crusoe's colonial efforts successful by justifying his continued domination of Friday as a moral inferior.

16. As G.A. Starr notes, in spiritual autobiographies of the period, one test of a person's conversion was "the urge to impart to others the benefits of one's conversion" (120).

17. Eric Jager argues that Crusoe feels no "concern for the other's spiritual welfare; Crusoe is thankful for the *personal* benefits of these exchanges" (328). Starr draws a similar, but more positive conclusion from Crusoe's remarks, which he claims indicate *Robinson Crusoe*'s place in the genre of spiritual autobiography. In that context, he suggests, "the lay convert was encouraged to share his discoveries with others not only for the good it might do them but for the value it must have for the self" (122).

Works Cited

Alam, Fakrul. "Religious and Linguistic Colonialism in Defoe's Fiction." *North Dakota Quarterly* 55 (1987): 116–23.

Armstrong, Dianne. "The Myth of Cronus: Cannibal and Sign in *Robinson Crusoe*." *Eighteenth-Century Fiction* 4 (1992): 207–20.

Backscheider, Paula R. "Defoe and the Geography of the Mind." *Tennessee Studies in Literature* 29 (1985): 41–65.

Bell, Ian A. "King Crusoe: Locke's Political Theory in *Robinson Crusoe*." *English*

88 *Andrew Fleck*

Studies 69 (1988): 27–36.

Bhabha, Homi K. *The Location of Culture*. New York: Routledge, 1994.

Blackburn, Timothy C. "Friday's Religion: Its Nature and Importance in *Robinson Crusoe*." *Eighteenth-Century Studies* 18 (1985): 360–82.

Brown, Laura. "Amazons and Africans: Gender Race and Empire in Daniel Defoe." *Women, "Race," and Writing in the Early Modern Period*. Ed. Margo Hendricks and Patricia Parker. London: Routledge, 1994. 118–37.

Carter, Margaret Anne. *Spiritual Rebirth in Robinson Crusoe: The Western Religious Search and Its Effect upon Friday*. Diss. Claremont Graduate School, 1995.

Cottom, David. "*Robinson Crusoe*: The Empire's New Clothes." *The Eighteenth Century* 22 (1981): 271–86.

Defoe, Daniel. *Robinson Crusoe*. London: Penguin, 1965.

Downie, J. A. "Defoe, Imperialism and the Travel Books Reconsidered." *Yearbook of English Studies* (1983): 66–83.

Gliserman, Martin J. "*Robinson Crusoe*: The Vicissitudes of Greed—Cannibalism and Capitalism." *American Imago* 47 (1990): 197–231.

Green, Martin. *Dreams of Adventure, Deeds of Empire*. New York: Basic Books, 1979.

Griffiths, Gareth. "The Myth of Authenticity." *The Postcolonial Studies Reader*. Ed. Bill Ashcroft, Gareth Griffiths, and Helen Tiffin. New York: Routledge, 1995. 237–41.

Hammond, J. R. *A Defoe Companion*. Lanham, MD: Barnes and Noble, 1993.

Heims, Neil. "*Robinson Crusoe* and the Fear of Being Eaten." *Colby Library Quarterly* 19 (1983): 190–93.

Jager, Eric. "The Parrot's Voice: Language and the Self in *Robinson Crusoe*." *Eighteenth-Century Studies* 21 (1988): 316–33.

JanMohamed, Abdul R. "The Economy of Manichean Allegory: The Function of Racial Difference in Colonialist Literature." "*Race," Writing and Difference*. Ed. Henry Louis Gates, Jr. Chicago: U of Chicago P, 1986. 78–106.

Jehlen, Myra. "Why Did the European Middle Class Cross the Ocean? A Seventeenth Century Riddle." *Discovering Difference: Contemporary Essays in American Culture*. Ed. Christopher K. Lohman. Bloomington: Indiana UP, 1993. 1–15.

Lloyd, David. "Kant's Examples." *Representations* 28 (1989): 34–54.

Maddox, James H., Jr. "Interpretive Crusoe." *English Literary History* 51 (1984): 33–52.

Richetti, John J. *Defoe's Narratives: Situations and Structures*. Oxford: Clarendon, 1975.

Ridley, Hugh. *Images of Imperial Rule*. London: Croom Helm, 1983.

Said, Edward W. *Culture and Imperialism*. New York: Vintage, 1993.

—. *Orientalism*. New York: Vintage, 1979.

Spivak, Gayatri Chakravorty. "Can the Subaltern Speak?" *Marxism and the Interpretation of Culture*. Ed. Cary Nelson and Lawrence Grossberg. Urbana: U of Illinois P, 1988. 271–313.

Stafford, Fiona J. *The Last of the Race: The Growth of the Myth from Milton to*

Darwin. Oxford: Clarendon, 1994.

Starr, G. A. *Defoe and Spiritual Autobiography*. Princeton: Princeton UP, 1965.

Tiffin, Helen. "Post-Colonial Literature and Counter-Discourse." *The Postcolonial Studies Reader*. Ed. Bill Ashcroft, Gareth Griffiths, and Helen Tiffin. New York: Routledge, 1995. 95–98.

7

Secularism, Satire and Scapegoatism in Chateaubriand's *Itinéraire de Paris à Jérusalem*

Syrine C. Hout

René de Chateaubriand once wrote: "polemics is my natural bearing . . . I always need an adversary, no matter where" (Peltier 68).[1] The problem regarding most critical reflections on this nugget of self-analysis, however, is that these have operated on the acceptance, as fact, of the notion that Chateaubriand's "adversary" was in actuality the binary legacy of the literature and philosophy of the French Enlightenment. Although Chateaubriand did, of course, make the style and *Weltanschauung* of the leading figures of the *Lumières* the targets for his criticism, the preoccupation with how and why he did so may have deflected critical attention from the author's view of his own immediate political and cultural milieu. The analysis of his views on the contemporaneous state of affairs, on issues related to domestic politics, religion, and culture, is almost always confined to his nonfictional pieces, which are often otherwise neglected.[2] Chateaubriand's own attitude towards the role of literature has probably strengthened this tendency among literary critics. In a letter to his friend Joubert he wrote that "one should not show the world except that which is beautiful" because he believed that the "beautiful" was on a higher plane and more authentic than the merely "true" (Clark 161). "One would secretly reveal to a friend one's flaws," Chateaubriand admits, "but one would hide them from the rest of the world" (Ages 233).

The question which comes to mind, of course, is whether or not a text, meant to appear purely literary, would be the ideal place to "hide" criticism, especially regarding one's own personal or, worse still, national "flaws." Naturally, some genres would provide better hiding-places than would certain others. Compared to other forms of writing, the travel account, whose setting must by definition change continually, has perhaps the greatest potential for disguising the targets of an author's criticism. Spatial displacement and temporary removal from the stage of action at home enable the traveler, should s/he so desire, to launch a subtle or muted attack. The third manner in which an author may further muffle an onslaught is by pretending to make a scapegoat of the "Other."

In this chapter I argue that Chateaubriand's *Itinéraire de Paris à Jérusalem*[3] is an example of muted satire.[4] More specifically, I will discuss the different ways in which the traveler/narrator cloaks his critique of European and particularly French cultural mores and political practices. To do so, emphasis must be placed on the narrative's essayistic and fragmentary nature by reading the text as a *journal sans date* whose critique of European cultural and political affairs is veiled precisely because it is rendered as an assault against an easier target, namely the non-European and the non-Christian represented by the Near East. It will be shown how Chateaubriand's approach to the Orient, often described as monological or manichean, i.e. non-dialogical, enables him to indulge in a clandestine critique of European affairs. In other words, we will see his monologue as more than just an attitude towards the Other: it is the strategy he follows to criticize the Self via the Other. In short, he satisfies his desire for cultural self-criticism by converting it, on the surface, into a politically and socially acceptable critique of a defenseless Other.

To begin with, it is necessary to reconsider the work's reception history in order to help explain why the *Itinéraire* has *not* thus far been perceived as a satirical work in disguise. To do so, I will consider four aspects: the text's immediate political impact, its ostensible *raison d'être*, its translation into English, and, lastly, its evaluation by modern literary critics. First, the political reaction to the *Itinéraire* was highly positive. In 1811, which "was one of the most remarkable [years] of [his] literary career," Chateaubriand was informed that Napoleon wished to offer him the *prix décennal* and make him a member of the *Académie* (Bassan, *Revue des Sciences Humaines* 112). Referred to as "the pilgrim," he became the center of attraction at the *salons*, especially that of Mme Récamier. Second, the author's declaration, in the *Préface* to the *Itinéraire* for the edition of his *Oeuvres complètes*, that he traveled to Jerusalem after "an anti-religious century [which] had lost its memory of the cradle of religion" (vol. 1, 1) caused the critics to see the work as a defense of Christianity, like *Le Génie du christianisme* (1802). Therefore, eighteenth-century irreverence for religion, the ostensible target of his attack, was seen as an *a priori* idea and an organizing principle for the narrative. Third, the fact that the last full-length English translation came out in 1814[5] must have made any interpretation of the *Itinéraire* a difficult task for Anglo-Saxon critics with little or no knowledge of the French language. Fourth, almost all critics agree that the *Itinéraire* broke new ground in the genre of travel literature. Its publication triggered waves of staggering success in France and abroad.[6] To begin with, Chateaubriand was admired for his risk-taking behavior, both in physical and financial terms. In 1806, at the time he took the trip, journeying in the Near East was still a frightening undertaking, fraught with peril. The security of French travelers in the Holy Land was not guaranteed until a peace treaty was signed by Henri IV and reconfirmed several times, notably in 1802.[7] At the end of the eighteenth century, Palestine had been almost *terra incognita*, and by Napoleon's time the tradition of Catholic pilgrimage was moribund (Shepherd 13). Thus, in traveling courageously as a pilgrim and a belated "Crusader" to the Holy Land, Chateaubriand was a pioneer. Furthermore, his trip was a great adventure because it cost him the equivalent of between fifty and a hundred thousand dollars, at a time when he had no financial resources of his own (Switzer 79).[8] Later, however, the revenues from the *Itinéraire* paid all of his debts (Shepherd 26).

As Edward Said puts it, the *Itinéraire* was one of the first "textual children" of Napoleon's expedition that was later rewritten by other pilgrims and travelers (Said 87–88, 177). "With Chateaubriand and Byron, the Orient almost becomes the obligatory passage of poets and artists. Lamartine, Nerval, Flaubert, among many others, observe the rite" (Hentsch 210). Chateaubriand's declaration that he was traveling in order to look for "images" for his project *Les Martyrs* (1809) establishes him as the first Romantic literary traveler. As Michel Butor has shown, *écriture* becomes the *raison d'être* for Romantic peregrinations (Butor 4–19). The *Itinéraire* marks a turning point in the history of travel writing because its exoticism is twin-faced: one is directed to the past, and the other to the future, but neither to the present, unlike most eighteenth-century travel accounts which focus on the here and now. It also introduces into the genre the new element of anecdote with "I" at the center, thereby instituting itself as the first subjective *Voyage en Orient* (El-Nouty 49).

Todorov explains that Chateaubriand invents the persona of the modern tourist because, being in a hurry, he prefers objects to human beings, imagery to language, sight to sound, and the dead to the living (Todorov 378). Seen in this light, Chateaubriand is paradoxically both the first bourgeois traveler and the last representative of the heroic type (Wolfzettel 85). Although I certainly agree that, for the most part, the *Itinéraire* signals a new direction in the evolution of the genre, I also believe that the critics' obsession with Chateaubriand's innovative style and approach has made them overlook a very significant dimension of the text, namely the traveler/narrator's pervasive, albeit mostly subtle, critique of European and particularly French politics and culture *via* the topos of the Orient. Since the *Itinéraire* is the polished version of Chateaubriand's earlier travel notes and letters, which reveal a fair amount of definite social and political criticism, it is surprising that critics should so far not have stressed the polemical nature of the text.

Chateaubriand is neither a romantic dreamer, nor is he totally oblivious to the present and lost in classical and medieval literary-historical scenes, as he has been portrayed in most interpretations of the *Itinéraire*. In fact, he is acutely aware of reality: "I am not at all one of these intrepid admirers of antiquity who are consoled for everything by a verse by Homer" (vol. 1, 328). Imagination and memory fade in the face of human reality. At the time of his departure in 1806, Chateaubriand was experiencing a personal crisis: his identity was being questioned by himself and others. "He is cut off from his past (the disappearance of his family, of Combourg, of the ancient frameworks of society), without a foreseeable future, without hope for conjugal happiness or a desire for procreation, without the possibility of political service, without an acquired fortune: he really lacks a place under the sun" (Berchet 108).

A main issue for which Chateaubriand holds France and particularly Napoleon responsible, without directly saying so, is the living conditions of the priests of the Holy Sepulchre in Jerusalem. Yet, he "beats around the bush" in two ways: he deflects his criticism by assailing several groups whose blame nobody would dispute and by making use of what I call the narrative technique of disruption, which relies on juxtaposition and deferral. The two groups which he openly and safely castigates are eighteenth-century antireligious thinker, on the one hand and the contemporaneous Muslim leaders, on the other. As if to prove that Arabs are still hostile towards European Christians, he describes how he was personally harassed by two spahis.[9] Fending for himself, Chateaubriand "gives him . . . an insult for an insult" (vol. 2, 148). Before doing so, however, he briefly reminds the reader of what is at stake: the necessary preservation of the Sepulchre. Chateaubriand's own language (of reprimand and not of prayer) needs deciphering as well because it is masked by intervening passages which distract the reader/censor from the author's major target of criticism: contemporaneous French foreign policy, especially that concerning the guardians of the Holy Tomb. He claims that "one thousand examples" culled from travel writings prove that Latin pilgrims have never been many. "If in 1589, at the moment when religion was very flourishing, one could only see seven Latin pilgrims in Palestine, how many could one estimate to have been there in 1806?" Clearly, therefore, it was not the Age of the *Lumières* which caused the number of pilgrims to dwindle: his point is that the priests of Jerusalem have been neglected by their countrymen for well over two centuries. He concludes that the money and goods for the priests were mainly provided by Jewish, Greek, and Armenian pilgrims (vol. 2, 171).

Having clarified this matter, and instead of now zeroing in on the Catholic government's responsibility towards the poor priests, he again deflects the censors' attention by giving detailed tables of his personal travel and lodging expenses. These reduce the tension which the preceding critical remarks may have caused, after which he picks up where he had left off. He reproduces several testimonies by earlier voyagers which corroborate his climactic thesis: "If these men of religion receive charity from Europe, then this charity, far from making them rich, is not enough for the preservation of the Holy Places which are crumbling everywhere, and which will soon be abandoned for lack of assistance. The poverty is therefore proven by the unanimous testimony of voyagers." His polemical voice is unmistakable: "I have already spoken about their suffering [in passages interspersed between longer "neutral" ones]; if more proof is required, here it is."

He cites several travelers' testimonies, including one by Deshayes. In doing so, he modulates his own angry voice. First, the Turks are blamed. "[The priests] must continuously give things to the Turk, if they want to live in peace; and when they do not have the means to satisfy their greed, they have to go to prison." Then, the blame begins to shift towards those who send the priests money in the first place. "Jerusalem is so far from Constantinople that the ambassador of the King, who resides there, is unable to receive news about their oppression until long afterwards. In the meantime they suffer and endure if they do not have the money to redeem themselves; and quite often the Turks are not satisfied by just tormenting them, but they also convert their churches into mosques." Defiantly, Chateaubriand warns that he "could provide entire volumes of similar testimonies deposited in the Voyages to Palestine," many of which point fingers at European authorities as the predominantly guilty parties in the matter.

Having these references to fall back on, Chateaubriand feels safe enough to step in and add one more piece of incriminating evidence. In the archives of the church, which had been set fire to by the Pasha a century earlier Chateaubriand finds a box filled with documents which he calls "a monument of iniquity and oppression, perhaps unique on earth, . . . an evangelical catalogue," one which he rescues from "eternal forgetfulness." He reproduces a few excerpts from longer documents with dates ranging between the years 414 and 609 in the Islamic calendar and concludes that the priests had been engaged "during several centuries in defending themselves, day after day, against all kinds of insults and tyranny." Of course, Oriental despotism and corruption must be shown to be the immediate causes of the guardians' suffering. The Western guise of insult is sheer neglect but, as such, it is here merely insinuated (vol. 2, 175–179). Most of the time, Chateaubriand prefers to find things out on his own. Occasionally, however, he listens to and reports on what others had to tell him when the contents or manner of their discourse can assist him in his silent Crusade against vice and corruption, especially those of a Western nature. What he consistently avoids, whether in the company of Western or Oriental characters, is dialogue in the sense of a verbal intercourse resulting in a concrete or, at least, potential change in one's previously held ideas.

Those with whom Chateaubriand is most often engaged, both verbally and emotionally, are the Jerusalemite priests.[10] But even they cannot exceed the limits that he sets for them. When one of them approaches him with the intention of talking about politics and the secrets of the Russian court, Chateaubriand exclaims: "Alas! Father, . . . where would you look for peace if you cannot find it here?" (vol. 2, 61). Since Chateaubriand is himself far from home, he can speak for himself, albeit in a convoluted style, about the issues that he deems important. As a cultural critic, he has to adopt his own "indirect speech" in order to bypass official chastisement in France.

One way of doing so is to rechannel his dissatisfaction with some travelers' reports about the living conditions of the priests by calling some of their testimonies to his aid. He holds a special grudge against Volney, who has falsely presented the priests as "small sovereigns" living in a "true paradise" and enjoying "the greatest honors" (vol. 2, 25). Furthermore, he contradicts the "imaginary and ridiculous paintings" which falsify the pilgrims' reactions upon setting foot for the first time in the Holy Land (vol. 2, 197). One priest opens up in response to Chateaubriand's questions.[11] When asked if he would like to go back to his country or write to his family in Mayenne, he gives a shocking answer which the author, posing as an interviewer, reproduces verbatim: "Who still remembers me in France? Do I know if I still have brothers and sisters? I hope to have the force, by the merits of the Crib of the Savior, to die here, without troubling anyone, and without thinking of a country where I am forgotten" (vol. 2, 56). The reason for the priest's complaint is specific and obvious: it is the deficient network of communication between the orders in France, or Europe, and their missionaries abroad. Left on their own, the latter turn not to the one who is supposed to be their living Savior, i.e. Napoleon, but the invisible one, Jesus Christ.

The harshest criticism of Napoleon comes from Père Bonaventure de Nola, the Guardian of the convent.[12] He says what would be for Chateaubriand too risky to say. Before letting him speak up against the Emperor, Chateaubriand poses as Napoleon's advocate: "One has to be in the position of the Fathers . . . to understand the pleasure that my arrival has given them. They believed they were saved by the presence of a single Frenchman." After handing Père Bonaventure a letter from the Ambassador to the Porte, Sebastiani, the Guardian ironically suggests that it be sent to the Pasha to make him "believe they are specially protected by the Emperor." Then, he temporarily suspends his condemnation of Napoleon by telling Chateaubriand about the Pasha's annual blackmail. In their case, paying off is the only means for survival, but money is scarce. "We will be obliged to sell the sacred vases; because we have not received for the last four years a single charity from Europe: if this continues, we will be forced to abandon the Holy Land, and to deliver to the Mohammedans the Tomb of Jesus Christ" (vol. 2, 43–44).

Undoubtedly, the priests are suffering at the hands of two culprits. Napoleon's crime, however, is far more damaging. By being indifferent to the guardians' financial needs, he gambles with the fate of the Christian presence in the Holy Land. The priests, poor in both the literal and figurative senses, are no more than bargaining chips which Napoleon is willing to offer up in exchange for secular, political hegemony in the region. It is he and not the *philosophes* who will deal the death blow to the Christian faith.[13] He is the Crusader who has defected from his army and betrayed his cause and calling. Naturally, however, Chateaubriand cannot explicitly denounce Napoleon as a traitor, and especially not in diplomatic circles.

Chateaubriand targets Napoleon on several other occasions and in various contexts. In Part I, "Voyage de la Grèce," he draws an analogy between him and a nameless tyrannical ruler in Turkey and states that the characteristics of all conquering nations are comparable. The Turks display "the abuses most common among the victorious nations." When Chateaubriand asserts that the "republican soldiers are not fairer masters than the satellites of a despot," and that "a proconsul is no less greedy than a pacha," it is difficult not to see the connection between this anonymous Turkish despot and Napoleon, first as a life consul (1802) and later as an Emperor (December 1804). In order to maintain some distinction between the two, however, Chateaubriand hastens to admit that, although "a proconsul could be a monster of shamelessness, avarice, [and] cruelty," not all of them enjoy destroying "the monuments of civilization and the arts." Only the Turks indulge in such public activities (vol. 1, 335–36).

In the final chapter, Part VII, "Voyage de Tunis et retour en France," Chateaubriand renews his attack on Napoleon. Here, he draws an analogy between him and Belisaire, one of the most famous generals of the Greek Empire. He argues that "in the century of Belisaire, the events were big and the men small. This is why the annals of this century, although full of tragic catastrophes, revolt us and tire us. In history we do not look for revolutions which control and crush men but for men who have control over revolutions, and who are more powerful than fortune." Belisaire could not produce a revolution because his noble soul was "foreign and isolated in the present" (vol. 2, 279). Originally a Corsican and thus a stranger, Napoleon took advantage of an ongoing revolution when he overthrew the *Directoire* in November 1799 upon his return from the failed expedition in Egypt.[14] "For the souls of a high nature to serve society, they have to be born in a nation which preserves the taste for order, religion and customs, and whose genius and character are in harmony with its moral and political position" (vol. 2, 279). Without ever mentioning the name of Napoleon, he indirectly delivers his opinions regarding the man's character and leadership, heartily disapproving of both.

Chateaubriand sharpens his critique of Napoleon at the end of Part V, "Suite du Voyage de Jérusalem," by making his comparisons more explicit. When taking leave of his hosts before embarking on his trip to Egypt, he exclaims: "I do not know a martyr comparable to these unfortunate men of religion; the condition in which they live resembles the one we were in, in France, under the reign of terror" (vol. 2, 203). Although the name most commonly associated with the Reign of Terror is that of Maximilien Robespierre, Napoleon was his accomplice.[15] Living under the reign of neglect (the terror being exercised by the Turkish officials), the priests now face their own possible extinction if no immediate action is taken on their behalf by the French government.

The Christian world as a whole is also irresponsible. "In the past all of Christendom would have rushed to repair the sacred monument." Unfortunately, however, his warning will fall on deaf ears because "to-

day nobody thinks about it, and the smallest charity extended to this
worthy project would seem a ridiculous superstition." The priests should
be saved, not only because they guard the Holy Sepulchre, but also
because they offer safe haven in a world of persecution and cruelty.
"Turks, Arabs, Greeks, schismatic Christians, all throw themselves under
the protection of some poor men of religion, who cannot defend themselves" (vol. 2, 202 & 204). Earlier, in a dream, Chateaubriand had
expressed his desire to grant asylum to all refugees trying to escape
from political oppression at home. By sharing the same wish if not the
same reality with the priests, his identification with them is obvious:
like them, he does not feel at ease at home, the principal difference
being that his home is France and not Jerusalem.

As I have shown, individuals are not permitted to change his precon-
ceived notions about Eastern habits. Were he to allow these to affect his
opinions, he would lose control of his privileged position as the "superior" French traveler but, more importantly, he would be negotiating
the "standardized" Orient required as a counter-image to subvert certain European practices. According to Chateaubriand, Louis IX is the
best ruler that France has ever known. The France that he is going back
to is no longer that of Saint Louis but that of Napoleon,[16] and
Chateaubriand is no longer the person he was at the outset of his journey.[17] Chateaubriand expresses regret for having left his country because his journey has only helped him see more clearly his nation's and
his own flaws and failings. In Madrid he is welcomed by the French
ambassador, Mr. Beauharnais, a friend of his brother's. The brother,
Jean-Baptiste, died on the scaffold with his father-in-law, Malesherbes,
in 1794. Although the Reign of Terror is over, his wounds have not yet
healed.

In the last paragraph of the *Itinéraire* Chateaubriand reminds us of
the previous twenty years of his life, filled with "chance" and "grief,"
during which he had to survive as an author. He promises that if "heaven"
should grant him the peace which he has sought but never enjoyed, then
he would erect "in silence" a monument for his country. If, on the other
hand, "providence" decides otherwise, then he can only hope that his
last days will be free of the "worries" which plagued his earlier life.
"Heaven" and "providence" (vol. 2, 304–05) represent the censors who
might disapprove of his work. However, he hopes that they will *overlook* the message of his text that he has so carefully wrapped up.
Chateaubriand writes that Saint Louis admonished his son by telling
him the following: "If any controversy or action takes place, inquire
until you reach the truth, whether for yourself or against yourself" (vol.

2, 298). This advice cannot be followed verbatim in 1811: unlike Philippe, Chateaubriand does not have the power to say or do openly what he wishes. As a writer, however, he can express his opinion about current issues indirectly by using different narrative and rhetorical devices. If his critical stance is discernible to even a very few readers, then he has indeed written enough; should it be impenetrable to all, then he has written far too much.

Notes

1. In this article I have provided my own English translations of all quotations in French from both primary and secondary literature sources. A much more detailed version of this article can be found in my book.
2. The study of the extremely diverse political writings of Chateaubriand is restricted to articles, speeches, pamphlets, and prefaces (Clément 43).
3. The composition of the *Itinéraire* did not begin until 1809, after Chateaubriand had completed *Les Martyrs* (1809). The writing was finished in July 1810. *L'Itinéraire de Paris à Jérusalem et de Jérusalem à Paris, en allant par la Grèce, et revenant par l'Egypte, la Barbarie et l'Espagne* was published by Normant in three volumes in Paris in February 1811.
4. I use the term "satire" here in its broadest sense possible, in accordance with the theoretical framework of satire postulated by George A. Test in *Satire: Spirit and Art*. He claims that "satire is no respecter of literary or artistic categories, it cannot be confined to or defined by social class, political, or economic system, type of culture, educational background, academic discipline, or historical period" (259). To illustrate his theory, he advances a quadripartite approach to satire by positing four basic elements—aggression, laughter, play, and judgment—and arguing that "some satire will be more aggressive, some funnier, others more playful, others more judgmental" (31). The special form of "social criticism shares with satire the elements of judgment and attack but lacks the elements of laughter and play" (34). Of course, Chateaubriand's brand of satire in the *Itinéraire* is social and cultural criticism.
5. The last translation of the *Itinéraire* was made by Frederic Shoberl in 1814 and reappeared in a new edition in 1835. The English title is *Travels in Greece, Palestine, Egypt, and Barbary, during the years 1806 and 1807* by F.A. de Chateaubriand.
6. The second edition came out also in 1811, and third in 1812, the fourth in 1822. Further editions came out in 1829, 1830, 1835, 1849, 1850, 1852, 1855, 1859 (4 times), 1860, 1863, 1865, 1866, 1867 (4 times), 1868 (3 times), and 20 times between 1869 and 1884. The *Itinéraire* was translated into English in London in 1811, 1812, and 1813, in New York in 1814; and a re-

edition came out in Philadelphia in 1815. It was translated into Dutch in 1811, into Spanish in 1817, into Italian in 1820–21, and into Russian in 1815. It was also translated into German and Polish.

7. English travel in Europe, of course, was more restricted than French travel. The Napoleonic Wars (1796–1815) canceled all bookings on the Grand Tour (Bassan, *Chateaubriand et la Terre Sainte* 32).

8. Chateaubriand's own figure of expenditure is 50,000 francs (vol. 1, 301).

9. In the course of the *Itinéraire* Chateaubriand is attacked three times, in Saint Saba (vol. 2, 59), Jerusalem (vol. 2, 147–48), and in a boat on the Nile (vol. 2, 229).

10. Bassan claims that it may have been the priests who, having greatly influenced his political beliefs, inspired him to write the *Itinéraire*. After returning to France, he maintained his relationship with them through correspondence (*Chateaubriand et la Terre Sainte* 78–79, 90–95).

11. Clément de la Noye arrived in Palestine, ironically enough, on the 14th of July 1805, the sixteenth anniversary of the fall of the Bastille.

12. He arrived in Palestine on October 23rd, 1773, and died in Naples on September 10th, 1822.

13. The Concordat with the papacy in 1802 backed away from the vaunted secularism of Revolutionary France and from Napoleon's own unreligious outlook. It created a host of problems for future statesmen by deeply embedding the Church in the fabric of French national life. Yet it was a recognition of the social utility of religion, and it made a contribution to the pacification of the country (Garraty and Gay 782).

14. The expeditionary force included 38,000 troops and nearly 400 ships, in addition to a "Commission of Arts and Sciences," consisting of over 150 scientists, engineers and archaeologists. When he set out for Palestine in 1799, he was accompanied by 13,000 men. In early August of 1798, a British fleet, commanded by Horatio Nelson, sailed into the harbor at Aboukir Bay, east of Alexandria, and destroyed the French fleet in the Battle of the Nile, cutting off Napoleon's forces and leaving them to be mopped up slowly by a British army. Napoleon escaped to France, arriving on October 13th, 1799 (Garraty and Gay 778).

15. During the Thermidorian reaction, Napoleon was in service with the army of Italy as a brigadier general. He was briefly imprisoned, but the distance from Paris and some helpful connections protected him from the logical consequences of his close association with the Robespierrists, who were guillotined in 1794 (Garraty and Gay 777). It was after Toulon that he became associated with Robespierre, with whose backing he became director of the planning of operations at the headquarters of the army of Italy. Robespierre went to Paris to urge the Committee of Public Safety to adopt Napoleon's schemes for an Italian offensive. After the execution, Napoleon was denounced as their planner (Markham 17).

16. As rulers of France, Saint Louis and Napoleon are particularly comparable. They both headed military expeditions to the Holy Land and North Africa,

where they were eventually defeated, improved relations between the French church and Rome and organized a new code of laws. In addition, their reputations peaked 27 years after their deaths in 1270 and 1821. Saint Louis was canonized in 1297; Napoleon became a messianic figure around 1848.

17. Even before embarking for Palestine, Chateaubriand exclaims: "How these two months have made me age!" (vol. 1, 371). In a letter to Mme de Pastoret (11 May 1807) he wrote: "I believe, Madam, that you will find me a little bit changed: ten months of tiredness and perils, the sight of the greatest ruins of the earth, the sun the Orient, the seriousness of the peoples that I have met, all these reasons have weighed on my spirit, and I naturally feel more serious and sadder" (O'Flaherty 83).

Works Cited

Ages, Arnold. "Chateaubriand and the *Philosophes.*" *Chateaubriand Today.* Madison: U of Wisconsin P, 1970. 229–41.

Bassan, Fernande. *Chateaubriand et la Terre Sainte.* Paris: Presses Universitaires de France, 1959.

—. "Chateaubriand, Lamartine, Nerval et Flaubert en Terre Sainte." *Revue des Sciences Humaines* 120 (1965): 493–513.

Berchet, Jean-Claude. "Un voyage vers soi." *Poétique* 53 (1983): 91–108.

Butor, Michel. "Le voyage et l'écriture." *Romantisme: Revue de la Société des Etudes Romantiques* 4 (1972): 4–19.

Chateaubriand, François-René de. *Itinéraire de Paris à Jérusalem.* Vols. 1 & 2. Ed. Emile Malakis. Baltimore: The Johns Hopkins UP, 1946.

Clark, Priscilla P. "Chateaubriand and Napoleon: History, Poetry or Both?" *Chateaubriand Today.* Ed. Richard Switzer. Madison: U of Wisconsin P, 1970. 161–68.

Clément, Jean-Paul. "Chateaubriand et la liberté." *Bulletin de Société Chateaubriand* 29 (1986): 43–50.

El-Nouty, Hassan. *Le Proche Orient dans la littérature française de Nerval à Barrès.* Paris: Nizet, 1958.

Garraty, John A., and Peter Gay. *The Columbia History of the World.* New York: Harper & Row, 1987.

Hentsch, Thierry. *L'Orient imaginaire: La vision politique occidentale de l'est méditerranéen.* Paris: Les Editions de Minuit, 1988.

Hout, Syrine C. *Viewing Europe From the Outside: Cultural Encounters and Critiques in the Eighteenth-Century Pseudo-Oriental Travelogue and the Nineteenth-Century 'Voyage en Orient.'* New York: Peter Lang, 1997.

Markham, Felix. *Napoleon and the Awakening of Europe: A Study of the Military, Political and Personal Elements of the Napoleonic Domination of Europe.* New York: Collier, 1965.

O'Flaherty, Kathleen. *Pessimisme de Chateaubriand: Résonances et limites.* Nanterre: Académie Européenne du livre, 1989

Peltier, Michel. "Chateaubriand le polémiste." *Ecrits de Paris: Revue des Questions Actuelles* (1983): 68–74.

Said, Edward W. *Orientalism*. New York: Vintage, 1979.

Shepherd, Naomi. *The Zealous Intruders: The Western Rediscovery of Palestine*. London: Collins, 1987.

Switzer, Richard. *Chateaubriand*. New York: Twayne, 1971.

Test, George A. *Satire: Spirit and Art*. Tampa: U of South Florida P, 1991.

Todorov, Tzvetan. *Nous et les Autres: La réflexion française sur la diversité humaine*. Paris: Edition du Seuil, 1989.

Wolfzettel, Friedrich. *Ce désir de vagabondage cosmopolite: Wege und Entwicklung des französischen Reiseberichts des 19. Jahrhunderts*. Tübingen: Max Niemeyer Verlag, 1986.

8

Remaking "Lawless Lads and Licentious Girls": The Salvation Army and the Regeneration of Empire

Troy Boone

The encounter between middle-class Christian social explorer and working-class "heathen" of the urban "underworld" dominates Victorian and Edwardian sociology and is, from Henry Mayhew's *London Labour and the London Poor* (1861–62) to Beatrice Webb's *My Apprenticeship* (1926), a generic norm of its characteristic literary manifestation, the social exploration text. A number of writers have examined how, in social exploration texts of the 1880s and 1890s, the urban poor of England transform from lazy paupers into impoverished underemployed, from wilfully immoral characters into helpless victims of a degenerating city environment, from savage racial others into outcast Britons.[1] *In Darkest England and the Way Out* (1890) exemplifies the power of these new representations: although conserving a disdain for laziness and immorality, William Booth, founder and first general of the Salvation Army, sounds an up-to-date alarm that consistent poverty might cause many English citydwellers to degenerate from useful citizens into useless "residuum."

Booth's resulting campaign to regenerate the urban poor echoes late-century worries about the decline of the British Empire and about the need to enlist the working class in halting this decline.[2] Although the sensational title *In Darkest England* clearly capitalizes on the publishing event of the summer of 1890, Henry Morton Stanley's *In Darkest Africa*, Booth quickly moves away from comparisons between working-class English and native African; insisting that an "analogy is as good as a suggestion" but "becomes wearisome when it is pressed too far" (18–19), Booth like many of his contemporaries resists clichés about the "urban savage" and imagines an incorporative English public unified by race, nationalism, imperial and industrial ambitions.[3] He not only argues that it is not "the inevitable and inexorable destiny of thou-

sands of *Englishmen* to be brutalized into worse than beasts by the condition of their environment" (22; my emphasis) but wishes to foster "a
sense of brotherhood and a consciousness of community of interest and
of nationality on the part of the English-speaking people throughout the
world" (151). Similarly, in 1886 Booth's friend Arnold White had
pointed out that the

> Transvaal and Zulu wars, and the Bechuanaland expedition,
> would have been unnecessary had Natal, the Transvaal, and
> the northern part of the Cape Colony been economically rein-
> forced by a peaceable army corps of God-fearing, hard-work-
> ing men and women from England and Scotland, sent out by
> the State. (White, "Common Sense" 379)

In an era of eager schemers, writers like Booth and White stand out for
the local and global sweep of their projects to clean out London and
buttress a sagging empire by relocating the poor in overseas colonies:
thus White proclaims, "Distress in London is not the distress of a great
city—it is the distress of a great empire . . . the conclusion is inevitable
that exceptional—because imperial distress—can be met only by exceptional—that is, by imperial measures" (White, *Problems of a Great
City* 226). Booth seeks to answer demands, such as White's, for a "peace-
able army corps of God-fearing, hard-working" British colonists by pre-
senting the Salvation Army as able to save not only the lost among the
poor but also the empire that many feared Britain was on the verge of
losing. Disturbed by the "disease-breeding, manhood-destroying character of . . . our large cities," Booth worries that members of the urban
working class, "their health sapped by their surroundings" (32), will
not be able to bear their share of the white man's burden: "Children
thus hungered, thus housed, and thus left to grow up as best they can
without being fathered or mothered, are not, educate them as you will,
exactly the most promising material for the making of the future citizens and rulers of the Empire" (73–74). Booth's social exploration
maps out "the malady" (23), a Dantesque cityscape that divides the poor
into "three circles, one within the other"—the "starving . . . but honest,
Poor," those "who live by Vice," and "those who exist by Crime"—all
three "sodden with Drink" and apparently escaping the surveillance of
middle-class observers except for Booth (32). His social scheme in
turn offers as a "remedy" (23) an interconnecting web of city, farm, and
overseas colonies—a system that transforms these devilish circles into

a Britain that is at once familiar (London supplies and is supplied by the kingdom that it unifies and the empire of which it is the "heart") and new in that it can be administered only by a strong Salvation Army. Booth's double campaign aims at remaking the concept of the English public by converting members of the working class into citizens who have a central role in the workings of empire; at the same time, he retains an essentialist notion of working-class character that subtly renders these converts "others" within the English public and demands that they remain subject to regulation by their betters.

Booth's call to arms is directed at the English middle class, which he seeks to commission in the larger project of regenerating the poor. Although Booth admits that the middle class also needs reformation, he establishes different registers with which to scrutinize and judge the different classes. By faulting his readers' lack of concern for the poor, Booth hopes to swell the ranks of beneficent public persons like himself, to solicit volunteers who will aid in the surveillance of British Empire and British workers, and yet to retain the sanctity of middle-class private life. As we will see, although Booth also hopes to recruit working-class subjects for service in his Army, he imagines their entry into public life in such a way that surveying power is withheld from them, that their domestic lives are always public issues, that their privacy is an impossibility. Regarding the chart-topping success of Stanley's *In Darkest Africa*, Booth wonders

> how strange it is that so much interest should be excited by a narrative of human squalor and human heroism in a distant continent, while greater squalor and heroism not less magnificent may be observed at our very doors . . . the stony streets of London, if they could but speak, would tell of tragedies as awful, of ruin as complete, of ravishments as horrible, as if we were in Central Africa. (19)

Implying that the streets speak only when their tales are interpreted by an attentive social surveyor, Booth charges his middle-class contemporaries with the sin of silent disengagement; he blames them, in effect, for abrogating their responsibilities as public persons, as socially concerned urban spectators. Few will realize, as Booth does, that East London "is the great Slough of Despond of our time," because "what a slough it is no man can gauge who has not waded therein, as some of us have done, up to the very neck for long years . . . with open eyes and with bleeding heart" (19).   In order to teach his readers to translate sympathy for the London poor into effective surveillance of this "residuum," to transform "bleeding heart" into "open eyes," he encourages all sorts of private gentlemen and gentlewomen to come forward with any resources that will propel his scheme—a million sterling (259), or information regarding how best to build colonists' cottages (235). Yet he asks these gentlefolk to go public only with those aspects of their lives (wealth, knowledge of engineering) that are already part of their public characters. Booth thus urges his middle-class readers into public affairs but nevertheless leaves middle-class private life privileged as an invisible norm, requiring no scrutiny.

Booth prefaces his book with a personal narrative that shows how public life offers middle-class subjects the visionary power of urban spectators and the spiritual power of social reformers, while not encroaching on middle-class domestic privacy:

> When but a mere child the degradation and helpless misery of the poor Stockingers of my native town, wandering gaunt and hunger-stricken through the streets droning out their melancholy ditties, crowding the Union or toiling like galley slaves on relief works for a bare subsistence, kindled in my heart yearnings to help the poor which have continued to this day and which have had a powerful influence on my whole life.

However great his "yearnings to help the poor," Booth's vignette establishes his power as middle-class urban spectator and social reformer through identification against rather than with the stockingers. Significantly, although Booth's many biographers insistently remind the reader that he grew up in considerable want, recalling the poverty of the helpless stockingers does not prod any reflection on his own youthful feelings of social and economic inferiority—what he later called his own "humiliating bondage" as an apprentice in a pawnbroker's shop, where he "was practically a white slave."[4] Booth's preface, with its spectatorial sweep and emphasis on the sympathy "kindled in" his heart, erases the fact that he viewed the Nottingham workers primarily from behind the counter of a pawnbroker's shop—a position that is at once stationary, conventionally viewed as parasitic, and "humiliating" for the aged Booth to recall.

Rather, the preface to *In Darkest England* describes the slavelike weavers as distant and essentially different from Booth the observer of their miseries. Although the stockingers are both pitiable and threatening—"gaunt" and "hunger-stricken," yet "wandering" and "crowding" like Mayhew's nomadic predators—the spectacle of the zombie-like poor testifies to Booth's visionary power, and their lack of it. Although wandering the streets, they do not possess the mobility of the urban spectator but are "like galley slaves," chained to the slums of Nottingham. In contrast, even though he is "a mere child," Booth is apparently able to survey (effortlessly, unperceived, and in perfect safety) a variety of city spaces (streets, Union, relief works). Finally, the placement of this childhood narrative at the beginning of the adult social reformer's text indicates that this contact with poverty does not taint Booth but becomes instead the foundation of the General's life work: erasing his own childhood limitations (economic, bodily, intellectual), Booth points us towards the epic survey of "darkest England" and the solution of its problems—the public man's "forty years of active service in the salvation of men" (Preface). Seeming to promise a description of the scene's psychological effects on the boy, autobiography here does not render the private person William Booth available for spectatorial scrutiny but instead proves that he is from childhood destined to powerful social observations, visionary social reforms, and national social status: the preface naturalizes the representation of middle-class subjects as able to be both private persons who engage in disembodied surveillance and public persons active for the nation's good.

Unlike this picture of his own childhood, with all its strategic omissions, Booth's exposure of the degeneracy of working-class youth—the "lawlessness of our lads, the increased license of our girls" (74)—is remorselessly frank. Like all Victorian and Edwardian social observers, male and female, Booth finds prostitution particularly fascinating,[5] and he summarizes its causes in a single melodramatic case history:

> The bastard of a harlot, born in a brothel, suckled on gin, and familiar from earliest infancy with all the bestialities of debauch, violated before she is twelve, and driven out into the streets by her mother a year or two later, what chance is there for such a girl in this world—I say nothing about the next? Yet such a case is not exceptional. There are many such differing in detail, but in essentials the same. (55)

Unfortunate birth, malnutrition, exposure to primal scenes, rape, and abandonment all reinforce the girl's victimization by environment rather than emphasize her faulty character; yet the insistent blaming of the girl's mother personalizes the degenerating environmental influence and begs the apparently too-immense question of what caused the mother to be "a harlot." Although Booth momentarily flirts with an uncharacteristically subtle economic analysis of prostitution ("there is no industrial career in which for a short time a beautiful girl can make as much money with as little trouble as the profession of a courtesan" [58]), even this sentence charges insistently toward imputations of laziness ("little trouble") and immorality ("courtesan"). His case studies seek to establish the environmental etiology of prostitution yet wind up leaving the characters of working-class subjects as much to blame as economic circumstances: "Some there are, no doubt, perhaps many, who—whether from inherited passion or from evil education—have deliberately embarked upon a life of vice, but with the majority it is not so" (58). Such cloudy renditions of "statistics" are quite strategic, and the difficulty of determining how many ("Some," "many," not the "majority") instances of degeneration result from environmental influences ("evil education") and how many from character traits ("inherited passion") simultaneously implies that degeneration is reversible and that most working-class subjects cannot help themselves. Booth's text raises this contradiction so as neatly to resolve it: if urban degeneration can be ameliorated, but the working class is incapable of accomplishing this improvement, the stalemate demands intervention by middle-class reformers.

The "essential" similarity of Booth's case studies posits that working-class culture itself is the degenerating force to be replaced by a more wholesome culture engineered and maintained by middle-class spectators, who can provide laws for lawless lads and restrict the license of licentious girls. Thus Booth treats the prostitute as a synecdoche for a supposed moral infirmity that disqualifies the working class from self-determination:[6] "untrained to labor, demoralized by a life of debauchery, accustomed to the wildest license, emancipated from all discipline but that of starvation," the "lost women of our streets . . . suffer from almost every fault that human material can possess" (271). Moreover, Booth defines this infirmity in terms of vision and thereby reinforces the qualifications, established in his preface, of the middle class, the Salvation Army, and its General to undertake the regeneration of the poor. Women fall into prostitution, he claims, because they "see the glittering bait" of riches, but the "penalty" of "disease, degradation and death" is "hidden" from their sight (59). The apparently less sinful young woman who is "driven out into the streets by her mother" (55) is similarly helpless, and her tale does not establish reader identification with her plight but with the visual power of the middle-class observer, who has the foresight to discern social consequences. The prostitute's "nature . . . is short-sighted" (59), but that of Booth—or anyone "who looks below the surface" (58)—is not.

Janet Wolff has influentially argued that the "rise and development of sociology in the nineteenth century was closely related to the growth and increasing separation of 'public' and 'private' spheres of activity in western industrial societies" (43–44) and that the power associated with the public realm—the urban spectator's "freedom to move about in the city" (39)—causes the invisibility of women and a "consequently partial conception of 'modernity'" (43). Wolff's analysis is most appropriate to a discussion of how Booth's text participates in such a separation of "the public world of work, politics, and city life" and "the 'private' sphere of the home and the suburb" (34); yet Wolff's claim that this separation of spheres divides power exclusively along the lines of gender—male public and female private—erases from the history of "sociology as a new discipline" (44) the very class issues that are so central to it. Whereas Wolff argues that the sociological literature of modernity is "primarily concerned with the 'public' spheres of work, politics, and the market place" (44), the dominant enterprise of nineteenth- and twentieth-century sociology is the investigation, classification, and reformation of every aspect of the domestic lives of the working class. The conception of modernity thus fostered is indeed partial: working-class privacy is an impediment to sociological knowledge, which must make such private affairs public so as to subject them to evaluation by middle-class men and women who are public figures but who nevertheless retain their status as private individuals. The very real asymmetries of power between middle-class men and women have been the subject of much rewarding feminist investigation but should not obscure the fact that, as a group with mutual class interests, male and female social observers unite in the project of maintaining spectatorial and discursive control over a population thereby rendered essentially "other" to them.

According to Booth, the mystery about what lies "below the surface" of working-class home life demands more middle-class investigation so as to make this dirty private realm a public issue, subject to regulation and reformation, before thirteen-year-olds become "public women." Booth implies that his visionary abilities qualify the Salvation Army for such a regenerating intervention, just as his prefatory autobiography opposes the narrative of the working-class girl's upbringing: the prostitute's career as a "public woman"—who "serves" men, according to Booth's logic, by damning herself and them—begins when she witnesses a degradation that is dangerous in that it is domestic, private, infectiously close; Booth's career as a "public person"—who "serves" men and women by saving them—begins when he surveys the public degradation of the stockingers from a distance that protects him from its effects. Booth's social scheme in turn removes working-class men and women from unregulated private spaces (brothels, gin-palaces, and bedrooms full of bestial debauchery) and replaces them in more salubrious open spaces (city, farm, and overseas colonies).

If the unregenerate prostitute "accepts her doom . . . and treads the long and torturing path-way of 'the streets' to the grave" (61), Booth offers a contrasting, upbeat narrative of what happens when such a woman joins the Salvation Army Slum Brigade—which is "composed of women" some of whom are "ladies born and bred" but most of whom, Booth insists, are "children of the poor" (166) who themselves engage in the "rescue of many fallen girls" (176). The women of the Slum Brigade have a very different experience of "the streets": "our . . . lasses go unharmed and loved at all hours, spending every other night always upon the streets" (63). *In Darkest England* here renders ambiguous the concept of "public woman" in order to imply that working-class women can inhabit the streets either as prostitutes subject to violence or as Salvation Army lasses protected from harm by the uniform they share with the General. Judith R. Walkowitz's study of the participation of late-Victorian women in such public events as Salvation Army spectacles has begun a useful revision of arguments, such as Wolff's, about the essential link between urban spectatorship and maleness.[7] Walkowitz argues that the Hallelujah lass represents "a new style of working-class woman" who "impinged on the civic spaces of her class superiors" and posed challenges to "conventions of gender," both of which were "contained and channeled . . . into obedience to a highly authoritarian institution" (Walkowitz, *City of Dreadful Delight* 73–74). However, by identifying the Salvation Army as the circumscribing institution, Walkowitz obscures how authoritative conceptions of essential working-class character much more efficiently limit such transgressions: the ability of working-class Salvationist women to revise "conventions of gender" is contained by exactly that mapping of "civic spaces" by their "class superiors"—by exclusive class divisions institutionalized partly through organizations like Booth's but certainly more diffusely throughout British culture.

Rather, in order to examine the Salvation Army's role in constructions of sexual difference, social class, and empire, it is crucial to consider the Army neither as the source of such constructions nor as the limit of challenges to them but as one space among many where constructions and challenges are discursively produced. The Salvation Army is a site where the socio-political power relations that Michel Foucault fortuitously describes as "discipline" can operate: "'Discipline' may be identified neither with an institution nor with an apparatus; it is a type of power" that "has its principle not so much in a person as in . . . an arrangement whose internal mechanisms produce the relation in which individuals are caught up" (*Discipline and Punish* 215, 202). Booth's disciplinary schemes (and the challenges to gender constructions they fostered) excite such controversy among his contemporaries because they contribute to the arrangement of capitalist and imperialist projects to regenerate the urban poor and the overseas empire. That is, even a bureaucracy like the Salvation Army operates most smoothly in the service of more massive institutions—as Booth's text implies throughout and as Booth's friend W. T. Stead makes explicit in an avid letter to Alfred, Viscount Milner: "You will be delighted to see that we have got the Salvation Army solid not only for Social Reform but also for Imperial Unity. I have written to Rhodes about it and we stand on the eve of great things."[8]

The Salvation Army should indeed be a cultural movement of great interest to feminists, not only because of the tremendous public authority and publishing success of Catherine Booth but because of the Army's controversial attempt to institutionalize equality between women and men. However, the history of the Salvation Army should remind us that feminist gains never necessarily imply the eradication of class difference. For example, Ann R. Higginbotham has revealingly detailed the divisions between Salvationist women, in particular how the Women's Social Services—founded in 1884 and administered, relatively independently of other branches of the Army, primarily by upper-middle-class women—"may well have appealed to Salvationist women who would have hesitated to lead a brass band or harangue a crowd in the slums of Whitechapel" (217). The history of the Women's Social Services demonstrates the difficulty of uniting middle- and working-class women within the Salvation Army and suggests that its incorporative ideals do not offer working-class women as much mobility as Walkowitz implies. If, by giving speeches to their class equals in the East End, working-class Salvationist women took on a public role most commonly available to wealthy women such as Octavia Hill and Beatrice Webb, this step into the "civic spaces" of the middle class is a significant moment in the history of working-class women. It is not, however, a radi-

cal shift in the balance of power between the classes that would allow
one to imagine, for example, working-class women investigating and
reforming the homes of their "betters."

Indeed, this new status publicizes a traditionally feminine and mater-
nal power to regulate equals and inferiors and places working-class Salvationist women between (on the one hand) the "unrespectable" poor
they observe and (on the other) the middle class that observes them.
Pamela J. Walker persuasively argues that working-class Salvationist
women were especially effective as critics of supposedly excessive drinking and gambling by men of their own class (101–09), and Catherine
Booth makes clear the benefits of this arrangement to middle-class reformers: according to her, the degenerate poor can only be led to regeneration "by people of their own class, who would go after them in
their own resorts, who would speak to them in a language they understood, and reach them by means suited to their own tastes" (qtd. in Inglis
176). Hardly bothering to disguise the aggressive policing implied in
"go after them," this enlistment of working class women in making
poor men's private lives a public issue is less an encouragement to trans-
gress class boundaries than a resonant example of the strategy of divide
and conquer that has long buttressed middle-class power.

Although the Salvation Army lasses might similarly advertise their
difference from prostitutes, their difference from middle-class women
is just as heavily marked. For instance, although William Booth claims
that the lasses "go unharmed and loved at all hours, spending every
other night always upon the streets" (63), his use of the word "loved"
and the phrase "spending every other night always upon the streets"
insinuates that the lasses bear the taint of the "licentious girls" from
which they have "evolved" and the traces of "outcast England" from
which they come. Although the Salvation Army uniform seems an equalizing costume[9] that makes it impossible to distinguish between "ladies
born and bred" who are slumming as lasses and those who are essentially "children of the poor" (166), the permanent inner marks of the
latter will, apparently, always penetrate any outer covering. Thus
Josephine Butler praises Catherine Booth for her training of "girl soldiers": "As a rule, the manners of the Salvation Lasses are beautiful, in
spite of occasional dropped h's, provincial accent, and other such de-
fects. As women, we cannot but rejoice that even a portion of our women
of the humbler ranks . . . is subjected to such a training as this" (Butler
648).

The dropped aspirates over which Butler so frequently worries[10] signal, for her, the more dangerous qualities of the working class that they

characterize—"a mass of creatures hardly human, debased through generations of misery, and ignorance, and vice, full of hatred—hatred of society and of everything which exists; wild beasts ready for vengeance" (Butler 646).[11] Throughout his book, Booth seeks to advertise the necessity and effectiveness of his scheme by negotiating between asserting and obscuring this threat of the "dangerous classes." Thus, in the lurid "Salvation Army Social Campaign" lithograph (see frontispiece), the city colony lighthouse directs the eye up from the urban morass, through the airy clouds of various Salvationist activities and the arboreal branches of the farm colony, to the heavenly colony across the sea; in answer to the worry that the undisciplined poor do not even "know how to bake a loaf or wash their clothes" (71), the illustration is capped by a lad and a girl, intent on baking and washing, who have apparently transcended the disciplinary maze contained by the social campaign arch. Yet their muscular industry is circumscribed by framing lines indivisible from the arch, which is heavily reinforced by ponderous statistics regarding their former evils.

Beatrice Webb's *My Apprenticeship* defines the spirit of the age with which I am dealing as "a new consciousness of sin among men of intellect and men of property," a "growing uneasiness . . . that the industrial organisation, which had yielded rent, interest and profits on a stupendous scale, had failed to provide a decent livelihood and tolerable conditions for a majority of the inhabitants of Great Britain" (154–55). Webb relates that this "class-consciousness of sin was usually accompanied by . . . a deliberate dedication of means and strength to the reorganisation of society on a more equalitarian basis," and among these forms of "devoted personal service" (157) she identifies "a theological category," including "General Booth" (155). His text might even seem to eschew the concept of "otherness" and to fantasize a classless society, entirely contained by the voraciously incorporative Salvation Army, and the very metaphor "army" seems at once hierarchical and egalitarian. Perfectly aware that the supposedly equalizing Army outfit would fascinate even his detractors, Booth uniformly appears—in the photographs for which he loved to pose—wearing the jersey and insignia that identify General, no less than rawest recruit, as subject to a Salvationist order that transcends any individual soldier. Moreover, despite his oft-criticized authoritarianism, Booth challenges the hierarchies of other armies and claims that his "makes every soldier in some degree an officer, charged with the responsibility of so many of his townsfolk, and expected to carry on the war against the streets, street, or part of a street allotted to his care" (Booth, "What Is the Salvation Army?" 178).

Booth's reform scheme thus seeks masterfully to resolve the contradictions between two claims with great power in liberal rhetoric about colonized and working-class subjects: converting these outsiders into upholders of the values and ambitions of the Western middle class is the least violent means of removing the danger of such "others"; reinforcing a belief that these converts retain signs of their "otherness" in turn entrenches the divisions on which imperialist and capitalist power depend.[12]

Yet—while acknowledging that Booth thus aims at the smooth functioning of power, and in spite of his disingenuous insistence that he offers "nothing Utopian in the presentation of remedies" (24)—it is important to recognize the utopian desire to reorganize society "on a more egalitarian basis," which makes the Army and its most famous literary product so much a part of his and Webb's liberal time: *In Darkest England* is a political conversion narrative driven by a tension between the longing to convert *fin-de-siècle* culture into a more wholesome form and the disciplinary terms in which this conversion is narrated.[13] Late-Victorian and early-Edwardian political and literary culture—dominated as it is by Charles Booth's projected labor colonies and Fabian Socialism, William Morris's *News from Nowhere* (1890) and H. G. Wells's *The Time Machine* (1895)—frustrates critical attempts to segregate literary romance and realism, reactionary and radical politics, social reform and social regulation. Such works wrestle for control of terms (degeneration, colonization, socialism) that are powerful discursive weapons in capitalist and imperialist culture in order to debate (between and often within texts) what sort of conversion these powers should be used to narrate. Such discursive complexities remind us that where "there is power, there is resistance, and yet, or rather consequently, this resistance is never in a position of exteriority in relation to power" (Foucault, *History of Sexuality* 95).

What is now the most famous response to the Salvationist movement, Bernard Shaw's *Major Barbara* (performed 1905, published 1907), dazzlingly rehearses both the utopian potential of Foucault's insight and the difficulty of converting narratives such as Booth's to alternative political ends. Although, like Booth the environmentalist and indefatigable fundraiser, Undershaft grasps both that "the worst of our crimes is poverty" caused by the bungling of Victorian industrialism (15) and that nothing can lift poverty "from Man's neck but money" (141), and although his Perivale St. Andrews village revises the rural colonies Booth imagined, it is difficult to conclude, as Stanley Weintraub does, that the comedy is "a theatrical *Darkest England*" (46) and

Undershaft its "most Boothian character" (49). Both the play and the character explode notions, which hold together texts like Booth's, of an essential bond between power and middle-class status. Eschewing back-to-the-land schemes, with which middle-class visionaries aim at rescuing the poor from their social selves by subjecting them to surveillance, Undershaft's model town scraps the "old moralities" (141) that exclusively separate labor and vision, public and private, middle and working class. Here capitalists "look after the drainage" so that workers may "find their own dreams" (141), and Undershaft is refreshingly bored with what goes on behind working-class doors: "When I speak to one of them it is 'Well, Jones, is the baby doing well? and has Mrs Jones made a good recovery?' 'Nicely, thank you, sir.' And thats all" (126–27). Undershaft need not "maintain discipline among" the workers because "every man of them keeps the man just below him in his place" (127); if Undershaft admits the benefits of this self-discipline according to social norms ("The result is a colossal profit, which comes to me" [127]), he denies neither that the benefits could accrue to labor nor that the power that upholds such norms could be used to change them.

This utopian possibility is inseparable from the play's unflinching observation, which causes critics such difficulties, that reform of capitalist culture must involve conversion of (and thus contact with) its powers—including the sanguinary products of Undershaft's warworks. Exposing capital and bombs alike as belonging essentially to no one group or class, as forms of a power that is "the only lever strong enough to overturn a social system" (143), Undershaft implies that Cusins will be able "to give the common man weapons . . . to force the intellectual oligarchy to use its genius for the general good" (150). Moreover, although the play is primarily concerned with class conflict, Undershaft's commodities are of course implicated in the military expansion of the British Empire: his partnership with Cusins similarly ignites the possibility that making such weapons equally accessible "to black man, white man and yellow man" (138) might be the means of attacking what Shaw's preface fleetingly refers to as "soul atrophy disguised as empire" (47). Yet this uncomfortable tension between romantic futurity and realistic present focuses attention onto the chief transformation that the play displays—the conversion of its central characters to new, productively conflicting, political identities—and onto an anti-essentialist concept not only of power but of identity. As power does not essentially belong to capital and empire, Cusins (who is both "a professor of Greek" and the illegitimate son of Australian "outcasts" [135]), Barbara (both "Mijor Earl's Grendorter" [112] and "daughter of a foundling" [151]), and

Undershaft (a millionaire "east ender" [143]) do not essentially belong to the class those institutions have historically served. Although the specifics of Booth's scheme appear primarily to be the whimsies of an elderly eccentric—except for an 1890 bestseller, the planet bears few traces of the farm and overseas colonies he envisioned[14]—the Boothian fantasy is more with us than the Shavian alternative. Particularly in the United States, the powers and problems of which, at the end of our century, often uncannily resemble those of late-Victorian Britain, the most intractable narrative of political progress involves regenerating middle-class institutions by converting a diversity of individuals to the values of those institutions, while insisting that those individuals retain an essential "other" identity. Promising no way out of all present difficulties, the alternative narrative—which might be the basis of a most supple political possibility—imagines the conversion of those institutions by individuals and groups, while recognizing that the politics of those individuals and groups are not reducible to their identities.

Notes

1. Jones, *Outcast London* 127–51, 262–314 describes how late-century degeneration theory (which argues that poverty causes the degeneration of the urban poor) gains prestige over earlier demoralization theory (which argues that paupers choose poverty and require moral training, for instance in self-help). Finch analyzes the shift from this "environmentalist" (8) reasoning (which "equates *behaviour* with *type*" and insists that "behaviour can be perfectly represented on a map of human types independent of social circumstances" [24]) to twentieth-century "psychological" reasoning (which seeks "an inner essence which behaviour could just as easily conceal, as reveal" [24] and identifies "individuals, or whole groups . . . as being a particular type, based upon psychic traits" [8]). Strategically blurring demoralization and degeneration, character and environment, Booth's text signals these shifting styles of sociological discourse and the power of even contrasting fashions to affirm essentialist differences between middle and working class. Booth's scheme also depends on the contemporary favor for ameliorist discourse—which, as Abrams notes, posits "reforms that would so ameliorate social conditions that individuals would be enabled, or forced, to improve themselves" (38) and presumes "a fundamental consensus and community of interest among individuals and classes" (9). Social imperialists such as Booth most obviously presume that a stable British Empire serves the interests of Britons of all classes (see Semmel 13–28, 234–39).
2. My use, throughout this chapter, of "working class" to refer to non-middle-

class English men and women is not meant to deny the differences between working-class individuals and groups but to oppose the nineteenth-century construction of "two distinct working classes . . . with a potential middle group which hovered between the two": "the respectable, a middle group who could go up or down depending upon environmental conditions, and the hopeless non-respectables" (Finch 34–35). Booth's text, with its determination to distinguish between "an uppercrust and a submerged tenth" (215), is among the most influential turn-of the-century contributions to this construction.

3. Nord, "Social Explorer" 122–34 usefully outlines the use of "urban savage" as a literary trope, though she underestimates the extent to which Booth's work diverges from those of earlier writers like Henry Mayhew. Mayhew's investigation presumes that the London poor constitute a "wandering horde," a race essentially different from but "intermingled with, and in a measure preying upon" the "industrious, provident, and civilized" middle class: the London poor are, for Mayhew, a race with "peculiar and distinctive physical as well as moral characteristics"—prognathous jaws, lozenge-shaped faces, and smaller brains, as well as violence, licentiousness, love of drink (1: 1–2). Contrasting desires, like Booth's, to imagine an English public unified by one racial, political, and imperial identity reach a jingoistic apex during the second Boer War (1899–1902).

4. Qtd. in Railton 6. The many biographies of Booth consistently narrate his early life as a Dickensian tale of middle-class drive for respectability frustrated by Booth's father—who (ironically) speculated in construction of cheap houses for Nottingham workers, ruined the family, and died when William was thirteen. Among biographies of Booth, which uniformly tend toward hero-worship, the liveliest account of his youth is Railton 1–15.

5. Walkowitz, *Prostitution and Victorian Society* compellingly demonstrates that Victorian assaults on prostitution exemplify the reformist desire to render working-class privacy an impossibility: the Contagious Diseases Acts of 1864, 1866, and 1869 were aimed, she argues, at "forcing prostitutes to acknowledge their status as 'public' women and destroying their private associations with the general community of the laboring poor" (5), at making it "impossible for a subject woman to keep her private and public worlds apart" (202); Walkowitz also details how feminists agitating for the repeal of these acts, as "mature, affluent women . . . enjoyed an unusual freedom to engage in public activities" (118), even as "more often than not their actual relationship with working-class women was hierarchical, controlling, and punitive" (131).

6. This characteristic representation, in Victorian sociological and novelistic discourse, of the prostitute as "emblematic" of the working class enables many of the most powerful constructions of this class (as licentious, criminal, infectious, feminine, physical and benighted), which in turn confirm the middle class in its self-representation (as continent, law-abiding, healthy, masculine, rational and knowing). Although I focus primarily on Booth's

treatment of "licentious girls" due to its centrality to this representation, which demands far more attention from scholars, Booth's less- extensive discussions of "lawless lads" similarly assume the inherent degeneracy of working-class culture:

> And with boys it is almost as bad. There are thousands who were begotten when both parents were besotted with drink, whose mothers saturated themselves with alcohol every day of their pregnancy, who may be said to have sucked in a taste for strong drink with their mothers' milk, and who were surrounded from childhood with opportunities and incitements to drink. (55)

Booth's gendering of deviance (girls become prostitutes, boys drunkards) is significant, but so is his implication that, between the two genders, the entire working class tends toward some sort of sensual excess. In turn, Booth's insistent focus on the *juvenile* origins of this tendency reinforces the possibility of reversing it, the childlike helplessness of the class it affects, and the need for paternalistic middle-class reforms.

7. Similarly, in her analysis ("Urban Peripatetic") of Beatrice Webb's undercover investigations into sweatshop conditions, Deborah Epstein Nord argues that "Webb's disguise, which freed her as a middle-class woman to enter into a working-class context, complicates the notion . . . that in urban space sex ultimately takes precedence over class in determining women's experience and consciousness within that space" (373). Certainly the discursive power of Victorian and Edwardian reformers such as Octavia Hill, Josephine Butler, Catherine Booth, Ellice Hopkins, and Webb should "argue for a subtler and more complex sense of how this relationship between sex and class figures in any given representation of the female spectator" (373–74).

8. Stead's 23 October 1890 letter to Milner is quoted in Whyte 2: 13. I do not address the much-debated issue of to what extent Stead co-authored *In Darkest England*: the long association of the Salvation Army and sensation journalism should raise more weighty concerns about how liberal constructions of working-class depravity operate on many discursive fronts.

9. This perception is a frequent motif in writings on the Salvation Army; in addition to Walkowitz, see Inglis's claim that "in a society where dress normally recorded the wearer's status, the clothing worn by a Salvationist was classless" (182).

10. In a different mood, Butler claimed that her "sympathies are wholly with the non-privileged, even when they drop every 'h'" (qtd. in Walkowitz, *Prostitution and Victorian Society* 115).

11. Similarly, even a sympathetic report on the Salvation Army Farm Colony at Hadleigh notes that "the denizens of the slums" conveyed to the Essex site "usually convert the rural scene into more or less of a slum during their

labors" (Bremner 155). Indeed, many of the waspish commentaries on the Salvation Army, which followed it from its founding in 1878 until well into the twentieth century, frequently imply that the Army itself is tinged by the inherent degradation of the slumdwellers it seeks to convert. Thus an 1884 *Saturday Review* writer complains of "a noisy mob rambling after a banner and a band, with a reformed housebreaker or converted potboy performing antics in front" and consistently describes the Army in terms lifted from inflammatory writings on the "dangerous classes"—as "a howling mob," "a heated and gabbling mob," "ignoble fanatics," "the stupidest of mankind," "coarse and ignorant" ("Rowdy Religion" 700).

12. Significantly, Army officers sent among the Zulus and Indians were ordered to learn their languages and customs so that, as Inglis says, "foreign sinners could be met as intimately as sinners at home" (194). Although *In Darkest England* never admits as much, the missionary goals of Booth's colonization scheme would seem to require that the urban poor sent overseas would receive this considerable education; yet Booth asserts that they would not need to vote in the elections of whatever country to which they were transported, as such people should not "bother their heads about politics" (qtd. in Inglis 200). In the context of the Reform Bill of 1884, which extended the vote to all males over twenty-one, Booth's fantasy of a realm where newly enfranchised working-class men would no longer need or desire to retain this right can only be described as regressive liberalism.

13. Victor Bailey's valuable work on the Salvation Army instructively demonstrates the liabilities of treating such an institution only in terms of either its disciplinary or its utopian operations. In an early essay, Bailey persuasively describes how Salvationist strategy—a massive conversion of supposedly degenerate working-class popular culture (music halls, pubs, penny dreadfuls) into equally entertaining but morally regenerating forms (Salvation Army brass bands, revival meetings, the *War Cry*)—represents a "moral imperialism" that "looked to colonise spaces in which 'savage' entertainments were performed" ("Salvation Army Riots" 238); however, Bailey's essay overstates the effectiveness of this disciplinary conversion and deemphasizes how, as Gareth Stedman Jones has compellingly demonstrated, the chief characteristics of working-class politics at the end of the century were invigoration of the cultural practices against which the Army directed its onslaught, and apathy toward militant imperial, especially anti-Boer, fervor (*Languages of Class* 179–238). Bailey's later reading of the Salvation Army ("'In Darkest England'") as "an expression of independent working-class cultural development, and not as an agency of middle-class domination" (134) goes to the other extreme: although he offers intriguing evidence for the similarity of Salvationist and socialist operations, to claim that these two movements together caused a "change in the social habits of the urban masses"—towards "self-discipline, self-respect and self-help" (149)—is to grant Booth's regeneration scheme the credit he so richly desires.

14. The Western cityscape, needless to say, extensively signifies the success of

Booth's plans to erect missionary city colonies in urban slums. The overseas colony project was never successful; yet, particularly in the United States, the Army relocated many working-class city families to farm colonies opened in 1898 at Fort Romie in California, Fort Amity in Colorado, and Fort Herrick in Ohio (see Spence 15–76). Although the development of the United States farm colonies is beyond the scope of the present chapter, that the site of the Fort Romie colony—four miles from Soledad, California—is now in the neighborhood of a penitentiary is an irony worth recording.

Works Cited

Abrams, Philip. *The Origins of British Sociology: 1834–1914.* Chicago: U of Chicago P, 1968.

Bailey, Victor. "'In Darkest England and the Way Out': The Salvation Army, Social Reform and the Labour Movement, 1885–1910." *International Review of Social History* 29 (1984): 133–71.

—. "Salvation Army Riots, the 'Skeleton Army' and Legal Authority in the Provincial Town." *Social Control in Nineteenth Century Britain.* Ed. A. P. Donajgrodzki. London: Croom Helm; Totowa, N.J.: Rowman and Littlefield, 1977:231–53.

Booth, William. *In Darkest England and the Way Out.* 1890, rpt. London: Salvation Army, 1984.

—. "What Is the Salvation Army?" *Contemporary Review* 42 (Aug. 1882): 175–82.

Bremner, C. S. "Hadleigh Farm Colony." *The Nation* (New York) 30 Aug. 1894: 154–56.

Butler, Josephine. "Catherine Booth." *Contemporary Review* 58 (Nov. 1890): 639–54.

Finch, Lynette. *The Classing Gaze: Sexuality, Class and Surveillance.* St. Leonards, New South Wales: Allen and Unwin, 1993.

Foucault, Michel. *Discipline and Punish: The Birth of the Prison.* 1975. Trans. Alan Sheridan. New York: Vintage-Random, 1979.

—. *The History of Sexuality, Volume 1: An Introduction.* 1976. Trans. Robert Hurley. New York: Vintage-Random, 1990.

Higginbotham, Ann R. "Respectable Sinners: Salvation Army Rescue Work with Unmarried Mothers, 1884–1914." *Religion in the Lives of English Women, 1760–1930.* Ed. Gail Malmgreen. Bloomington: Indiana UP, 1986. 216–33.

Inglis, K. S. *Churches and the Working Classes in Victorian England.* London: Routledge; Toronto: U of Toronto P, 1963.

Jones, Gareth Stedman. *Languages of Class: Studies in English Working Class History 1832–1982.* Cambridge: Cambridge UP, 1983.

—. *Outcast London: A Study in the Relationship Between Classes in Victorian Society.* Oxford: Clarendon, 1971.

Mayhew, Henry. *London Labour and the London Poor; a Cyclopædia of the Condition and Earnings of Those That Will Work, Those That Cannot Work, and Those That Will Not Work.* 4 vols. London: Griffin, Bohn, 1861–62. Rpt. New York: Dover, 1968.

Nord, Deborah Epstein. "The Social Explorer as Anthropologist: Victorian Travellers among the Urban Poor." *Visions of the Modern City: Essays in History, Literature, and Art.* Ed. William Sharpe and Leonard Wallock. Baltimore: The Johns Hopkins UP, 1987. 122–34.

—. "The Urban Peripatetic: Spectator, Streetwalker, Woman Writer." *Nineteenth-Century Literature* 46 (1991). 351–75.

Railton, G. S. *The Authoritative Life of General William Booth, Founder of the Salvation Army.* New York: Hodder and Stoughton; George H. Doran, 1912.

"Rowdy Religion." *The Saturday Review of Politics, Literature, Science, and Art,* 31 May 1884: 700.

Semmel, Bernard. *Imperialism and Social Reform: English Social-Imperial Thought 1895–1914.* Cambridge: Harvard UP, 1960.

Shaw, Bernard. *Major Barbara.* 1907. Ed. Dan H. Laurence. London: Penguin, 1960.

Spence, Clark C. *The Salvation Army Farm Colonies.* Tucson: U of Arizona P, 1985.

Walker, Pamela J. "'I Live But Not Yet I for Christ Liveth in Me': Men and Masculinity in the Salvation Army, 1865–90." *Manful Assertions: Masculinities in Britain since 1800.* Ed. Michael Roper and John Tosh. London: Routledge, 1991. 92–112.

Walkowitz, Judith R. *City of Dreadful Delight: Narratives of Sexual Danger in Late-Victorian London.* Chicago: U of Chicago P, 1992.

—. *Prostitution and Victorian Society: Women, Class, and the State.* Cambridge: Cambridge UP, 1980.

Webb, Beatrice. *My Apprenticeship.* 2nd ed. London: Longmans, Green, 1926.

Weintraub, Stanley. "Bernard Shaw in Darkest England: G.B.S. and the Salvation Army's General William Booth." *Shaw: The Annual of Bernard Shaw Studies.* Vol. 10. Ed. Stanley Weintraub and Fred D. Crawford. University Park: Pennsylvania State UP, 1990. 45–59.

White, Arnold. "The Common Sense of Colonization and Emigration." *Contemporary Review* 49 (Mar. 1886): 375–82.

—. *The Problems of a Great City.* London: Remington, 1886.

Whyte, Frederic. *The Life of W. T. Stead.* 2 vols. London: Jonathan Cape; New York: Houghton, 1925.

Wolff, Janet. *Feminine Sentences: Essays on Women and Culture.* Berkeley: U of California P, 1990.

• 9 •

Cross-Cultural Dress in Victorian British Missionary Narratives: Dressing for Eternity

Susan Fleming McAllister

British missionaries in the nineteenth century served as very important agents of cultural communication; many of them, such as David Livingstone and James Hudson Taylor, were often controversial personalities both at home and abroad, testing the limits of their own culture in ways that their contemporaries questioned. For example, David Livingstone's involvement in business ventures as what he thought to be the "progress" of civilization troubled some contemporary Evangelicals who argued that trying to "civilize" indigenous people first and proselytize them later was not biblically valid. Another famous missionary and the founder of the China Inland Mission, Hudson Taylor, was accused of "going native" because he wore Manchurian attire (then the standard dress of the Chinese empire), ate with chopsticks and at one time lived in the same house with his wife and several other single women active in the China Inland Mission.

Large audiences were attentive to the dangerous, adventurous episodes the missionaries reported. Livingstone's narrative of his experiences in Africa, *Missionary Travels and Researches in South Africa,* was considered one of the important readings for prospective missionaries and went through many editions; Taylor's narrative, *A Retrospect,* equally popular, had gone through at least six editions by 1909. The missionaries' knowledge of the cultures and languages of foreign people and their heroism as bearers of European civilization and the gospel to distant, remote lands gave to their narratives tremendous authority. Throughout the nineteenth century, the narratives of missionaries were the primary lens through which Western Evangelical Christians viewed the indigenous people of Asia, the Middle East, India, Africa, and the Carribean and South Sea Islands.

The authority of these narratives is derived in part from the idealist vision of missionary work held by many Christians in nineteenth-century Britain. For instance, Henry Martyn, an early missionary to India, was highly influential in Britain and is believed by many critics to have been the model for St. John Rivers in Charlotte Bronte's *Jane Eyre*. St. John, the pious prospective missionary who proposes marriage to Jane, formulates the requirements for the "good" missionary: "to bear [the gospel] afar, to deliver it well, skill and strength, courage and eloquence, the best qualifications of soldier, statesman, and orator, were all needed" (388). Bronte's representation of the missionary figure through St. John, though questioned on a personal level by Jane, is reiterated at the end of the novel in idealistic terms. He is "Firm, faithful, and devoted, full of energy and zeal, and truth, he labours for his race; he clears their painful way to improvement; he hews down like a giant the prejudices of creed and caste that encumber it" (477). As the regulator and mediator between and across cultures, Bronte's missionary must be willing to die for the Indians and at the same time participate in purging their culture of those parts of "creed and caste" that hinder "improvement."

The narratives of the missionaries who went to China create a similar description of the life of the missionary. Yet many of these narratives question the positive impact of the so-called "improvement" of Chinese culture resulting from Western contact. Instead of being hearty reinforcers of imperialist policies and racial stereotypes, many of the missionaries disputed and reshaped many of the contemporary ideas the British had about the Chinese culture, and also about their own culture. By *culture* here I mean a loose structure by which people usually with a common language and geographical origin associate themselves within a recognizable context through social, ethical, religious, or political practices.

Culture is constantly in flux, so that the contact between two or more cultures usually produces an interminable reevaluation or reassessment of the values, ideals and goals of the individuals within those cultures. I am interested in the places of cultural intersection that produce or serve as a catalyst for reassessments of perceptions between and among cultures. I also want to explore how and why these reevaluations are made. My notion of the contact between cultures differs, however, from Mary Louise Pratt's idea of "contact zones" which she defines as the

> social spaces where disparate cultures meet, clash, and grapple with each other, often in highly asymmetrical relations of domination and subordination—like colonialism, slavery, or their aftermaths as they are lived out across the globe today . . . .

> [The] space of colonial encounters . . . in which peoples geo-
> graphically and historically separated come into contact with
> each other and establish ongoing relations, usually involving
> conditions of coercion, radical inequality, and intractable con-
> flict. (6)

Pratt's definition here from *Imperial Eyes* focuses on the effects the
Spanish introduction of Catholicism and foreign trade had on the indigenous cultures of Central and South America. Although Pratt concedes
that the movement of domination and subordination can go both ways
between colonized and colonizer, her study does not include, for example, a careful consideration of the precarious position of missionaries within the indigenous culture and their representations of cultural
communication and exchange. From her belief that the contact between
cultures will necessarily involve domination and subordination, she
necessarily concludes that the dominant culture will be primarily exploitative, while the subordinate culture will be exploited, able to "resist" only through creative reworkings of the colonizer's cultural materials; hence, her scholarship tends to oversimplify the complex interactions between cultures. In working out her ideas about the contact zone,
Pratt describes "transculturation" as the way "subordinated or marginal
groups select and invent from materials transmitted to them by a dominant metropolitan culture . . . . [and] determine to varying extents what
they absorb into their own, and what they use it for" (6). While Pratt
focuses on the representations of marginal groups, I believe an equally
important counter-study to be an exploration of the writings of the imposing culture as it represents its interactions with other cultures.

It is in the changes resulting from communications and interaction
between different peoples where *culture* both occurs and exists as a
differentiating process. *Reculturation* results when two or more cultures keep close contact and the effects of such contact resonates in the
writing of both the imposed on and the imposing cultures. These points
of change occur as cultures come into the evaluative process of redefinition when they encounter other cultures. In this evaluative process
of redefinition, the members of one culture must reconsider not only
the members of another culture, but they must also reconsider themselves in relation to and perhaps as a part of that other culture. This
reculturation emanates from the communication between cultures that
is recorded by representatives from the impinging culture, such as the
missionaries. I want to consider the way the missionaries represent this

reculturation by first looking at the way they codify "Britishness" and then by looking at the ways this "Britishness" breaks down at points of cultural interaction. One particular point in the narratives where *reculturation* is most evident occurs in discussions of conversions, both of Chinese people to Christianity and of the missionaries to the cultural habits of the Chinese. This particular study will deal primarily with the latter of these conversion episodes.

Both the autobiographies and biographies of missionaries such as Robert Morrison, James Hudson Taylor, W. H. Medhurst, John MacGowan an Geraldine Guinness convey a wealth of insight into the places where British culture and selfhood manifested itself through the written narrative, because they many times found themselves in situations that forced them to renegotiate their own prejudices about the Chinese. These narratives suggest that British economic ventures in China often created a hostile environment for missionaries. Britain controlled much of the money flow in banks, and the Chinese discovered that British companies paid them far less than their work was worth in the home market.

The missionaries believed many potential converts were lost because the Chinese associated them with this imperial exploitation of their land and resources. For the sake of their Christian mission, the missionaries wanted to clarify their stance concerning the British manipulation of the Chinese economy for their own political and monetary gain. In his autobiography, *Christ or Confucius, Which?*, John MacGowan represents both his own frustration and the frustration of the Chinese in attempting to understand the missionary's message in the midst of economic subjugation and abuse:

> They [two Chinese men, both potential converts] . . . asked how a people that grew and sold opium could be moral or benevolent. Besides, was it not a tradition, graven deep into the heart of the nation by many a bitter experience in the history of the past, that the barbarian was ever the foe of China, whose lands and riches he coveted? Was it conceivable that his nature could ever change? Impossible! He was but changing his tactics. Instead of lance and spear, and wild and bloody inroads, he came as he pretended for purposes of trade, and to preach doctrines which he said would benefit the people, whilst he was really laying deep schemes, when he had won the affections of the people, for possessing the Em-

pire for himself. (57–58)

MacGowan here reports two Chinese men's criticism of British involvement in the opium trade; only one of these men eventually becomes a Christian. MacGowan highlights what he believes are the
disparate objectives of British imperialism and the missionary enterprise: the former operates for the end of material gain through the exploitation of Chinese people and land, while the latter operates for the
end of eternal (spiritual) gain for the Chinese. He implies in this excerpt that had the British not been involved in the opium trade, which
consequently stigmatized the reputations of all British foreigners in
China, the number of Chinese converts would have been much higher.
MacGowan also concedes to the Chinese that the long experience of
their culture with foreign invasion, coupled with the savageness of the
opium trade and other exploitative business enterprises, justify the opinion of the Chinese men that the British and, indeed, all Europeans are
"barbarians."

MacGowan demonstrates the missionaries' reluctance to convert to
the economic policy that Western powers were wielding in China; his
narrative suggests that he identifies himself so much with the Chinese
people that he has in essence been converted to the Chinese tradition of
being suspicious of the motives of foreign involvement in China. Implicit in this passage, too, is MacGowan's anxiety that the missionary
enterprise will never quite be free of the fetters of an association with
business ventures, especially since some of the ships which transported
the missionaries had once carried opium. His representation of the difficulties the missionaries faced as the result of their assumed complicity
with capitalist imperialist enterprises, however, suggests that the issue
of missionary involvement in imperialist relations is more complicated
and conflicted than many post-colonial explanations and analyses of
missionary involvement such as Pratt's *Imperial Eyes* and Homi K.
Bhabha's *Location of Culture*. Such evidence from missionary narratives contests the more prevalent view from new historicists such as
Jerome Ch'en's *China and the West, Society and Culture 1815–1937*,
Raymond Dawson's *The Chinese Chameleon: An Analysis of European Conceptions of Chinese Civilization*, and Colin Mackerras's *Western Images of China* that tend to negatively stereotype missionaries and
their involvement in imperialist economic policy.

The missionary narratives also deal with the ramifications of another
more overt conversion—that of the missionaries to Chinese dress and

etiquette. In nineteenth-century England, dress and manners were the outward marker of Victorian cultural and social expression. The missionaries often depict the strangeness and exoticism of Chinese dress; more interestingly, many missionaries also defend their choice to wear Chinese dress at a time when dress codes were at their strictest for Victorian society.

Many missionaries tried to overcome the negative image of being foreigners (and thus associated with the violence and abuse of imperialist venturers) by accommodating themselves to Chinese dress and manners. They believed that this negative image and certain cultural barriers such as European dress created extra tension in their relationships with the Chinese and often elicited unwanted excitement or abuse from the crowds that came to hear them speak. They also believed the best way to navigate around the inevitable "foreignness" of their appearance was to adopt Chinese dress and manners. Hudson Taylor, for example, adopted the native dress of the literati, and, through his success, also convinced countless other missionaries, even those not working for the China Inland Mission, to do the same. Wearing Chinese dress, however, was not without its drawbacks from a physical standpoint. Taylor complains of the discomforts of having his head shaved and dying his hair black; he also regards the Chinese dress as highly peculiar at first. He explains in a letter to his sister that the native socks are coarse, and the breeches are "oh, what unheard-of garments," with a waist two feet too wide and short legs just below the knee which arc tucked into long white socks (*Hudson Taylor in Early Years* 319).

Yet even the discomforts of wearing Chinese garb would not deter Taylor from converting to native dress; he was willing to cross culturally boundaries and challenge the dogma of strict Victorian codes of dress and etiquette for the sake of making Jesus Christ's message of eternal salvation clear to the Chinese. Although Pat Barr believes that Taylor and the China Inland Mission missionaries wore native dress mainly as "a gracious gesture of conciliation" (27), Taylor emphasizes the practical benefits for his ministry: Chinese dress enables the missionary to enter the domestic realm of the Chinese more readily and thus has greater opportunity to teach and preach the gospel more intimately. He also concedes that Chinese dress is in fact more suitable than European clothing for the severe seasons in China. In his *Retrospect*, Taylor explains the positive experiences of wearing native dress when traveling to the countryside with a friend to preach and hand out tracts and books:

> Mr. Burns at that time was wearing English dress; but
> saw that while I was the younger and in every way less
> experienced, I had the quiet hearers, while he was fol-
> lowed by the rude boys, and by the curious but careless;
> that I was invited to the homes of the people, while he
> received an apology that the crowd that would follow pre-
> cluded his being invited. After some weeks of observa-
> tion, he also adopted the native dress, and enjoyed the
> increased facilities which it gave. (59)

Taylor has adopted the literati's dress which demands respect in Chinese society; he has given the Chinese a visible symbol with which they
can identify and so are more inclined to invite him to take part in their
domestic intercourse. Because he has outwardly demonstrated his respect and interest in Chinese culture, Taylor believes he attracts the
more "civilized" boys. On the other hand, because Burns has chosen
not to participate in the etiquette of Chinese dress and manners, he has
no common ground with the respectable Chinese citizens; instead, his
inappropriateness attracts only rowdy, crude boys. After seeing the
benefits of native dress, Burns never wears European dress again. One
historian writes of Burns' ministry, "He lived more among the Chinese
than any previous worker had done, dressing as a Chinaman and eating
Chinese food; and he took the risk of itinerating widely beyond the
stipulated limits of the treaty ports" (Graham 149).

   This example demonstrates, then, that proper or appropriate dress for
the nineteenth-century person, and especially for the missionary, was
not merely a matter of private, individual preference but rather was a
matter of dramatic cultural and social significance. To the nineteenth-
century mind, dress represented a deep concern with boundaries, both
spiritual and cultural, obvious in popular books of etiquette from the
period like Sarah Jane Hale's *Manners; or Happy Homes and Good
Society All the Year Round*. Hale argues that in his pitying love for the
fallen Adam and Eve, God provided clothes to cover their sin, just as he
gave Christ as the covering or propitiation for sins. She considers dress
as "something more than necessity of climate, something better than
condition of comfort, something higher than elegance of civilization."
For Hale dress is "the index of conscience, the evidence of our emotional nature. It reveals, more clearly than speech expresses, the inner
life of heart and soul in a people, and also the tendencies of individual"
(39).

Etiquette books like Hale's suggest that dress was essentially a public demonstration of the inner self. *The Habits of Good Society,* an etiquette book published in Britain and America, credits Christ's "greatest follower," St. Paul, with leaving "many injunctions to gentleness and courteousness of manner, and fine passages on women's dress, which should be painted over every lady's toilet table in the kingdom" (27). The writer later warns in a chapter concerning dress that people who rebel against fashion are vain, while those who feign simplicity are vulgar. The only position that remains suitable for the Victorian middle-class person is "to follow fashion so far as not to make [one]self peculiar by opposing it" (139). This preoccupation of dress as the covering of the soul is evident in more canonical texts such as Thomas Carlyle's *Sartor Resartus.* Carlyle speaks of the importance of dress in representing the spirit of the person in *Sartor Resartus*: "All visible things are emblems; what thou seest is not there on its own account; strictly taken, is not there at all; Matter exists only spiritually, and to represent some Idea, and *body* it forth. Hence *Clothes*, as despicable as we think them, are so unspeakably significant." For the Victorian, clothes were important precisely because they were the outward representation of the state of the soul; clothes also marked the spiritual state of other people.

In Victorian Britain, the idea of dress as clothing for the spirit derives from the Christian value or Golden Rule to "love thy neighbor as thyself." By dressing in well-fitted, fashionable clothes, men and women visually express their love for others. Modesty and class appropriateness in dress are also part of this expression of respect for others' sensibilities. Such rules of dress are a common concern in many nineteenth-century novels. Characters who dress appropriately and modestly demonstrate their spiritual willingness for self-sacrifice; novelists also use dress to demarcate boundaries of social and cultural appropriateness. Inappropriate dress was not only considered a violation of the Golden Rule, but also of the cultural and social boundaries of upper and middle-class England. Jane Eyre, for instance, reluctantly allows Rochester to purchase only two new dresses for her before their first attempt to get married. Rochester wants to buy "a rich silk of the most brilliant amethyst" and "a superb pink satin," but Jane insists on a "sober black satin and pearl-gray silk." She vehemently opposes Rochester's preference for the amethyst and pink dresses; they are inappropriate for someone of her social and economic position. She explains, "I told him in a new series of whispers, that he might as well buy me a gold gown and a silver bonnet at once: I should certainly never venture to wear his choice" (296). Through her symbolic refusal of the brighter, richer-looking dresses, Jane maintains her self-sacrificing image and her social status through her rigid quaker dress. Her dress has served to condition and define her lower middle-class status, and what we see is Jane's adherence to the social conventions of Victorian rules of dress; she knows she is not yet Rochester's social equal, and to allow him to buy fancy dresses for her would break rules of etiquette and make her a laughing stock, "'glittering like a parterre'" (296).

Bertha, Rochester's insane wife and Jane's counterpart in the novel, disrupts the dress codes of the Victorian period; her dress suggests the confusion of her soul. When she first sees Bertha in a waking dream, Jane cannot tell whether she is wearing a " gown, sheet, or shroud." Later when Jane discovers that Bertha is indeed Rochester's wife and goes to see her in the attic, Jane reports that she is "like some strange wild animal . . . covered with clothing" (321). The only thing that distinguishes Bertha from an animal is the fact that she does wear clothes. But these clothes are never described in any way; Bertha is a "clothed hyena," incapable of partaking in the etiquette of the Golden Rule because she is wild at heart.

For Dinah Morris in George Eliot's *Adam Bede*, dress becomes a social enabler. She wants to dress simply and modestly so the crowd will focus on her message rather than her looks. But the simplicity of her dress becomes exciting in the very plainness of its style; the people in the countryside come to hear her because they are curious about "the quaker-like costume and odd deportment of the female Methodists" (64). They are captivated by the "net quaker cap" which serves to keep her luxurious hair in check. The conservative attire, however, accentuates and mystifies Dinah's beauty, making her more intriguing.

Like Dinah, some missionaries believed that in adopting Chinese dress, they were following the Golden Rule of dress. Wearing Chinese dress would be a conservative move; it would enable the women missionaries, especially, to travel more freely and be heard more readily. Other missionaries believed that wearing European dress would attract more Chinese interest; if they could get the Chinese to pay attention to them through dress, they could get the Chinese to listen to the gospel. Lottie Moon, an American Southern Baptist missionary, for instance, never wore Chinese dress. She believed that converting to Chinese dress would endanger the moral integrity of the Westerners (Hunter 138).

A British woman who did adopt native dress risked being treated as a

Chinese peasant or prostitute because of her big feet. In his book of etiquette *"Ways That Are Dark,"* Gilbert Walshe explains that women with big feet in China were either peasants (nearly like slaves) or prostitutes. Luella Miner, an American missionary, also expresses the shortcomings of native dress in enabling her to assimilate into Chinese society:

> I had, as I thought eschewed all foreign articles of attire, going bare-headed and looking as much like a Chinese woman as big nose, big feet, and light hair would permit, but still my long robe of fine cotton cloth was quite different from their homespun short garments and my umbrella now and then proved more interesting than the difference between the true God and the temple idols. (quoted in Hunter 19)

The British women's big feet and the refusal of many British men to wear a real queue continued to hamper the assimilation of missionaries into Chinese culture and society. Geraldine Guinness explains the difficult transition of adopting native dress in her autobiography *In the Far East*:

> Picture to yourself your missionary, dressed in the full costume of this extraordinary land, surrounded by an eager interested group of Chinese, sitting in the stern of a fine river-steamer . . . making rapidly towards the interior of this great empire . . . . Really in China! though not yet quite Chinese, as we long and hope to be. Witness, for instance, the discomfort we experience from the novel costumes to which as yet we find it impossible fully to reconcile ourselves . . . . More and more come crowding round; . . . . They seem quite kind and friendly these men, with their queer awkward garments and long tails. (34–35)

Guinness here expresses both the thrill and novelty of her experience in being interrogated by Chinese curiosity. She has previously imagined Chinese dress will minimize the shock of her difference but discovers that in this instance, it makes her more noticeable. Guinness is like Dinah: they both discover that their complicity with rules of dress within one culture will not achieve the same effect when applied to another culture. Despite its inconvenience, Chinese dress *does* make close contact with the Chinese possible; Guinness is intrigued with the Chinese man's demeanor and becomes curious about the oddness of *his appearance.* The reactions of the Chinese indicate to Guinness that she is as much of an oddity, a "marvelous spectacle," to the Chinese as they are to her. She ends this episode by stressing her desire to speak Chinese so that she can tell these people of "the good news" (35). The urgency of her gospel message enables Guinness to rise above the strict dress codes of her Victorian middle-class background in order to attempt to assimilate more quickly into the Chinese culture.

In becoming like the Chinese in dress and manners, the missionaries believed they could elide their own boundaries of culture and class and the fear they had of the Chinese culture itself. They also believed they could allay the negative image that opium trade had given all foreigners. While the first generation of Evangelical Christians enforced rules and regulations which made dress the outer expression of inner righteousness, the new generation of Evangelicals manipulated these rules to suit the needs of their spiritual strategies for spreading the gospel. By donning Chinese attire, Guinness and other missionaries were not adopting the Chinese way of thinking about matters of the spirit; instead, they were able to see dress as a rhetorical means to the end of sharing their message of the empire of eternity. Even the writer of *The Habits of Good Society* concedes that in certain climates, the British should relinquish their strict dress codes for more comfortable clothing: "Can anything be more painfully ridiculous than an Englishman wearing a black silk hat and frock-coat of cloth under the sun of the equator? Yet such is our want of sense, or our love of national costumes, however hideous that it is the etiquette in our colonies, whether in the tropics or the arctic regions, to wear precisely the same stiff hot court dress as at St. James" (149).

The missionaries who converted at least outwardly to Chinese dress and etiquette had to endure criticism from home and skepticism from other missionaries in the field who continued to wear European dress. Despite such criticism, those missionaries who chose to wear Chinese dress did so in order "to get close access to the hearts of the people . . . to win their confidence and love." Taylor explains: "To effect this we seek as far as possible to meet them, in costume, in language, in manners" (321). His narrative suggests a different way for measuring conversion and its success or failure. His repeated proclamation was that the healing power of Jesus Christ could overcome any cultural difference; this power, he believed, was demonstrable in his reports of the success of dressing like the Chinese. For in doing so, Taylor and other missionaries were dressing for eternity. The missionaries' reculturation, represented in their writing about their conversion to wearing different clothing and casting off the old rules of Victorian etiquette, was the outward expression of their deep concern to bring every soul into eternal life through the Gospel of Jesus Christ. In the end they hoped that their outward conversion would result in the inward conversion of Chinese souls for eternity.

Works Cited

Barnett, Suzanne Wilson and John King Fairbank, eds. *Christianity in China: Early Protestant Missionary Writings.* Cambridge: The Committee on American-East Asian Relations of the Department of History, 1985.

Barr, Pat. *To China with Love.* London: Secker & Warburg, 1972.

Bebbington, D.W. *Evangelicalism in Modern Britain.* London: Unwin Hyman, 1989.

Bhabha, Homi K. *The Location of Culture.* London: Routledge, 1994.

Bronte, Charlotte. *Jane Eyre.* London: Penguin,1966.

Carlyle, Thomas. *Sartor Resartus.* Oxford UP, 1987.

Ch'en, Jerome. *China and the West, Society and Culture 1815-1937.* London: Hutchinson, 1979.

Dawson, Raymond. *The Chinese Chameleon.* London: Oxford UP, 1967.

Deane, David J. *Robert Moffat: The Missionary Hero of Kuruman.* London: S.W. Partridge, c1890.

Eliot, George. *Adam Bede.* Penguin, 1980.

Gates, Henry Louis, ed. *"Race," Writing and Difference.* Chicago: U of Chicago P, 1986.

Guinness, Geraldine. *In the Far East: Letters from Geraldine Guinness.* London: Morgan & Scott, 1889.

—. *The Story of the China Inland Mission.* London: Morgan & Scott, 1900.

Hale, Sarah Josepha. *Manners; or, Happy Homes and Good Society All the Year Round.* Boston: J. E. Tilton, 1868.

Hunter, Jane. *The Gospel of Gentility.* New Haven: Yale UP, 1984.

Livingstone, David. *Missionary Travels and Researches in South Africa.* London: J. Murray, 1857.

MacGowan, Rev. John. *Christ or Confucius, Which? Or the Story of the Amoy Mission.* London: London Missionary Society, 1889.

Mackerras, Colin. *Western Images of China.* Hong Kong: Oxford UP, 1989.

Medhurst, W.H. *China: Its State and Prospects.* London: John Snow, 1838.

—. *The Foreigner in Far Cathay.* New York: Scribner, Armstrong, 1873.

Morrison, Robert. *Dr. Morrison's Sermons and Discourses on China: A Parting Memorial.* London: W. Simpkin and R. Marshall, 1826.

Pratt, Mary Louise. *Imperial Eyes: Travel Writing and Transculturation.* London and New York: Routledge, 1992.

Robson, William. *Griffith John: Founder of the Hankow Mission.* London: S.W. Partridge, 1888.

Taylor, Dr. and Mrs. Howard. *Hudson Taylor in Early Years.* London: The China Inland Mission, 1940.

Taylor, J. Hudson. *A Retrospect.* 6th edition. New York: Gospel Publishing House, c.1909.

The Habits of Good Society. New York: Carleton, 1865.

Tompkins, Jane. *Sensational Designs.* New York: Oxford UP, 1985.

Townsend, W.J. *Robert Morrison: The Pioneer of Chinese Missions.* New York: Fleming H. Revell, 1901.

Walshe, W. Gilbert. *"Ways That Are Dark."* Shanghai: Kelly and Walsh, c1900.

"I Did Not Make Myself So . . . ":
Samson Occom and American Religious Autobiography

Eileen Razzari Elrod

> Christians are some times worse than the Savage Indians.
> —Samson Occom, 1769[1]

In 1772, Samson Occom composed what LaVonne Ruoff calls the "first Indian best-seller": an execution sermon before the hanging of his fellow Christian Mohegan, Moses Paul (62).[2] The most famous student of Eleazar Wheelock—a New England preacher turned Indian educator—Occom himself became a missionary, teaching and preaching to Native Americans, and raising significant sums of money on a British tour on behalf of missionary efforts with Native Americans.[3] An articulate and persuasive speaker, Occom was successful in ministry and marketing, inspiring jealousy in white colleagues (who worried that his popularity undermined theirs) and generosity for "Wheelock's Indians" in British audiences (who marveled at the civilized Christian savage). Occom preached over 300 sermons while in England, and raised over twelve thousand pounds. Funded significantly by that revenue, Wheelock's educational venture in New Hampshire was subsequently transformed into Dartmouth College; its mission of Indian education dissolved. Occom vigorously, angrily, opposed Wheelock in this venture, which he viewed as a violation of the trust of the donors to whom he had appealed, and a betrayal of the Indians for whose education he was concerned.[4] Occom's inadvertent role in the founding of Dartmouth and his sermon vilifying his fellow Indian both for the crime of murder and for drunkenness—a vice he himself had been accused of—are merely the beginnings of the perplexing story of Samson Occom and the New England missionaries.[5] In order to begin to appreciate the complexity of Occom's situation, and, by extension, the stories of thousands of other non-European Christian converts in early America, we need to examine his fascinating autobiographical piece, "A Short Narrative of

My Life."[6] Occom's brief account (which he began to compose years before his final break with Wheelock over Dartmouth) provides readers with a kind of rhetorical map of the muddied notion of self wrought by Occom's conversion, and of the complexities and contradictions of, for example, values of justice and compassion—crucial to Christianity— and the practice of racism—entrenched in the Christian tradition.

Moreover, Occom's story challenges the assumptions underlying much of the religious life-writing in the early period of American literary history; his story, and, in particular, his interesting and unfinished rendition of that story in "A Short Narrative," interrogates a traditional Protestant (and here, specifically Puritan) set of answers about how and why one composes a life story. The differences in tone, style, and structure between Occom's narrative and those of many of his contemporaries, with whom he shared a great deal, most notably a bedrock of pious Calvinism, reveal what is unspoken and unquestioned in some of the texts more familiar to readers of early American religious autobiography. Occom's alternative narrative undercuts what becomes the dominant mode of discourse in early American religious autobiographical writing: the story of the interior self in its spiritual progression toward rebirth and sanctification, the approved Puritan narrative. If some late twentieth-century readers of, for instance, Jonathan Edwards' "Personal Narrative," wonder, as my students always do, what actually "happened" in the Puritan writer's life—that is, what were the actual life circumstances that accompanied, even caused, the interior narrative, then Occom's narrative provides them with a telling counterpoint, as he focuses entirely on the material circumstances resulting from the racist treatment he experienced at the hands of his fellow Christians. Occom's "Short Narrative," along with other early autobiographical texts by women, by African American, and Native American writers, interrogates the autobiographical mode of writing, requiring readers to "enlarge the frame" around early American autobiography, and to reconsider religious autobiography, particularly the conversion narrative, that form that has been viewed as the "center" of religious autobiography in the early period (Shea, "Prehistory" 31, 42).

A discussion of Samson Occom must begin with the circumstances that shaped his story. Occom remained within the tradition whose vicious practices he experienced firsthand. In his own words, he was "Born a Heathen and Brought up In Heathenism," and he remained a faithful Christian for the rest of his life after his conversion, eager to introduce Western civilization, literacy, and Christ to his fellow Indians.[7] Despite his split with Wheelock over the founding of Dartmouth, and his anger over his own mistreatment by white missionaries (expressed in the "Short Narrative," and in many personal letters), Occom remained loyal to Christianity, completing his missionary effort by establishing the Brothertown community of Christian Indians in New York near the end of his life. His adherence to traditional Protestantism notwithstanding, Occom was held suspect throughout his career by white ministers who accused him both of having too strong an allegiance to his kinsmen, and of arrogance.

Samson Occom's preliminary move toward an autobiographical account seems to have been provoked by specific accusations (in a string of ongoing troubles Occom had with church and mission authorities) concerning his identity and character.[8] As he prepared to leave on his fundraising tour of England in 1765, Occom was again attacked, this time by the Boston commissioners of the London missionary society sponsoring the tour. There were rumors that he was Mohawk, rather than Mohegan, that he had been converted immediately before (and purposely *for*) the British tour, and that he drank. Discouraged by accusations that he was not who he seemed to be, Occom wrote to Wheelock in 1765:

> [T]hey think it is nothing but a Shame to Send me over the great Water, they Say it is to Impose upon the good People . . . Some say I can't Talk Indian, orthers say I can't read . . . O that God would give us grace and Wisdom to conduct aright before him and before all men,—I have a Struggle in my Mind At times, knowing not where I am going, I dont know but I am Looking for a Spot of ground where my Bones must be Buried, and never to see my Poor Family again . . . (Richardson 75)

Occom roused himself to respond to the attacks; he had to defend himself for the good of his cause—Indian education—and for the sake of his reputation. He first drafted a preliminary narrative prior to the English tour in 1765, then expanded and completed it after his return, in 1768, in a climate of even greater controversy and accusation. Occom's English and American friends were wary of his confidence and self-direction—more pronounced than it had been before his great success in England. He was carefully watched, and Wheelock and others reminded Occom of his humble origins and proper place under their authority. In spite of their corrections, Occom took the part of his fellow Mohegans in yet more disputes, clashing with Wheelock and others in increasingly vigorous disagreements that resulted, finally, in Occom losing his only source of steady income (Blodgett 105–09).[9] And there were other, more personal, troubles, as well: in addition to being accused of public drunkenness, one of his many children was rebellious. His wife Mary became seriously ill, while he himself suffered a shoulder injury which prevented him from riding a horse. Compounding all of these troubles, rumors about Occom spread throughout the community, so that, increasingly, he had very little credibility with other missionaries and ministers, especially Wheelock (Blodgett 109–11). It is in this context—of accusation, suspicion and terrible discouragement—that Occom returned to the task of setting down the circumstances of his life experience. He must have felt pressure to defend himself and to correct the misconceptions fostered by years of direct accusation and rumor.

In contrast to more extensive, formal and internally focused personal narratives of other early American Puritan writers, Occom's is shaped by these constraints of experience, and, indeed, by the larger cultural and religious constraints which he specifically addresses in his narrative. In defending himself, Occom might have been expected to defend the New England missionary enterprise with Native Americans, with which he had had so much to do. But he did not. Instead he wrote a scathing indictment of his white missionary colleagues. In the process, he calls into question his own sense of identity—as it was inextricably linked to New England Christianity—just as he means to assert his authentic self in the face of accusations of inauthenticity (that he was not a Mohegan, that he was not a proper Christian). The focus of the narrative seems to shift over the course of the text: rather than insisting on his own actual identity in the face of the lies being told about him, Occom progressively focuses his attention on exposing the lies around him, on the hypocrisy of his missionary colleagues. In the end he not only presents his own understandably decentered self, he decenters the model religious self of many of his contemporary religious writers.

I want to situate Occom's account historically by acknowledging the personal narrative of one of his near contemporaries, Jonathan Edwards.[10] Both men were important participants in the Great Awakening of the 1740s: Edwards as both preacher and interpreter of the "Surprising Work of God" he witnessed, Occom as one of the model converts during what he describes in his narrative as the time of "Strange Concern among the White People."[11] The two men knew many of the same people, and held many beliefs in common. But by comparing them, I do not mean to elide the significant differences between these texts, or to suggest that there is a sameness of purpose, tone or circumstance. Indeed, what interests me here are the important differences between the two. Occom had neither the spiritual leisure nor the relative security of circumstance of Edwards. Surely the differences in the levels of introspection and tone between these two works result, in large part, from the differences in situations, and, just as importantly, purposes, of their writers. Edwards' narrative reflects its pensive, earnest author, who endeavors to get closer and closer to the ultimate meaning of his own spiritual journey, and to represent that journey in a way that will bring glory to God. Occom, in contrast, sees his own troubles, and their cause, most clearly.

Edwards's "Personal Narrative" recounts his progression from an unenlightened spiritual condition to a state of increasing spiritual confidence. At every turn and every reversal (and there are many in this brief narrative), Edwards reevaluates the spiritual state that he had, only sentences before, found, if not satisfactory, at least a marked improvement over his former state. Each reevaluation brings new insight into his own sinfulness, and a deeper sense of joy in the sovereignty of God. And Edwards's narrative (and plenty of other seventeenth and eighteenth-century American religious autobiographical writing) is almost entirely focused on his internal condition, with very few references to his life circumstances. This is not to say, however, that the external world is not present in Edwards's narrative. Edwards comes to depend upon the spiritual meaning inherent in the natural world, a dependence, as so many readers have noticed, that anticipates the transcendentalism of Emerson. Edwards looks at the sky from his father's pasture and the meaning of the sovereignty of God becomes clear to him; Emerson crosses a bare common at twilight and is transformed into a "part or particle of God," one who sees all clearly without the distractions of egotism (*Nature* 10). Still, the beauty and spirituality of the natural world notwithstanding, ultimate meaning in Edwards's narrative depends upon a mode of progressive internal revelation, which is characteristic of other early American religious autobiographical writing. Edwards weights the end of the account with interpretive authority. The reader, who has all along been asked to reevaluate each of Edwards's "former" states, must depend upon the end of the narrative for the most authoritative vision of Edwards's self and God.[12] Edwards presents his religious self in a recursive way, circling back into the narrative, with a deepening, increasingly certain, sense of spiritual development.

In Occom's text, too, the reader can observe a progressive revelation, with the authoritative interpretation occurring in the final paragraphs.

But there the comparison to Edwards and most other New England autobiographical writers must end. While Edwards's narrative depends
upon internal revelation and upon a natural world imbued with spiritual
meaning, Occom's spiritual revelations are prefatory—almost paren-
thetical—and the rest of the meaning of the text is inextricably bound to
and by the very specific, discrete, difficulties of his everyday life. While
Edwards resides in a natural world that catapults him into a spiritual
reality of abstract doctrines, Occom lives in a relentlessly material world
of circumstance shaped by his racist brethren.

Occom's introductory paragraph consists of a very brief account of
his "Heathenish Ways" when he could neither read nor write, and was
"unacquainted with the English tongue." From the beginning then,
Occom clearly and emphatically speaks from the perspective of the acculturated Native. This makes sense in light of his purpose: in order to
justify himself to his audience he needs to identify himself as one of
them. Moreover, throughout the account Occom presents other Indians
as "other," using the third person, referring, repeatedly, to "these Indians" and to "them," language consistently suggestive of a profound separation between his current and original selves, between his religious
and racial identity. Indeed, despite the increasing anger toward white
Christians that his letters take on in this same time period, the sense of
identification with white Christianity is fairly consistent. In fact, Leon
Richardson in his 1933 account describes Occom as the only one of
Wheelock's Indian charges who seemed to bear out his theories that a
properly Christianized Indian would be distinguishable only by color
from white New England Puritans: "in attire, in mannerisms, in language, in habits, even in mental attitude, Occom, upon superficial observation, was hardly distinguishable from the traditional New England
divine" (12–13).[13] One might argue that Arnold Krupat's observation
of William Apess—that his "sense of self . . . [is] deriv[ed] entirely
from Christian culture"—could be said of Samson Occom as well (*Voice*
145).

What is most surprising here, however, is that Occom's conversion
to Christianity—the main stuff of so many contemporary religious figures' autobiographical accounts—occurs only briefly in the second paragraph of the narrative. After providing some necessary details concerning the religious climate of the Great Awakening—"there were Extraordinary Ministers Preaching from Place to Place and a Strange Concern
among the White People"—Occom mentions, but only briefly and in a
subordinate clause, his conversion to Christianity: "These Preachers
did not only come to us, but we frequently went to their meetings and

Churches. After I was awakened & converted, I went to all the meetings, I could come at; & Continued under Trouble of Mind about 6 months; at which time I began to Learn the English Letters; got me a Primer, and used to go to my English Neighbours frequently for Assistance in Reading . . ." (13). The initial account of his conversion to Christianity consists of a preliminary mention, a quick fact embedded in his acquisition of habits of churchgoing and literacy. Occom does go on briefly to say that he had a "discovery of the way of Salvation," and to describe a deepening of his spiritual state, a time in which he "found Serenity and Pleasure of Soul, in Serving God"(13). But again the focus is only very briefly on his spiritual awakening, and these comments seem buried in descriptions of his continued educational progress, and earnest declarations of concern for his "Poor Brethren." Much of the subsequent narrative consists of a recounting of the details of Occom's life and ministry: how he kept school, how he held religious meetings, how he served as an arbiter in disputes.

Even though in the introductory paragraphs Occom clearly aligns himself with European Christians—as eager as they are to christianize the Natives—he also consistently presents himself in subsequent paragraphs as one under the unfortunate control of white church leaders and missionaries. He emphasizes the ways in which he has no control over his circumstances, the way decisions are made for him, by using passive constructions repeatedly, saying "I have been obliged" or "I was obliged," and explaining how he "was allowed" to supplement his inadequate income. The emphasis throughout the piece is on Occom's lack of control, and on his dependence on authorities who mistreat him and then fail to exercise compassion concerning his circumstances. He is not an agent of action here; rather, he is consistently acted upon. Interestingly, this same stylistic feature (frequent use of passive voice) occurs in a number of other early American religious autobiographies, including Edwards' "Personal Narrative." But most often in these other texts, the agent is God, with the narrator being acted upon by the divine. In contrast, Occom is acted upon by other missionaries, resulting in hardship and discomfort for himself and his family. Occom doesn't name those who do the obliging and allowing, nor does he directly accuse his colleagues of mistreatment. Instead he catalogues his own extraordinary need, along with his faithful service, in increasing detail. It is not until the very end of this catalog, the end of the narrative, that he begins to present his conclusions regarding the meaning of his misfortune.

Occom describes his hardships and the ways he has been mistreated by quoting the Apostle Paul in the Second Letter to the Corinthians. In the biblical text Paul himself speaks as an angry missionary, confronting his Corinthian readers with claims that they have mistreated him. He places his faithful service in the context of those he calls "false apostles" and "deceitful workers," arguing further, in words that Occom literally repeats, that he speaks "like a fool" (2 Cor. 11).[14] Because Occom actually quotes Paul here, it is difficult to imagine that he would not have been identifying with the angry, accusatory tone of this section of the biblical epistle. And as Occom cataloged the particulars of his hardship, he must have recalled Paul's litany of peril from the same passage, in which he recounts beatings, imprisonment, stonings, and shipwrecks. Occom, for his part, recalls how he has lived in a Wigwam, traveled two miles for wood and eighteen miles for meal; he has had to "contrive every way" to feed his family as a result of his meager pay: fishing, keeping pigs, raising corn, potatoes, and beans, binding books, selling feathers, and making pails and spoons. Like Paul, Occom establishes his authority by listing his hardships. And he establishes his virtue by describing the vicious behavior of others. Occom confronts the missionaries with rhetoric from their own authoritative text, using the language and circumstances of the apostle to draw a parallel to his own. And in his reconfiguration of things here, the missionaries are the ungrateful and recalcitrant Corinthians, while he is the faithful, and long-suffering apostle, the "true" missionary. Occom's audience would have heard the language of the biblical text, particularly in the Pauline description of the angry, ranting fool, constrained to name the vile behavior of brethren who have, for the moment, become adversaries.

Just as many early American writers of spiritual autobiography present themselves as travelers who arrive, by reflective turns, at an increasing sense of revelation in their narratives, so Samson Occom, after reflecting on his own experience of financial need and oppression, moves toward an ultimate revelation at the end of his narrative. He begins to accuse his audience of intentional racist abuse:

> I Can't Conceive how these gentlemen would have me Live. I am ready to impute it to their Ignorance, and I would wish they had changed circumstances with me but one month, that they may know, by experience, what my Case really was; but I am now fully convinced, that it was not Ignorance . . . . (17)

Though he asserts that it *was not* ignorance that lead to his mistreatment, Occom stops short of naming the cause in precise terms: he will not explicitly name the race issue until the final paragraph of the narrative. Instead, Occom goes on to contrast the vast difference in pay between himself and white missionaries who have fewer qualifications. "[W]hat can be the Reason that they used me after this manner?" he rhetorically asks his reader (18).[15] And then, in an intriguing response to his own previously repeated assertions concerning his relationships with and position in regard to the white missionaries, Occom asserts that "I am not under obligations to them"(18). Occom probably means financial obligation here, but his word choice, his repetition of the earlier "obliged," which he had used to describe the extraordinary constraints of circumstance, all caused by the "gentlemen" to whom he now says he is not obliged, is notable. He reveals a distinct sense of self , one that must be separated from his audience, from those who have mistreated him so severely.

The final revelation that Occom presents in his "Short Narrative" is one that would have had a profoundly discomfiting effect on his audience. In an attempt to answer his own questions (concerning why those with whom he has faithfully worked for years have abused and exploited him), he recalls a story told by a "Poor Indian Boy," whose white master regularly beats him (18). When asked to explain the violence of his master, the boy says that his master might beat him because of his poor performance, or he might beat him because he is inclined to do so, but finally, that he "Beats me for the most of the Time 'because I am an Indian'" (18). Occom follows his fable of abuse with his own reflection, explaining, finally, the meaning of his own experiences, which parallel the boy's beatings:

> So I am *ready* to Say, they have used me thus, because I Can't Influence the Indians so well as other missionaries; but I can assure them I have endeavoured to teach them as well as I know how;—but I *must Say,* "I believe it is because I am a poor Indian." I Can't help that God has made me so; I did not make my self so.— (18)

In this, the remarkable conclusion, Occom defends himself by aiming directly at his accusers, attributing years of hardship to the overt racism of his Christian colleagues, a racism that occurs in the context of a racist culture, one that spawns the story of the Indian boy and fuels the repeated mistreatment of Occom.

Occom's life narrative becomes a list of grievances. And it is as if over the course of the text Occom comes to the conclusion, the final insight or truth, that he presents to readers. But Occom's truth, in contrast to Edwards' and others, is not a revelation about the state of his soul, but rather an insight concerning others and the meaning of his own circumstances. His defense of himself, finally, rests not on his authentic identity, but on the authentic identity of his audience, which has fostered ongoing abuse of Occom in particular, and of other "poor Indians" in general. While other narratives progress toward an accumulation of spiritual insight, with the end result of a self-revelation designed to encourage and challenge the larger religious community, Occom's narrative ends with a damning revelation about the community, an unmasking of the community ethos that has legitimated the calculated cruelty and false accusations to which Occom was subject throughout his career.

In the end Occom's account of his life effectively undercuts the expected form of religious autobiographical narrative from the early period of American literary history. The truth that Occom presents here opposes the assumption at the foundation of most of those texts: that one can tell the truth of one's life in a vacuum of spiritual reality, without recourse to the larger social and political realities that shape one's notions of spiritual truth. While many of Occom's contemporaries and seventeenth-century predecessors in their life-writing present hardship as God's chastening hand, sanctifying them, deepening their experiences of faith, Occom's halting, listy, narrative insists on the hard human truth of his daily experience, reminding readers that the conventional approach of other Christian autobiographers depends upon the identities of the tellers who are not in the margin, but in the mainstream of the Anglo-Christian community. There are, of course, very important exceptions, early American religious autobiographical writers who set their own self-knowledge in the context of a larger, not exclusively internal, reality. John Woolman, for instance, the great eighteenth-century American Quaker journal writer, describes how he comes to realize the injustice of slavery, and then lives a life of such alarming integrity as to make those around him (who cooperate, even unwittingly, with an unjust society) profoundly uncomfortable. But Woolman's Quaker social and political awareness concerning the rights of slaves, Indians and poor workers, which he sees as part of his spiritual development and which dominates his text, serves as a contrast to Puritan autobiographical writing—the tradition that Occom, as a Great Awakening convert, participates in—where notions of conscience, for the most part, are limited to purely personal moral and ethical concerns.

By articulating his final angry complaint against the missionaries, Occom severely qualifies the certain definition of himself that he presented at the beginning of the narrative, where he took pains to distinguish himself from his Indian origins. By exposing race as the grounds for the inequity he has endured, he realigns himself with the Mohegan community. Moreover, Occom's use of the story of the Indian boy as a template for his own experience effectively dismantles not only his own earlier assertions of identity, but also the tidy dualism of "heathen" and "Christian," the terms that had given meaning to Occom's life as an Indian missionary to the Indians, and Indian spokesman to the Christians. By describing the racism he has experienced, Occom challenges the assumptions of the superiority of the Christian culture, assumptions that he seems, at other times, to share with his audience.

The shifting, uncertain location of the self presented here distinguishes Occom's text, and places it in company with other autobiographical writing. In discussing early American autobiographical texts by Sewall, Byrd, and Carter, Shea says that the "'I' in their writing is confident that it speaks from the center of the real world, whereas, in the autobiographical succession from Anne Hutchinson, the 'I,' finding itself set out at an apparent margin, disputes the given real and invents a text that acknowledges a journeying rather than a fixed center" ("Prehistory" 37). Occom participates in this tradition; his "Brief Account" reads as a preliminary description of his movement toward the discovery that has shaped his life: not the discovery of Christ, but the discovery of the vicious racism of Christians.

Occom describes himself as a man who has been thoroughly changed by cross-cultural contact, but he presents himself, consistently and unmistakably, as an Indian as well. Still, this is not quite the synecdochic self that Arnold Krupat posits as a model for later Native American autobiography, that is, a "narration of personal history . . . marked by the individual's sense of himself in relation to collective social units or groupings" ("Autobiography" 176). Occom describes his own ideological and cultural distance from non-Christianized Indians, and yet he can not derive the full meaning from the tradition that he would/does embrace: the "sweetness" of the Sovereignty of God that overcomes Jonathan Edwards, for instance, can not impress Occom. Instead he experiences the harshness of the sovereignty of his white missionary coworkers. And he is prevented from experiencing what had been by his own reports one of the primary appeals of Christianity, that is material gain and financial security. In the end the self Occom presents is, as Elliott describes it, permanently "liminal," deriving its power and meaning finally from fluidity, from the threshold that Occom inhabits (234).

Finally, though, what should contemporary readers make of Occom's seeming self-hatred in the last two sentences of his narrative, when he explains the reason for his own mistreatment by quoting the story of the Indian boy: "'I believe it is because I am a poor Indian.' I Can't help that God has made me So; I did not make my self so.—" The tone of this last bit of Occom's text seems pathetic; Occom's self-figuring as "poor"—a modifier not present in the boy's original self-description at the end of the story—and helpless (in the face of God's choice of his racial identity) seems apologetic, even pitiful. It may be.[16] But there are other nuances to Occom's concluding sentences as well. By insisting that he is not who he is by his own making, he confronts his contemporaries with their own self-making: in Occom's and his audience's view of things, race may be God-ordained, but human behavior, or what Occom calls "use" in this passage, is, emphatically, not. Furthermore, by describing himself as "poor," he reminds readers of the rest of his narrative, of the poverty imposed upon him by mission authorities. God may have ordained his racial identity, but the missionaries have ordained his impoverished circumstances. And both circumstances occur— equally, it seems—outside of Occom's power. Perhaps it isn't self-hatred at all, but instead a chafing against the powerlessness he has experienced, against the religious sensibility that continues to insure his powerlessness. His "I did not make myself so" is as much an indictment of the missionaries who have shaped his experience as it is an appeal to the sovereign God who ordained his race.

Notes

1. From a letter to Eleazar Wheelock, reprinted in Blodgett (110). Occom refers here specifically to "White people" who had called him a "drunkard."
2. Occom is referred to as a "first" by others as well: Murray calls him the first Indian writer of significance (44); Peyer says Native American literature in English begins with Occom (208); Elliott notes that he is the first Native American ordained as a Christian minister (233). The sermon for Moses Paul went through nineteen editions and was translated into Welsh in 1827 (Ruoff 62). The execution sermon, an important early American genre, was usually delivered before the execution of a convicted criminal. The purpose,

generally, of these sermons was to impress hearers with the seriousness of the crimes of the condemned, and to provoke them, in the face of one criminal's guilt and certain death, to reflect on their own morality and mortality and to repent. See Bosco, Minnick. Murray discusses the particular power of this (Occom's) sermon's orchestration—a virtuous Indian preaching a warning about a wicked Indian, calling it a "moral tableau." Noting the way he speaks to several separate audiences within the sermon, he suggests that Occom's overall intent, as he allows each component to "overhear" the other audience's parts, is marginally subversive (45–47).

3. Wheelock ran a private school and was the Pastor of the Second Congregational Church of Lebanon, Connecticut. Occom entered the school in December, 1743, and remained under Wheelock's instruction for four years, until his poor eyesight and ill health caused him to abandon his studies. Occom was an excellent student, whose performance prompted Wheelock to concentrate his educational efforts on other Native Americans, by founding the famous Indian Charity School (Peyer 209–10).

4. See Axtell on Wheelock's founding of Dartmouth.

5. Elliott notes that accusations of drunkenness followed Occom throughout his career, and were repeated by later writers such as Timothy Dwight even though he believed they were unfounded. Elliott also distinguishes between early American notions of "drunkard" and "being overtaken with strong drink" as he discusses the pervasive stereotype of the drunken Indian in early New England and now (251, 239).

6. Occom's narrative remained unpublished until 1982, when Bernd Peyer included it in his anthology. I use Peyer's translation here. The typescript is located at the Dartmouth College Library Special Collections.

7. See Lonkhuyzen for a discussion of the role of goods and technology, including literacy, in the conversions of Native Americans in New England in the early period. Occom's letters indicate a special concern for literacy and for improving his own and other Indians' material circumstances via Christianity. Weinstein attributes Occom's interest in religion, and his loyalty to Christianity, entirely to these concerns.

8. For instance, Occom was a participant in a long-running land dispute (the Mason Controversy) between Native Americans and colonists. A group of Mohegans, sponsored by the Mason family, lobbied for compensation for or the return of stolen Mohegan lands. After charges from a schoolmaster, Robert Clelland and his patron, Rev. David Jewett, pastor of the North Church of New London, Connecticut, and others that he was inappropriately involved, Occom withdrew himself from the dispute with an apology for misconduct in 1865. (For more on the Mason controversy, see Weinstein.) Occom's quarrels with Jewett and Clelland lasted many years, and were renewed even after his return from England. Before their complaints about his involvement in the Mason affair, Occom had accused Clelland of favoring the English over the Indians in his school (Blodgett 78–80). A year earlier Jewett had complained that, first, Occom did not attend his sermons, and second,

that Occom held his own Sunday meetings in his schoolhouse, which Jewett
felt had an immediate effect of depleting the attendance at his (Jewett's)
sermons. After his return from England, when Wheelock and others repeatedly complained that Occom had become arrogant and independent, his
troubles in getting along with his Christian brethren worsened dramatically.
See Richardson and Bodgett.

9. Wheelock wanted Occom to settle in the wilderness with the Iroquois; Occom
refused. And this is the point at which Occom and Wheelock clashed over
the founding of Dartmouth.

10. Occom's dates are 1723–92; Edwards's are 1703–58. Edwards's "Personal
Narrative" was written in 1739, then published posthumously in 1865, three
years before Occom wrote his "Short Narrative."

11. Edwards's first discussion of religious awakening occurs in his 1737 "Faithful Narrative of the Surprising Work of God," an account of his experiences
with his own congregation at Northampton in 1734–35. His 1746 work, "A
Treatise Concerning Religious Affections," provides a fuller analysis of the
revival known as the "Great Awakening."

12. There are many notable discussions of style in Edwards's narrative. See,
for example, Scheick, and Shea.

13. Wheelock baldly described his attempts to "purge all the Indian out" of
another one of his students when speaking about Indian education (qtd. in
Axtell 98, Elliott 241).

14. Others, including David Murray and Bernd Peyer, have noted the strong
tone of this line, but have not heard the Pauline resonance. Corinthians, and
the Apostle Paul's anger, may have had a particular appeal for Occom: Elliott
notes his use of another section of the same epistle in a confrontational letter
to Wheelock concerning the founding of Dartmouth (245–46).

15. Wheelock in fact called for the training of Indian missionaries, in part,
precisely because he saw them as needing only half the pay of English missionaries (Elliott 241).

16. Elliott includes a discussion of a similar moment in one of Occom's letters
(to Wheelock) in which he describes himself as "good for nothing" (242–
43).

Works Cited

Axtell, James. *The European and the Indian: Essays in the Ethnohistory of Colonial North America.* New York: Oxford UP, 1981.

Blodgett, Harold. *Samson Occom.* Dartmouth College Manuscript Series 3.
Hanover: Dartmouth College, 1935.

Bosco, Ronald A. "Lectures at the Pillory: The Early American Execution Sermon." *American Quarterly* 30 (1978): 156–76.

Edwards, Jonathan. *The Works of Jonathan Edwards.* Ed. Perry Miller, John E.

Smith and Harry S. Stout. 13 vols. to date. New Haven: Yale UP, 1957—.

—. "Personal Narrative." *A Jonathan Edwards Reader.* ed. John E. Smith et al. New Haven: Yale UP, 1995. 281–96.

Elliott, Michael. "'This Indian Bait': Samson Occom and the Voice of Liminality." *Early American Literature* 29 (1994): 233–51.

Emerson, Ralph Waldo. *Nature. Essays and Lectures.* New York: Library of America, 1982.

Krupat, Arnold. *The Voice in the Margin: Native American Literature and the Canon.* Berkeley: U of California P, 1989.

—. "Native American Autobiography and the Synecdochic Self." *American Autobiography: Retrospect and Prospect.* ed. Paul John Eakin. Madison: U of Wisconsin P, 1991. 171–94.

Minnick, Wayne C. "The New England Execution Sermon, 1639–1800." *Speech Monographs* 35 (1968): 77–89.

Murray, David. *Forked Tongues: Speech, Writing and Representation in North American Indian Texts.* Bloomington: Indiana UP, 1991.

Nelson, Dana. "Reading the Written Selves of Colonial America: Franklin, Occom, Equiano, and Palou/Serra." *Resources For American Literary Study* 19 (1993): 246–259.

Occom, Samson. *A Sermon Preached at the Execution of Moses Paul, an Indian.* Bennington: William Watson, 1772.

—. "A Short Narrative of my Life." *The Elders Wrote: An Anthology of Early Prose by North American Indians 1768–1931.* ed. Bernd Peyer. Berlin: Reimer, 1982. 12–18.

Peyer, Bernd. "Samson Occom: Mohegan Missionary and Writer of the 18th Century." *American Indian Quarterly* 6 (1982): 208–17.

Richardson, Leon Burr. *An Indian Preacher In England.* Dartmouth College Manuscript Series 2. Hanover: Dartmouth College, 1933.

Ruoff, A. LaVonne Brown. *American Indian Literatures: An Introduction, Bibliographic Review, and Selected Bibliography.* New York: MLA, 1990.

Scheick, William J. *The Writings of Jonathan Edwards: Theme, Motif, and Style.* College Station: Texas A&M UP, 1975.

Shea, Daniel B. Jr. "The Art and Instruction of Jonathan Edwards' *Personal Narrative.*" *The American Puritan Imagination.* ed. Sacvan Bercovitch. New York: Cambridge UP, 1974. 159–72.

—. "The Prehistory of American Autobiography." *American Autobiography: Retrospect and Prospect.* ed. Paul John Eakin. Madison: U of Wisconsin P, 1991. 25–46.

Van Lonkhuyzen, Harold W. "A Reappraisal of the Praying Indians: Acculturation, Conversion, and Identity at Natick, Massachusetts, 1646–1730." *New England Quarterly* 63 (1990): 396–428.

Weinstein, Laurie. "Samson Occom: A Charismatic Eighteenth-Century Mohegan Leader." *Enduring Traditions: The Native Peoples of New England.* ed. Laurie Weinstein. Westport, Connecticut: Bergin and Garvey. 91–102.

Woolman, John. *The Journal and Major Essays of John Woolman.* ed. Phillips P. Moulton. New York: Oxford UP, 1971.

• 11 •

'Our Glory and Joy': Stephen Riggs and the Politics of Nineteenth-Century American Missionary Ethnography Among the Sioux

Edwin J. McAllister

Stephen Return Riggs (1812–83) was a Presbyterian missionary to the Dakota Sioux Indians from 1837 until his death. Like countless other American missionaries in the nineteenth and early twentieth centuries, Riggs took up the pen to describe for Christians at home the people among whom he lived and worked. The works of these missionaries were widely read, and in a culture that valued Christian piety and self-sacrifice, their words had tremendous authority. Consequently, their effect on American attitudes toward Native Americans and dark-skinned foreigners carried tremendous weight and performed a powerful type of cultural work.

Riggs's representations of the Dakota in many ways exemplify the agendas and assumptions of the "mainstream" American ethnography centralized in the Smithsonian during the middle and late nineteenth century. For example, the successful assimilation of Native Americans into patterns of settler culture and the destruction of Native American social institutions would be the aim of most ethnography produced during these years, and Riggs's is no exception. Yet it is also true that Riggs's Christian beliefs produce a significantly different sense of "otherness" in his ethnographic writing. The narrative of conversion that characterizes much missionary writing necessitates a construction of an easily bridgeable distance separating red man and white; a former state of savagery is contrasted with a present elevated moral and social state. Like most missionaries, Riggs produced representations of the Native Americans that focused on the saving power of the gospel to lift the red man from savagery to civilization, representations designed to show the "civilizing" power of conversion at work, not only in the lives of notable individuals, but also in the life of the Dakota community.

When Riggs first travelled to Minnesota in 1837 to work toward the

evangelization of the Dakota Sioux Indians, he did so under the auspices of the American Board of Commissioners for Foreign Missions,
an ecumenical umbrella organization that from its inception in 1810
oversaw the distribution and work of American foreign missionaries.
That Minnesota Indian territory would have been considered "foreign"
in 1837 is perhaps not so surprising as it seems initially. Minnesota
would be a territory rather than a state for twenty more years. More
importantly, the Native Americans living in Minnesota Indian territory
were far removed from centers of white population. Over the course of
the next forty years as the American frontier was pushed more and more
rapidly westward, Riggs would find himself less and less isolated from
his countrymen. Finally, recognizing that the domestication of the West
was to a large extent a *fait accompli*, the ABCFM would give up its
jurisdiction over the Dakota mission, the last of its Native American
enterprises, relegating control over them to domestic mission boards.

Governmental bureaucracy was also responsive to the shift in status
of the "Indian problem" from a foreign to a domestic issue. In 1874,
Major John Wesley Powell, a Civil War veteran, recognized authority
on anthropology, and, four years later, the first head of the newly-formed
Bureau of American Ethnology, warned the U.S. Congress that the disappearance of the American frontier was substantially narrowing the
choices available for dealing with the Native Americans: "There is
now no great uninhabited and unknown region to which the Indian can
be sent. He is among us, and we must either protect him or destroy
him" (quoted in Hinsley 145). Powell's recognition that the Native
Americans were now "among us" found its bureaucratic corollary in
the gradual shift in the administration of Indian affairs from the Department of War to the Department of the Interior. With the Native Americans now a domestic issue, public administrators found themselves
forced to confront the "Indian problem" not as a military concern, but
instead as an issue of domestic policy and control, of how to properly
integrate the red man into civilization. The central question they faced
was how to do so most quickly and efficiently.

It was quite explicitly out of the need for information on how to make
decisions regarding the assimilation of Native Americans that the discipline of ethnology in America was born. In the Introductory section of
the First Annual Report of the Bureau of American Ethnology, Powell
would, after noting the achievements of his newly formed bureau during the past year, observe that:

Edwin J. McAllister

> In pursuing these ethnographic investigations it has been the endeavor as far as possible to produce results that would be of practical value in the administration of Indian affairs, and for this purpose especial attention has been paid to vital statistics . . . the progress made by the Indians toward civilization, and the causes and remedies of the inevitable conflict that arises from the spread of civilization over a region previously inhabited by savages. I may be allowed to express hope that our labors in this direction will not be void of such useful results. (xiv)

Certain assumptions are obvious in the passage: the inevitability of the conflict between savages and spreading civilization, the usefulness of ethnographic knowledge for assimilating Native Americans to civilization, that Native Americans *could* be civilized, and that such civilization represented not simply a difference, but a natural upward progression beyond their savage state.

In its study of this savage state, the Smithsonian, and later the Bureau of American Ethnology, relied for its ethnographic information on those who knew the Indians best: army officers and missionaries, men who had lived and worked among Native Americans over a span of years. It was enthusiastic amateurs like these who formed the core of the field workers for the newly emerging science of ethnology, collecting and recording information in the field, eventually using systematized forms produced by the central authorities in Washington (Hinsley 48). Riggs, who had little formal educational training other than his years in seminary, would be a model data collector for the budding new science and a significant contributor to the methodological standardization of linguistic information gathering. Riggs's first substantial publication was his tremendous Dakota dictionary and grammar, compiled after eighteen years of patient effort. He at first attempted to have the dictionary published by subscription, but the work was brought to the attention of Joseph Henry, the General Secretary of the Smithsonian Institution (which would later oversee the Bureau of American Ethnology), who, after consulting with William W. Turner, the Smithsonian's most prominent philologist, decided to print the dictionary as one of the first of the Smithsonian's "Contributions to Knowledge" series in 1851. Riggs would proudly report that it had "obtained the commendation of literary men generally, and it was said that for no volume published by the Smithsonian Institution up to that time, was the demand so great" (Riggs 1880: 121). He would also call it "a missionary contribution to science" and perhaps "the means of perpetuating the remembrance of the Dakotas, beyond the time when, as a distinct people, they shall have disappeared from the continent" (Riggs 1869: 415).

For later generations of ethnologists, the idea of an untrained, and, worse, unscientific missionary producing ethnographic data might have been repugnant, but for Riggs and his contemporaries, the enthusiastic amateur as data-gatherer made perfect sense. Believing that the science of ethnology was following a natural upward course of development, most practitioners in the first half of the nineteenth century were prepared to admit that the discipline was in an early stage compared with more standardized and professionalized disciplines like natural history, an assumption that justified the numbers of amateurs involved in the collection of ethnographic data. Missionaries seemed in fact to be better positioned to collect this data than almost anyone else. W.W. Turner, the man who recommended Riggs's dictionary to Joseph Henry, felt that the missionaries were the only group of men "qualified by education and sustained by motives of benevolence" to spend the necessary years studying the "mental idiosyncracies of our red brethren" (quoted in Hinsley 50).

The discipline was professionalized very quickly by its association with the Smithsonian. By 1869, Joseph Henry would be ready to claim that ethnology had "passed from the period of pure speculation . . . into that of the active collection of materials preparatory to the next —that of deduction and generalizations" (quoted in Hinsley 35). Riggs would, in fact, help to produce the methodology that later came to characterize professionalized ethnology; his article entitled "Illustration of the Method of Recording Indian Languages" would be published in the B.A.E.'s first Annual Report in 1879. Riggs's first formal ethnography of the Dakota Sioux, entitled "Dakota Texts, Grammar, and Ethnography," would be published posthumously by the B.A.E. in 1893.[1]

If Riggs's ethnographic work exemplifies the tendency toward increasing methodological rigor and professionalism in nineteenth century American ethnology, there are other components of Riggs's ethnographic program that place him in a less exemplary, more ambiguous relationship to the established mainstreams of ethnographic thought, components related directly to assumptions and agendas of his evangelical Christianity. Mainstream ethnology in America was to a certain extent molded by pietist Christian assumptions, particularly the assumption of the unity of man. Joseph Henry's distaste for the work of physical anthropologists like Samuel G. Morton (whose *Crania Americana* and *Crania Aegyptica* purported to show that the races had been separate since their origins and that nonwhite races lacked the brain size to participate in civilization) was a sentiment he shared with most nineteenth century American Christians.[2] As a consequence, such work had no place at the Smithsonian or later in the B.A.E. Riggs's representations of the Dakota Sioux without question exemplify the participation of ethnology in the mainstream attempt to assimilate the Native Americans to the "civilization" of nineteenth century bourgeois America. But it is also true that Riggs's representations of Native Americans are significantly different, that the narratives of conversion in much missionary ethnography implicitly (and sometimes explicitly) resist certain pessimistic assumptions coded into much late nineteenth century developmental ethnology about the possibility for assimilating Native Americans.

Developmental ethnology of the sort practiced by B.A.E. ethnologists generally located the central "difference" between civilized and savage man as a question of temporal disjunction, mapping "civilization" along a single horizontal axis and assuming that all societies progressed along the same pathway. Nineteenth century American ethnologists did not think of human societies as part of a broad spectrum of different cultures. Most did not imagine "cultures" as plural at all. The opening sentence of E.B. Tylor's germinal *Primitive Culture* (1871) exemplifies the common sense that culture was a singular phenomenon: "Culture or Civilization, taken in its ethnographic sense," Tylor writes, "is that complex whole which includes knowledge, belief, art, morals, law, custom, and any other capabilities and habits acquired by man as a member of society." Thus, the term "culture" was normative rather than descriptive (Sattlemeyer 107). Native American and other primitive "tribes" or "nations" or "races" were part of the same creation as white men but had developed more slowly. Both travelled along the same upward path that terminated in the culture of the ethnographer. Given enough time, savage nations would end up in the same place.

If the monogenist assumptions behind developmental ethnography worked against "scientific" justifications for the destruction or enslavement of dark-skinned peoples produced by physical anthropologists, it could also be very easily used as its own justification for institutionalizing grotesque inequalities between "savages" and their civilized brethren. Savages who had not developed the capacity for higher forms of government on their own clearly could not be expected to participate fully in the "civilized" decision-making process, even in decisions regarding their own welfare. For instance, James Mill, John Stuart Mill's father, in his *History of British India* (1817), argued that the Hindus were only "half-civilized." As such, despotism was the only mode of government appropriate to their "level of civilization," and the best form of that they could hope for was the "enlightened despotism" of British rule. Only for the enlightened European were the radical politics of utilitarianism appropriate (Stocking 32–33). The same thinking lay behind the paternalistic policies of Congress and the Bureau of Indian Affairs, for example the decision in 1871 to stop treaty making with the Indians, after some three hundred seventy treaties, and the later decision to privatize Indian land holdings with the 1887 Dawes Act (Feit 112).

Developmental ethnologists, even those most optimistic about the eventuality of Native American participation in American culture, suggested that the process could be a lengthy one. Assimilation depended on programs of uplift and education that might take many generations to effect. Even if the natives' natural progress toward civilization could be hastened by the benevolent intervention of more civilized people, it was only natural to assume that several generations at the very least would have to pass before Native Americans could fully participate as citizens in civilized American life. Given the widespread belief among Americans (and the official policy of the B.A.E.) that conflict would inevitably arise "from the spread of civilization over a region previously inhabited by savages," such assumptions had dangerous implications, dooming the savage to extinction regardless of the good intentions of his civilized white brothers.

Riggs and other missionary ethnographers had good cause to reject temporal disjunction as the grounding point of difference between savage and civilized man; while the missionaries were at the time a driving force behind efforts at education and "uplift" for the red men, their principal reason for being among the Native Americans was the salvation of souls, an operation that for them had far greater implications for the project of assimilation than it had for those who assumed that Christianity was merely one element in the panoply of civilized institutions. For most missionaries in the nineteenth century, true civilization and Christianity were synonymous. Christianity was not just one element of civilized life; it was the very rock on which civilization was grounded, and those who did not embrace it would never be civilized. Stephen Riggs insisted on the temporal priority of salvation before civilization. Adopting the rhetoric of progress and advancement for his cause, he would proclaim that the idea "that uncivilized heathen nations should *first* be civilized, and *then* Christianized, is a sentiment of the past. Now it is coming more and more to be acknowledged that *the Bible is the great civilizer of the nations*" (Riggs 1869: 386). Like savage peoples, ethnographic knowledge was itself developing toward a more perfect grasp of the real grounding point of difference between civilized and savage nations: "But what makes us to differ from them? Chiefly we are indebted to the Bible for our superior intelligence and more civilized habits" (1869:338). Riggs would demonstrate the truth of this maxim in his representations both of individuals and of the Dakota people generally, choosing as his codes for denoting the assimilation of them into a civilized state certain outward manifestations of nineteenth century respectability: adoption of agriculture and a sedentary mode of life in a house, cutting off long hair, and wearing white men's clothes. Again and again, Riggs shows that the Dakota who accept the gospel also accept the necessity it entails of becoming civilized—in other words, of behaving like white nineteenth century middle-class Americans.

Riggs's accounts of the behavior of his early converts work to confirm his insistence on the temporal priority of salvation to civilization, and the natural emergence of one from the other. He tells the story of Simon Ana-wang-mani in both *Mary and I*, a book produced for a general public audience, and more fully in *Dakota Ethnography*, but in each case the message is the same: conversion will make of the savages good, domestic, hard-working, lower middle-class Americans. Simon was the first full-blooded Dakota male to "come out on the side of the new religion" (1880: 65) and is the first Dakota mentioned by name in any of Riggs's work.3

Pre-salvation Simon is a Dakota warrior "known for recklessness . . . . There was in him a strong will, which sometimes showed itself in the form of stubbornness. His eye, even in a later day, showed that there had been evil, hatred, and maliciousness there. He was a thorough Indian" (1893: 219). Simon's first acts as a convert are to officially marry his wife and to take to himself an English name. Simon puts on white men's clothes, cuts his hair, and plants a garden by the mission fields, inspiring Riggs to remark: "By dressing like a white man and going to work, he showed his faith by his works . . . . He built for himself a cabin, and fenced a field and planted it. For this his wife's friends opposed and persecuted him" (1893: 221). Ridiculed in his own village, Simon goes to another Dakota village, where he is briefly honored, but having no Christian company, falls prey to the evils of alcohol. Tempted with fire water, "He fell! . . . He put off his white man's clothes and for some time was an Indian again." However, Simon eventually comes to his senses, and so "in 1854 he returned to the dress and customs of the white men and to his profession of love to Jesus Christ.

Since that time he has witnessed a good confession before many witnesses as a ruling elder and class leader, and recently as a licensed preacher" (1893: 222–23). Riggs clearly makes no distinction between Christian belief and nineteenth century middle class American social practices, and the latter serve as a certain signifier of the former. It is clearly Simon's conversion to and practice of Christianity that civilize him and not the amount of education he has. If the durability of that civilizing power is in doubt, it is so only briefly, and then only because Simon has so little Christian company.

The pattern repeats itself as the Riggs find more converts, underlining the inevitability of post-salvation assimilation to civilized behavior, which includes the rejection of uncivilized company of the sort that caused Simon's temporary fall: "We began to have more young men in the church, and they began to separate themselves more and more from the village, and to build cabins and make fields for themselves. Thus the religion of Christ worked to disintegrate heathenism" (1880: 114). Here Christian conversion is directly equated with a very specific set of social practices and, importantly, it happens quickly. If certain developmental ethnographers like James Mill theorized that vast amounts of time would be necessary to "civilize" the natives, Riggs would work explicitly against such an assumption by showing the speedy conversion of the Indians to social practices considered universally to denote civilized behavior by most nineteenth century Americans.

In his accounts of the formation of the Hazelwood Republic, Riggs quite explicitly makes a case for the ability of the Christianized Dakotas as a body to participate immediately not only in a broadly defined range of "civilized" practices, but in a very specifically American range of practices as well. If Native Americans could participate in agriculture, sedentary home-building, and church life, Riggs also shows that they are ready to take on the political responsibilities necessary to participate as citizens in the public life of the U.S. In the late 1850s, having a number of Dakota converts, Riggs and his fellow missionaries determine to establish a "settlement of the civilized and Christianized Dakotas" (1880: 131) apart from the Dakotas living on the agency. "We had now such a respectable community of young men, who had cut off their hair and exchanged the dress of the Dakotas for that of the white man, and whose wants were now very different from the annuity Dakotas generally, that we took measures to organize them into a separate band, which we called the Hazelwood Republic" (1880:133). This group organizes themselves democratically, signing a constitution, electing a president, and voting on important matters of state.

In a sketch that Riggs says will illustrate both "the Dakota beliefs in regard to diseases, and the common way of treating them, as well as the progress of thought, and changes of practice, consequent upon the introduction of Christianity," we see the citizens of Hazelwood at work in a dispute over the "rightness" of treating the sick using traditional shamanistic practices. A Christianized native is upbraided by his fellow converts for calling in a traditional medicine man to treat his dying wife. Unsure of how to respond to this reversion to uncivilized practice, the Dakotas ask Riggs for his guidance, but he refuses, instead instructing them to call together an assembly of elders. The elders "were told that the Gospel of Christ molded the customs and habits of every people by whom it was received. There might be some wrong things in a national custom which could be eliminated, and the custom substantially retained. Or the custom might be so radically absurd and wrong, that it could not be redeemed. In that case, Christianity required its abandonment" (1869: 216). The members of the Hazelwood Republic, after discussing the matter fully, vote overwhelmingly to give up traditional practices for treating the sick. Clearly, this group of native Americans is ready to take on the challenge of civilized, Christian democracy. Riggs even attempts to have the senior members of the Hazelwood Republic made citizens of the state, but they are refused on the grounds that their English is not good enough for them to understand the law.

Perhaps the central incident in Riggs's missionary life was the 1862 Dakota uprising. The uprising seems to have been caused by several factors. A loosely related group of Dakotas had killed forty white settlers earlier in the year at Spirit Lake, and the Bureau of Indian Affairs insisted that the agency Indians themselves undertake a punitive expedition against them. In addition, the BIA decided in 1862 that rather than giving cash annuities to agency Indians, they would pay the equivalent in goods. However, neither the cash or the annuities were on hand at the agreed time and the several of the Dakotas, near to starving, broke into the government warehouse and took flour. Subsequent misunderstandings finally culminated in a pitched battle that lasted several weeks and caused many deaths among whites and Native Americans alike. A group of four hundred Dakota males were captured. After a series of quick trials in which the burden of proof was placed on the accused, over three hundred of these were sentenced to death. Most of the sentences were later commuted, but thirty eight accused by white eyewitnesses of murder were hung together in front of the other Dakotas.

To give Riggs his due, he seems to have recognized that the discontent of the Dakotas had a certain legitimacy. He includes in his autobiography an excerpt from a newspaper article written by 'his daughter Martha for the Cincinatti Christian Herald recounting the uprising which blames most of the trouble on the behavior of whites:

> The Indians have not been without excuse for their evil deeds. Our own people have given them intoxicating drinks, taught them to swear, violated the rights of womanhood among them, robbed them of their dues, and insulted them! What more would be necessary to cause one nation to rise against another? What more, I ask? And yet there are many who curse this people, and cry, Exterminate the fiends." Dare we, as a nation, thus bring a curse upon ourselves and on future generations? (quoted in 1880: 178)

In *Tah-Koo Wah-Kan; or, the Gospel Among the Dakotas* (1869), Riggs would provide a similar list of causes behind the 1862 uprising (and in much the same order) but would, however, conclude by tracing the source of the conflict to the inevitability of conflict between heathen savages and civilized Christians: "And last, but not least, among the causes which produced the Sioux outbreak must be mentioned *the antagonism of heathenism to Christianity and Civilization*" (1869: 331–32). One is reminded of John Wesley Powell's remark (quoted earlier) regarding "the inevitable conflict that arises from the spread of civilization over a region previously inhabited by savages." Riggs adds Christianity to the equation, but the justification for the assimilationist agenda is obviously the same for professional ethnographers or for missionaries: we can only save the Indians by destroying their institutions (which will otherwise inevitably cause conflict with spreading civilization) and by assimilating them to our patterns of acceptable behavior. Riggs goes on to quote approvingly Mr. Pond (a fellow missionary), who conflates assimilation, salvation, providence, and manifest destiny: "'They [the Dakotas] hoped to be able to roll back the providential wheel of Almighty God'" (1869: 331).

Riggs also uses his depictions of the 1862 uprising to strengthen his claim that salvation must come before civilization. The Dakotas have all been exposed to education and encouraged to take up the plow and put on white men's clothing, yet it is only the church members who do not participate in the violence—more, they protect the white settlers. Again, from Martha Riggs's newspaper account: "It must be remembered that the church members, as a whole, have had no hand in it.

One, John Otherday, guided a party of sixty-two across the prairies. Two others . . . have recently brought into Fort Ridgly three captive women and eleven children" (1880:178). Translators from the Hazelwood Republic are used by the army to ransom white captives. Clearly, only those Indians who have been converted to Christianity can truly be relied on to behave in acceptable ways; the rest will continue in savagery.

Riggs's providential vision of salvation and civilization moving in lockstep westward across the frontier is realized in the mass conversion of the captive Dakota men, who make their decision regarding conversion based on their rational assessment of the outcome of the uprising.

> In one aspect, the question was Shall the Indian or the white man rule?" But in another and more important one it was, Shall the Kingdom of Christ be set up among the Dakotas, or shall the worship of stones be continued?" So especially thought those three hundred and thirty prisoners, who were wearing chains on their ankles in Mankato in the winter of 1862–63, and they regarded the question as having been settled by the events of the last few months. The power of the white men had prevailed; and the religion of the Great Spirit, or the white man's god, was to be supreme. (1869: 341–42)

Riggs insists that the 1862 conflict is only secondarily of civilization versus savagery. The primary relevance of the event for Riggs and for his Dakota charges is the triumph of Christianity over heathenism, the deep truth made plain by the military victory of the whites. "Their own gods had failed them signally, as was manifest in their present condition" (1880: 187). Not surprisingly, these converts, like all Riggs's converts before them, begin displaying the behaviors associated with civilization. If their current situation makes agriculture and home-building impossible and the wearing of white man's clothes unavoidable, there are still behaviors within their control that they can choose to adapt or reject. Riggs shows the miraculous birth of interest in education among the Dakotas: "The prisoners asked for books . . . . From this time on the prison became a school . . . . They were all exceedingly anxious to learn. And the more their minds were turned toward God and His word, the more interested they became in learning to read and write" (1880: 187).

In the years following the uprising, the Dakotas, converted and unconverted, are moved to the Crow Creek reservation. Upon their arrival, the Hazelwood Republic converts are dismayed by the decision of the US Bureau of Indian Affairs to allow the unconverted Dakotas to keep their old system of tribal government on the reservation, having reasoned that as they had been electing their church officers, so they would elect the necessary civil officers. In other words, the converts are ready to continue the democratic practices they established earlier in the Hazelwood Republic, but are prevented from doing so by the decision of the BIA that recognizes the pre-conversion heathen power and social structures of Dakota society.

Riggs represents the reservation system as the land base on which traditional communal economic and governance practices, practices he has already associated with savagery, can be continued. Riggs's opinions here are much the same as those of the scientific establishment in America. Major Powell of the BAE would use a similar argument only a few years later to support the passage of the General Allotment Act of 1887, also known as the Dawes Act, which provided for the allotment of reservation lands into individual holdings. Appealing directly to Lewis Henry Morgan's *Ancient Society,* which argued that the recognition of private property rights was one of the necessary sequential steps on the march toward civilization, Lewis urged passage of the act, claiming it would aid in the transformation of "communalistic" Indians into "individualistic" Americans (Feit 112–13). Clearly, though, for Morgan and Powell, the institutionalization of private property among Native Americans is only one of a series of perhaps very slow steps toward civilization. For Riggs, it is all that remains necessary to make citizens of the Dakotas.

Arriving at Crow Creek, the Hazelwood Republicans, who had come to associate owning their own land and houses, working their own farms, and electing their own leaders as not only civilized, but Christian behaviors, find that they "must be Indian or starve!" One of the converts remarks sadly that "I could not bear to have my children grow up nothing but Indians" (1880: 238–39). Riggs's converted Dakotas themselves voice these arguments against communal tribal structures and land holdings, pointing to the reestablished Hazelwood Republic as the model for Dakota behavior. Riggs has one Dakota argue:

> If when we are hungry we cry out to our Great Father, give us food," or when we are cold we say, Send us clothes," we become as little children—we are not men. Here at this place we

see that each man takes care of himself; he has a farm and a
house, and some cows and a few chickens. We go into their
houses and we see tables and chairs, and when they eat they
spread a cloth over the table, as do white people, and there are
curtains to the windows, and we see the women dressed like
white women—here we find men. (1880: 282–83)

The Dakota move out of savagery to civilization is part of a natural
progression like growing up. Clinging to traditional institutions would
be as shameful as keeping the toys of childhood after becoming an
adult. Riggs suggests that the assimilation of the Native Americans,
the making of them into something other than mere "Indians," will be
retarded by allowing them to keep any of their old institutions or by
setting up paternalistic economic structures to care for them until the
develop into civilized beings.

A stern believer in the Protestant work ethic, Riggs's rejection of an
annuity system based on government handouts must be seen in light of
his insistence on the *ability* of Native Americans to fend for themselves
in the face of encroaching white settlements, an argument predicated
entirely on his belief in a quickly bridgeable gap between savages and
civilized men. Riggs was not arguing that the Native Americans should
be ignored, rather that they should be (and *could* be) assimilated as
quickly as possible into the social, governmental, and property structures of white nineteenth century America. "The men who would have
their hair cut, and put on pantaloons, should have their fields plowed
and houses built for them; and they would be furnished with work,
cattle, wagons, etc" (1869: 397); "But give them a chance," Riggs
wrote, "and hold out proper inducements to them. Make it possible for
them to become men . . . not by feeding and clothing them, except for
the present necessity, but by showing them that work is honorable . . .
and that the law of labor is one from which no people are exempt"
(1869: 400).

Riggs is no multiculturalist hero. He was working very consciously
and unapologetically toward the eradication of Native American customs, beliefs, and institutions of every sort. In doing so Riggs did not
imagine that he was assimilating them into a *different* culture, but rather
that he was assisting them to take their rightful place within culture
itself, and not as developmental inferiors but as full participants. Seen
in the context of the pervasive mindset that figured culture as a single
ladder upon which the nations of man were placed at higher or lower

positions, Riggs's assimilationist program emerges, lamentably short-sighted by our current standards, but relatively enlightened for its own time: "The Indian tribes of our continent may become extinct as such; but if this extinction is brought about by introducing them to civilization and Christianity and merging them into our own great nation, which is receiving accretions from all others, who will deplore the result? Rather let us labor for it, realizing that if by our efforts they cease to be Indians and become fellow citizens it will be our glory and joy" (1893: 167). In calling for the cultural assimilation of Native Americans, and insisting upon the easy possibility of that assimilation, Riggs was responding to an alternative even less attractive by contemporary standards: Extermination at its worst, or a paternalistic refusal to treat the Native Americans as developmental equals at best.

Notes

1. I have some doubt as to whether Riggs intended to publish a formal ethnology at all. He was producing a letter" for the BAE to be entitled Unwritten Laws," which his son Thomas had published when it was found among Riggs's papers after his death. In a letter to J.C. Pilling (then chief of the BAE) dated April 20, 1881, Stephen Riggs wrote of his planned article: This letter, I think, will cover Ethnology. But I do not profess to be skilled in Ethnology as a science, and shall be glad of any suggestions from Maj. Powell and yourself." (quoted in Riggs 1893). The letter is interesting in that it clearly shows that Riggs was aware of the inappropriacy of his producing a formal ethnography, suggesting that the discipline had become professionalized enough by the 1890s to make even one of its pioneer amateurs feel unqualified.

2. William Stanton's *The Leopard's Spots: Scientific Attitudes Toward Race in America 1815–59* is a fascinating introduction to physical anthropology," branch of ethnology that argued that different races were actually separate species. Popular in the pre-Civil war south, scientists like Samuel George Morton would employ the numerical precision emerging in other scientific disciplines to prove" the natural and unchangeable intellectual inferiority of other races, particularly through craniometric measurements. Morton's Crania Americana, published in 1839, used graphic tables to show that whites had, on the average, a substantially larger craniometric volume—in other words, bigger brains. According to Hinsley, Joseph Henry apparently felt some discomfort with physical anthropology, not only because he felt that it was politically unwise to encourage highly controversial research at a time when he was attempting to construct an objective" scientific community,

but also because he thought it was damaging to Christian piety. For whatever reason, it had no place at the Smithsonian or the Bureau of American Ethnology, and consequently was largely left out during the construction of respectable ethnology. (It is worth noting, though, that Henry's refusal to allow physical anthropologists to lecture under the auspices of the Smithsonian was a discourtesy he also extended to abolitionists, so perhaps political expedients outweighed pietist in the decision.) Riggs clearly and specifically sets up his own work in opposition to it—on numerous occasions stating very explicitly that the Dakota are human beings just like us and subject to the same religious dispensation. However, I chose to leave it out of this chapter not only because it is a tremendous and complicated matter, but also because craniometry was not really a part of "mainstream" ethnology at the time that Riggs was writing.

3. This despite the fact that Riggs recounts having saved numbers of Dakota women and half-breeds long before Simon is converted. As far as I know, Riggs never mentions a Dakota woman by name anywhere in his work.

Works Cited

Bureau of American Ethnology. *First Annual Report of the Bureau of American Ethnology to the Secretary of the Smithsonian Institution 1879–80*, J.W. Powell, Director. Washington, D.C.: Government Printing Office, 1881.

Feit, Harvey. The Construction of Algonquin Hunting Territories: Private Property as Moral Lesson, Policy Advocacy, and Ethnographic Error," in *Colonial Situations: Essays on the Contextualization of Ethnographic Knowledge*. Ed. George W. Stocking, Jr. Madison: U of Wisconsin P, 1991.

Hinsley, Curtis M., Jr. *Savages and Scientists: The Smithsonian Institution and the Development of American Anthropology 1846–1910*. Washington, D.C: Smithsonian Institution, 1981.

Riggs, Stephen R. *A Dakota-English Dictionary* (edited reprint of 1851 edition), James Owen Dorsey, ed. in Contributions to North American Ethnology, vol. 7. Washington, DC: Government Printing Office, 1890.

—. *Dakota Grammar, Texts, and Ethnography*, ed. James Owen Dorsey. in Contributions to North American Ethnology, vol. 9. Washington, DC: Government Printing Office, 1893.

—. "Illustration of the method of recording Indian languages: from the manuscripts of J.O. Dorsey, A.S. Gatschet, and S.R. Riggs" in *U.S. Bureau of American Ethnology First Annual Report, 1879–80*. Washington, DC: Government Printing Office, 1881.

—. *Mary and I: Forty Years Among the Sioux*. Chicago: W.G. Holmes, 1880.

—. *Tah-Koo Wah-Kan: or, the Gospel Among the Dakotas*. Boston: Congregational Publishing Society, 1869.

Sattelmeyer, Robert. *Thoreau's Reading: A Study in Intellectual History.* Princeton, NJ: Princeton UP, 1988.

Stanton, William. *The Leopard's Spots: Scientific Attitudes Toward Race in America 1815–59.* Chicago: U of Chicago Press, 1960.

Stocking, George. *Victorian Anthropology.* New York: The Free Press, 1987.

Tylor, Edward B. *Primitive Culture: Researches into the Development of Mythology, Philosophy, Religion, Language, Art, and Custom.* 2 vols. London: Murray; New York: Putnam, 1920.

12

Encountering Christ in Shusaku Endo's Mudswamp of Japan

John T. Netland

The history of Christianity in Japan offers an instructive example of how difficult multicultural rapprochement can be. In spite of a Christian presence for over 400 years, Christianity remains an overwhelmingly miniscule piece of Japan's religious mosaic, its adherents amounting to little more than one percent of the population. Explanations for this phenomenon demonstrate part of the cultural impasse which has made Christianity so problematic in Japan. A Christian reading of this history might frame the narrative as a simple tale of persecution and resistance by a cynical political order which saw the foreign religion as a threat to its power. On the other hand, a Japanese reading of this history might frame it as a story of an undesired western ideology that could never be successfully imposed on a culture so ill-suited to it.

Both readings concede that the history of Christianity in Japan has been a less than successful venture. It began auspiciously enough. St. Francis Xavier landed in Kagoshima in 1549, introducing Christianity to Japan where it flourished for the rest of the century. The Christian mission, however, never did entirely shed its western cultural and political trappings and therefore courted suspicion of its political allegiances. Finally, in 1614, the Shogun Ieyasu reversed previous policies of toleration by issuing his Edict of Expulsion, which set the stage for a brutal persecution of Christians and in the process cut off Japan from the west for over two centuries.[1]

Actually, neither Europe nor Japan was at that time very conducive to a depoliticized, cross-cultural dialogue. For most of the sixteenth century, Europe was dealing with the political repercussions of the Reformation and the Counter-Reformation, complex movements in which religious polemic became enmeshed in the commercial and political interests of most European nations. These interests followed the maritime powers on their voyages around the world. Both the European Catholic missionaries and merchants often dragged their old world disputes into their relations with the Japanese authorities, lending credence to suspicions that the religious mission of the Church might merely mask political reorientation, transforming Japanese society from its feudal parochialism into an ambitious modern nation organized around the centralized military authority of the shogun. One result of this political transformation was to make the stability of the state the preeminent social objective, sanctioned even by the Japanese religions, which emphasized obligations to the social order. Christianity, however, insisted that ultimate allegiances belong to God rather than to the secular state. The Japanese authorities thus began to feel that "Christianity was a disease which infected their subjects with disloyalty" (Elison 3). The Edict of Expulsion had accused Christians of seeking "to make Japan into 'their own possession' . . . [and] to 'contravene governmental regulations, traduce Shinto, calumniate the True Law, destroy righteousness, corrupt goodness'—in short, to subvert the native Japanese, the Buddhist, and the Confucian foundations of the social order" (Elisonas 367).

It is within this historical setting that the distinguished Japanese novelist Shusaku Endo works out the multicultural implications of his Christian faith. Thoroughly Japanese, persistently Catholic, he has had to reconcile what he calls "a Japanese and a Western (Christian) self" (Endo, qtd. Higgins 415). Likening his baptism at the age of eleven to the forced imposition of a "'ready-made suit,' a Western suit, ill-matched to his Japanese body," Endo seeks in his fiction to reshape "the Western suit into a Japanese kimono" (Higgins 416). This tension between Japanese culture and Christian faith is most pronounced in his historical fiction, with its imaginative retelling of crucial episodes from the history of Christianity in Japan. *Silence* is set in the fierce persecution initiated by Ieyasu, while *The Samurai* recounts an obscure, seventeenth-century Japanese trade mission to the New World. These historical novels, written eleven years apart, frame Endo's attempt to reconcile Christianity and Japanese culture.

To some extent the history of Christianity in Japan seems to confirm a central tenet of post-colonial theories, that virtually all European dealings with other cultures are masks for the political exercise of power. Postcolonial theories, by definition, take their frame of reference from the troubled history of western colonialism. They often lament the suppression of indigenous cultures and honor the silenced victims of imperialism. Beyond the colonial context, other strains of multiculturalism give voice to peoples whose histories have been muted within the dominant discourses of European and North American cultures. Central to these approaches is the desire to understand these cultures on their own terms, apart from the intellectual paradigms presumably imposed upon them by Euro-American cultures. This theoretical reorienting of cultural history owes much to Edward Said's *Orientalism*, which documents the European imperial imagination and its inscription of an Oriental "otherness" onto such cultures. Orientalism is for Said "the corporate institution for dealing with the Orient . . . , a Western style for dominating, restructuring, and having authority over the Orient" (3). Travel narratives, linguistic and anthropological scholarship, missionary activities, the popularization of "Oriental" fashions and motifs—all are deeply implicated in power structures of an expansive European civilization whose every relationship with the "Orient is a relationship of power, of domination, of varying degrees of a complex hegemony" (Said 5).

While Said's paradigm has considerable relevance for nineteenth-century Europe, when the balance of power decidedly favored Europe, the historical context of the early Christian mission to Japan reveals a crucial difference. While the exercise of power is certainly present in that context, it is not the story of a hegemonic, colonial power imposing its will upon a powerless people. Japan has never been colonized by the west, nor was the cross implanted on Japanese soil by force. Rather, secular power has generally been the prerogative of the Japanese state. That difference is crucial for our understanding of Endo's historical fiction. While these novels honestly portray the often troubling relationship of religion and power, they resist the reductionism of attributing this complicity solely to western hegemony. Instead they portray a radically Christian alternative to the worst impulses of both eastern and western political ambition. In so doing, they hint at a divine order that both acknowledges and transcends cultural particularity.

Silence tells the story of Father Sebastian Rodrigues, a fictional 17th-century Jesuit missionary, who is drawn to Japan by a combination of spiritual fervor, romantic idealism, and curiosity about the alleged apostasy of his seminary instructor, Father Christovao Ferreira. In spite of his idealism, Rodrigues's apostasy seems inevitable virtually from his arrival in Japan. He has come to assume the mantle of the heroic martyr, to lay down his life for the Church. His early meditative reveries, in the tradition of Ignatian meditation, are heavily laden with western iconic ideals—Christ as benevolent conqueror, Christ as King, Christ as the Good Shepherd. Little by little, that idealism gives way under the relentlessly de-romanticized suffering he sees. He witnesses the horrifyingly banal deaths of Japanese Christians, whose martyrdoms scarcely disturb the oppressive silence of the natural order. His longing to hear the voice of God and to see the Gospel triumph in Japan gradually dissipates in the face of a relentless silence, a silence dramatically broken when Rodrigues himself apostatizes.

Beyond the universal theme of faith and doubt, the novel problematizes the historical confrontation of East and West during the seventeenth-century, a confrontation the Japanese authorities characterize as undesired aggression. The magistrate Inoue crudely likens the Christian missionaries to an importunate woman. "Father," he says, "I want you to think over two things this old man has told you. One is that the persistent affection of an ugly woman is an intolerable burden for a man; the other, that a barren woman should not become a wife" (*Silence* 124).[1] His interpreter accuses Rodrigues of wanting "to impose [his] selfish dream upon Japan" (*Silence* 134). In arguing that the Christian faith is a selfish religious ideal, undesired by and ill-suited to Japanese society, these authorities reduce the Christian mission to the discourses of power.

Conspicuously absent from that argument is any reference to the respective truth claims of Christianity and Japanese religions, an absence that calls attention to profoundly different cultural sensibilities about the nature and place of truth in religious expression. For the Christian missionary, the imperative to preach the Gospel is based on particular claims about the nature of God, the created order, and the human condition. Call it dogmatic or propositional, the Christian faith is based on absolutist claims about the person of Jesus Christ, claims which do not offer much middle ground between belief and disbelief. Such is the understanding of the faith that Father Rodrigues proclaims. During his interrogation, Rodrigues consistently defends his faith by appealing to universal truth. Interestingly, the interpreter willingly accepts the challenge. Having "learned Christian doctrine in the seminary," the interpreter is eager to refute western misunderstandings of Buddhism and to turn the metaphysical problem of evil against the Christian world view. Yet Father Rodrigues holds his own, eventually making the interpreter angrily change the subject. It is a contest whose rules reflect the Christian worldview and which plays to the rhetorical strengths of the priest. The interpreter has accepted the standard of truth to settle questions of competing religious claims, and his angry dismissal of the argument at the end indicates that he knows he has not refuted Christianity on rational grounds.

On the other hand, Inoue demonstrates his Japanese religious sensibilities in quietly displacing universal truth claims with a more pragmatic and particularist notion of truth. "Father," he quietly insists, "we are not disputing about the right and wrong of your doctrine. In Spain and Portugal and such countries it may be true. The reason we have outlawed Christianity in Japan is that, after deep and earnest consideration, we find its teaching of no value for the Japan of today" (*Silence* 108). Rodrigues responds again with a compelling defense of universality: "It is precisely because truth is common to all countries and all times that we call it truth. If a true doctrine were not true alike in Portugal and Japan we could not call it 'true" (*Silence* 109). Inoue merely nods in polite acquiescence, never disputing the priest's defense of universality, and Rodrigues begins to believe that he is "winning the controversy." But though his defense of universal truth is never refuted, he does not win anything, for the debate about truth is virtually irrelevant to Inoue's pragmatic particularism. In the abyss separating the religious sensibilities of the sixteenth-century Japanese from the European Christian, there is virtually no common ground, other than the exercise of power, on which to adjudicate competing religious claims. Christian appeals to reason, evidence, and truth claims mean little to the Japanese state intent on establishing its political stability. The religious debate is simply a pretext for the exercise of power, a power designed to eradicate the otherness of Christianity from penetrating a homogenous Japanese culture.

In pressuring Rodrigues to apostatize, Inoue refrains from direct refutation, opting instead to undermine Christianity by manipulating its very ideals. Far more insidious than the threat of unspeakable tortures is the nagging suspicion—suggested by the apostate Ferreira and brilliantly exploited by Inoue—that Japanese culture inevitably subverts Christianity from within. Ferreira presents himself to the imprisoned Rodrigues as "an old missionary defeated by missionary work," convinced that the Christian "religion does not take root in this country" (*Silence* 146). It is he who introduces the swamp metaphor that implies an incompatibility of east and west: "This country is a swamp . . . . Whenever you plant a sapling in this swamp the roots begin to rot . . . . And we have planted the sapling of Christianity in this swamp" (*Silence* 147). Inoue adds, "The Christianity you brought to Japan has changed its form and has become a strange thing . . . . Japan is that kind of country; it can't be helped" (*Silence* 188). Ferreira's apostasy is based on a grudging acquiescence to Inoue's cultural particularity, the belief that eastern and western cultures are fundamentally incompatible and that the Christian Gospel is too culture-bound to be adaptable to the swamp of Japan. Ferreira's defeatism is thus more disturbing to Rodrigues than is Inoue's persecution, for while the latter does little to deny the claims of Christianity (persecution, after all, confirms a prominent Scriptural theme), the former undermines the Christian claim to universality. It challenges the trans-cultural normativity of Christianity, suggesting instead that Japanese culture inevitably syncretizes and hence distorts Christianity.

This clash of Christian faith and Japanese culture is prominent throughout the novel. Rodrigues frequently wonders about the cultural barriers to Christianity and is troubled by the excessive veneration the Japanese have for the icons (*Silence* 45). Later, while marveling at the cunning of Inoue's plan to make the Christians spit on the crucifix and declare the Blessed Virgin a whore, he worries that the "peasants sometimes seem to honor Mary rather than Christ" (*Silence* 56). These are not idle concerns, for such excesses of a proper Catholic veneration suggest an eclectic blend of Shinto animism and Christianity, raising troubling questions about whether such eclecticism assures cultural relevance or undermines Christianity's integrity. Language barriers, too, create problems for the missionaries. Rodrigues recalls Xavier's linguistic problem of confusing Deus with Dainichi, "the sun which the people of this country had revered for many generations" (*Silence* 70). Ferreira concludes that this linguistic confusion in fact reveals a profound irreconcilability between Christianity and the Japanese mind:

> From the beginning those same Japanese who confused 'Deus' and 'Dainichi' twisted and changed our God and began to create something different. Even when the confusion of vocabulary disappeared the twisting and changing secretly continued. Even in the glorious missionary period you mentioned the Japanese did not believe in the Christian God but in their own distortion. (*Silence* 148)[2]

The view that Christianity has been co-opted by the swamp of Japan is reinforced by Inoue's strategy to make Rodrigues apostatize. Were Rodrigues given the choice of apostasy or his own life, he likely would choose martyrdom over apostasy. But Inoue does not give him that choice. Rather, the priest is asked to apostatize to save the lives of the Japanese Christians hanging in the pit. A brilliant strategy, this choice appeals directly to Rodrigues's Christian love and sense of mission. Throughout his time in Japan, he frequently questions whether he has accomplished anything beyond merely troubling the Japanese Christians: "He had come to this country to lay down his life for other men, but instead of that the Japanese were laying down their lives one by one for him" (*Silence* 133). The night before the apostasy takes place, he is grieved by "his inability to love these people as Christ had loved them" (*Silence* 158). His nagging fear that he is not useful to others is exploited by Ferreira, who proclaims defensively that he, at least, is still useful to others even as an apostate. To Rodrigues, then, the command to apostatize comes not primarily as an invitation to escape suffering, but paradoxically as an appeal to his deepest Christian values. What is more Christ-like than to lay down one's life for others? Certainly the apostasy means a death to his public life of service to God, a life more precious to him than anything he can imagine. This strategy of appealing to Rodrigues's Christian virtues is rendered explicit when Ferreira tells him, "Certainly Christ would have apostatized for them . . . . You are now going to perform the most painful act of love that has ever been performed" (*Silence* 169–70).

This manipulation of Christian virtues on behalf of a nationalistic strategy to eradicate the faith seems to confirm Inoue's contention that Japan inevitably changes Christianity. Yet Endo is not content to give Inoue or Ferreira the last word. It is not, finally, Ferreira who leads Rodrigues to trample on the *fumie*. It is the emaciated Christ in the bronze image who breaks the silence and cries out to Rodrigues's heart: "Trample! Trample! I more than anyone know of the pain in your foot. Trample! It was to be trampled on by men that I was born into this world. It was to share men's pain that I carried my cross" (*Silence* 171). The apparent defeat of Christianity by the mudswamp of Japan ironically validates the very Kingdom it seeks to destroy. It is the moral authority of the suffering Christ that confirms Rodrigues's act, as if to say that the topsy-turvy Kingdom of God, in which the first are last and the last first, can take even Inoue's cynical manipulation of Christian ideals and use it to keep the spark of faith flickering.

Jean Higgins sees *Silence* as a transitional novel for Endo, indicating "the end of confrontation and the beginning of reconciliation" between Christianity and Japanese culture (417). This transition is signalled by the transformation of the "Rodrigues of the West" into the "Rodrigues of the East." The former constantly recurs to images of "the risen Christ, serene in conquest; a Christ of glory, whose example calls for heroism in his followers . . ." while the latter is drawn to the "weak and powerless Christ who shows himself understanding of the weak, who has compassion with the betrayer" (Higgins 421). By framing this transformation as the displacement of a Western for an Eastern paradigm of spirituality, Higgins may be overstating its cultural dimension, for Christ's identification with the dispossessed surely belongs to western spirituality as well. Nevertheless, it is true that Rodrigues consistently imagines

Christ in terms of western iconography—until the emaciated image of the bronze Christ stares up at him in its eastern starkness. This transformation of Rodrigues's religious imagination, from the idealized portraits of Christ as shepherd and king to Christ as fellow sufferer, suggests less of a displacement of west with east than a diminishment of all cultural particularity. Van C. Gessel notes that "the faith of Rodrigues and his companions has to be stripped of its cultural trappings before they can comprehend the true nature of Christ" (447). The effect is to present an image of Christ stripped of the triumphalism of western Christianity, thus bringing the central—and universal—themes of the Gospel into sharper focus. It is a conversion that negates rather than affirms the cultural particularity of either east or west, leaving the cross-cultural tension, in Gessel's words, in "a tentative truce," a "struggle in which there can be no victors" (447). Although it is not uniquely eastern, the concluding affirmation of faith presents Christianity in terms that Endo believes to be culturally comprehensible to the Japanese: "The religious mentality of the Japanese is . . . responsive to one who 'suffers with us' and who 'allows for our weakness,' but their mentality has little tolerance for any kind of transcendent being who judges humans harshly, then punishes them" (Endo, *Life of Jesus* 1). This image of a fellow sufferer resonates with the Japanese psyche, perhaps because it is free of any offensive cultural overtones of western triumphalism.

The narrative ends with the paradoxical affirmation of faith in the two most unlikely characters: an apostate priest hearing the confession of the betrayer, Kichijiro. Rodrigues reflects that even if this improper administration of the sacrament "was betraying [his fellow priests], he was not betraying his Lord. He loved him now in a different way from before. Everything that had taken place until now had been necessary to bring him to this love. 'Even now I am the last priest in this land. But Our Lord was not silent. Even if he had been silent, my life until this day would have spoken of him'" (*Silence* 191). But these expressions of faith involve cultural losses. Kichijiro, the ignoble coward, remains a social pariah without a place in his community. Rodrigues, too, affirms a private faith that comes in the wake of his giving up the only cultural expression of Christianity he has ever known. Gone forever is his place in the institutional Church, his vocation as priest, and even his national identity, now that he has been given a Japanese name and family. Left unanswered is the troubling question of whether the ecclesiastical institutions Rodrigues has forsaken can ever be adapted to Japanese culture or whether they are too intrinsically embedded in western culture to be a viable mediator of Christian faith in Japan.

If *Silence* offers only a tentative reconciliation of Christ and culture, *The Samurai* testifies in a more confident voice to the power of the suffering, rejected Christ not only to transcend cultural differences but to even to affirm elements of both cultures. The context of this novel differs significantly from that in *Silence*. For one thing, the cross-cultural setting is reversed, with a Japanese delegation of trade envoys journeying to the Christianized West. Gessel calls the novel "a remarkably faithful account of a voyage to Mexico and Europe undertaken in 1613 by envoys of the powerful Sendai daimyo Date Masamune" (445). In the novel the Japanese delegation consists of thirty-eight merchants in addition to the four low-ranking samurai who function as the official ambassadors—Hasekura, Nishi, Tanaka, and Matsuki. Guiding the Japanese is a Franciscan missionary, Father Velasco, whose spiritual zeal is exceeded only by his dubious ambition "to be appointed Bishop of Japan so that he may win the hearts of the Japanese people" (Gessel 445).

In spite of their samurai status, the four envoys share the burden of genteel poverty, their destitute family fortunes compelling them to accept the mission. Tanaka tells Hasekura: "I didn't take on this mission because I was ordered to by the Council of Elders. I took it because I wanted to get back our old fief at Nihonmatsu" (*The Samurai* 148). Hasekura, too, has been made vague promises by the Council of Elders about disputed family lands should the mission succeed. The merchants, on the other hand, simply have one objective in mind—to open up lucrative trade opportunities with the west. They thoroughly live down to Inaze Nitobe's contemptuous depiction of an amoral merchant class, particularly in their eagerness to convert to Christianity in order to sell their wares.[3]

The delegation is sent first to *Nueva España*, where it seeks to negotiate with the secular rulers in Mexico City. It is there that Velasco's machinations begin in earnest. Convinced that parading a group of converts from a field notoriously resistant to conversion would bolster his standing in the Church, and persuading the merchants that their economic goals could be thereby advanced, Velasco produces a group conversion in the chapel of the Franciscan monastery. Blithely untroubled by professing Christ in order to serve Mammon, the merchants return to Japan, enriched by the fruits of their conversion. At this point, the envoys split up. Matsuki presciently suspects that this mission masks ulterior purposes, and he chooses pragmatically to seek his political fortunes back in Japan, while the other envoys continue the mission. Rebuffed by the Viceroy in Mexico City, they are persuaded by Velasco to proceed to Spain where he promises an audience with the King. This promise, too, proves hollow. Driven to desperation, they finally succumb to Velasco's persistent entreaties and convert to Christianity, hoping that this action will grant them a sympathetic audience before their last resort, the Council of Bishops in Madrid. Nevertheless, the mission fails, and the group returns to an altered political situation in Japan. The Shogun has expelled the Christians and is ruthlessly crushing political dissent.

The conversions create the central dramatic and ethical tensions in the novel. Except for the young idealist Nishi, none of the group shows genuine interest in Christianity. Tanaka and Hasekura are caught in a complicated cultural dilemma. They have been told that their mission is of utmost importance and are given enormous latitude to accomplish it:

> "In the land of foreigners," Lord Shiraishi added abruptly, "the ways of life will probably be different from those here in Japan. You must not cling to Japanese customs if they stand in the way of your mission. If that which is white in Japan is black in the foreign lands, consider it black. Even if you remain unconvinced in your heart, you must wear a look of acquiescence on your face." (*The Samurai* 49)

This invitation from his lord surely would seem to justify an expedient conversion. Yet, as Nitobe points out, *Bushido* expected more from the samurai than from the merchants. "Lying or equivocation were deemed equally cowardly. The bushi held that his high social position demanded a loftier standard of veracity than that of the tradesman" (Nitobe 62). In addition, one of the cardinal samurai virtues, *giri*, "meant duty, pure and simple," the duty owed "to parents, to superiors, to inferiors, to society at large" (25). Whether that duty in this case meant— as Tanaka believed—the absolute obligation to recover his family lands whatever the cost, or whether that obligation demanded fidelity to the culture and religious institutions of his community remains ambiguous. As Nitobe points out, the obligation of the samurai is not just to the immediate community, but also "a higher sense of responsibility to his ancestors and to Heaven" (38). Hasekura recognizes this responsibility: "To become a Christian was to betray the marshland . . . . So long as the Hasekura house continued, the samurai's deceased father and grandfather would be a part of the marshland. Those dead souls would not permit him to become a Christian" (*The Samurai* 160). For Hasekura, converting to Christianity could hardly be a mere matter of form. As it turns out, Tanaka's and Hasekura's conversions eventually cost them their lives, Tanaka through the samurai recourse to *seppuku* (ritual suicide) and Hasekura through Christian martyrdom. What was entered into as a mere formality becomes, in the eyes of the Shogun's court, a genuine conversion, for which Hasekura must die. But it is not just this political betrayal that creates a "Christian" out of Hasekura, for very much in spite of his will he comes to believe in the Christ whom he has previously despised. Though the betrayal triggers his identification with Christ, Hasekura's journey to Christian faith proceeds not outside of, but very much within, his cultural landscape.

Like *Silence*, this novel explores cultural differences. The Japanese samurai, who have lived in parochial isolation, react both with suspicion and sympathy to the immensity of western civilization. The young samurai, Nishi, responds to his companion's question as to whether he will convert by commenting on how much this trip has expanded his vistas:

> "I don't know. I'll have to give it a lot of thought as we travel to Madrid. But on this journey I've realized how huge the world is. I've learned that the nations of Europe surpass Japan in wealth and grandeur. That's why I'd like to learn their languages. I don't think we can simply close our eyes to the beliefs of all of the people in this vast world." (*The Samurai* 148)

Whereas in *Silence* much of the cross-cultural debate is used by the authorities to argue that Christianity is ill-suited to Japanese society, *The Samurai* turns that cross-cultural dynamic around by associating Japanese homogeneity with parochialism. Nishi represents that enthusiastic idealism which sees cultural difference not as something to fear, but as a beckoning horizon to explore.

At the same time, the novel is hardly an apology for the west, nor even for Christian missions. Setting the novel in the New World allows Endo to critique the Church's sorry complicity in imperial conquest. A renegade priest in Mexico tells the envoys,

> "Atrocious things happened here in Nueva España before the padres came. The foreigners snatched away the lands of these Indians and drove them from their homes. Many were brutally

murdered; the survivors were sold into slavery . . . . The padres who came to this country later on have forgotten the many sufferings of the Indian people . . . . They pretend that nothing ever happened. They feign ignorance, and in seemingly sincere tones preach God's mercy and God's love. That's what disgusted me." (120)

Having seen what he has of this exploitation and distrusting Velasco's opportunism, Matsuki undoubtedly speaks for the group when he pleads with Velasco to leave Japan alone. "The happiness you padres preach is poison to Japan. That has been very clear to me since we arrived in Nueva España. This country would have lived in peace if the Spanish ships had not come. Your version of happiness has disrupted this country" (*The Samurai* 112–13). This echo of Inoue's anti-Christian polemic in *Silence* gains in credibility given that it is corroborated by the history of *Nueva España*.

But the novel is not primarily about the Church's moral culpability. The indictment of Christianity's complicity in imperialism is not used by Endo to dismiss categorically the Church or the West, for both eastern and western political ambitions are sharply undermined in *The Samurai*. Velasco remains unsympathetic for most of the novel, his shameless opportunism tainting his rare moments of self-reflective honesty. Likewise, the Tokugawa regime is equally indicted for its cynical exploitation of the samurai Hasekura, whose only sin has been an unwavering fidelity to his mission. It turns out that Matsuki is right: the mission is a ruse, the envoys unsuspecting decoys in the Shogun's geopolitical ambitions. He explains to his erstwhile mates:

> "Edo [present-day Tokyo] and our domain never had trade with Nueva España as their main object . . . . Edo used our domain to find out how to build and sail the great ships . . . .That's why they didn't choose qualified people as envoys. Instead they appointed low-ranking lance-corporals who could die or rot anywhere along the way and no one would care." (*The Samurai* 236)

Although it is the samurai's lot to follow his lord's will even to death, the Shogunate's cynical exploitation of the envoys shows greater kinship with Machiavelli than with *Bushido*. Nitobe explains that the obligations between lord and retainer are not entirely one-sided. The ruler must not only earn the respect of his subjects, he is also "a father to his subjects, whom Heaven entrusted to his care" (Nitobe 38). He is obliged to demonstrate benevolence, without which the feudal relationship "could easily degenerate into militarism . . . [and] despotism of the worst kind" (37).

Where then does Christ fit into this cynical world of political ambition? For the two main characters, Hasekura and Velasco, it is through the demise of their worldly ambitions—the betrayal of Hasekura's loyalty and the crumbling of Velasco's schemes—that they come to a genuine encounter with Christ. Martyrdom demonstrates in Velasco that final conversion of self-interest to the selfless pursuit of Christ's kingdom. Hasekura's betrayal makes him reconsider his antipathy toward the "wretched, emasculated figure" he has previously despised (*The Samurai* 84). The thought of worshipping this man once filled him with shame. He could "detect nothing sublime or holy in a man as wretched and powerless as this" (*The Samurai* 160). Only when he has been condemned to death as an expedient scapegoat for the political regime does he begin to empathize with the despised and rejected Christ. Even before he is willing to declare himself a believer, he tells his servant, Yozo, of his newfound appreciation for Christ:

> "I suppose that somewhere in the hearts of men, there's a yearning for someone who will be with you throughout your life, someone who will never betray you, never leave you—even it that someone is just a sick, mangy dog. That man became just such a miserable dog for the sake of mankind." (*The Samurai* 245)

Before being led off to his final interrogation before the Council of Elders, Hasekura has another moment with Yozo, who haltingly reminds his master that there is one who "will be beside you . . . . He will attend you" (262). With an emphatic nod of his head, Hasekura concurs as he sets off to meet that One. Gessel concludes that these affirmations of faith demonstrate a further development in Endo's reconciliation of cultural differences. Neither east nor west triumphs, but both are validated:

> Velasco, once he has cast off his unseemly pride, is allowed to

worship and serve his image of a glorified Christ with a rational and aggressive faith. Captured when he returns to Japan
following Hasekura's death, Velasco is burned at the stake; his
martyr's death becomes an unsullied reflection of his dynamic,
Western beliefs. Hasekura, by contrast, accepts the compan-
ionship of Jesus almost passively. His faith is primarily non-
rational and thoroughly internalized . . . . Endo in *Samurai* grants
both men a place in the eternal mansions of heaven. (Gessel
447–48)

If the cultural conflict between Christianity and Japanese culture has
been diminished in this novel, as Gessel suggests, one reason for this
reconciliation may well be that culture figures positively as well as negatively in Hasekura's conversion. Throughout the novel, Endo draws
the reader's attention to comparisons between the samurai relationship
between lord and retainer and the relationship of the Christian disciple
to Christ. Velasco marvels at the "bonds in this relationship that go
beyond mere personal interest," the "almost familial sense of love."
This cultural relationship inspires the veteran missionary that he "must
serve God the way these Japanese retainers serve their lords" (*The Samurai* 134) . It is also this samurai relationship which, when breached by
Hasekura's superiors, draws Hasekura to an identification with One
whose loyalty is beyond question. A deep longing for the kind of com-
panionship and reciprocated loyalty that *Bushido* affirms characterizes
Hasekura's newly-found appreciation for Jesus.[4] Hasekura never makes
a dogmatic profession of faith, his faith in Christ remaining largely non-
rational. What he does articulate about Christ often retains Buddhist
overtones. For instance, we are told that the samurai has discovered
"the desperate karma of man," above which "hung that ugly, emaciated
figure with his arms and legs nailed to a cross, and his head dangling
limply down" (*The Samurai* 245–46). Just before he meets the Council
of Elders, he considers his situation in language with a decidedly Buddhist flavor: "Everything had been decided from the outset; he was simply running along predetermined tracks. Falling into a dark, empty
void" (262). Hasekura's non-dogmatic faith hardly resolves the doctrinal conflicts between Christianity and Japanese culture, but Endo has
always been more interested in dramatizing the human experience of
faith than in doctrinal precision. In this novel he dramatizes the conversion of a simple Japanese warrior who comes to Christ in the only way
that makes sense to him.

In both novels, Endo explores the complicated relations of Christ and culture. Endo acknowledges that Christianity cannot entirely escape its cultural inscription, and in *Silence* he wonders whether Christianity can take root in the mudswamp of Japan without being radically neutered of institutional and cultural norms. In that respect, *Silence* never entirely answers Inoue's multiculturalist critique of the western Church. *The Samurai*, on the other hand, makes some cultural accommodations while also reminding the reader of Christ's transcendent critique of all human cultures—east and west inclusively. Somewhere within that ambivalent middle ground between cultural particularity and trans-cultural universality, Endo presents to us the most unlikely representatives of faith— the betrayer, the apostate, the pragmatically insincere convert, the manipulative power broker—who all discover in the Man of Sorrows their hearts' deepest desire.

Notes

1. For readers unfamiliar with Japanese history, William Johnston's "Translator's Preface" to *Silence* offers a succinct synopsis of the Christian presence in Japan. For a more detailed account of early modern Japan, the reader is referred to volume four of the *Cambridge History of Japan*.
2. Jurgas Elisonas explains that Xavier was ill served by his interpreter, Yajiro, a man whose Christian zeal exceeded his theological grasp. It was Yajiro who told Xavier that "the Japanese religious preached that 'there is only one God, creator of all things'" and that this God was known by the name of "de ny chy" (*Dainichi*). In fact, *Dainichi* refers to the central Buddha of the Shingon sect of Buddhism and is understood to be "the ultimate reality that is identical with the total functioning of the cosmos and also identical with the enlightened mind" (Elisonas 307–08), a conception of the divine considerably different from the Christian belief in the personal Creator of the universe.
3. In his classic exposition of *Bushido*, Nitobe calls a "loose business morality . . . the worst blot on our national reputation," and devotes considerable attention to the ethical and social chasm separating the merchants from the samurai in feudal Japan (64).
4. One should not infer, however, that the entire samurai ethic can easily be appropriated within Christianity. There are still considerable differences between the Christian valuation of the individual self and the non-individualistic conception of the self implicit in *Bushido*. Such tensions between Christianity and *Bushido*, and the possibilities of reconciling them, are lucidly explored by Inaze Nitobe, himself a Japanese Christian.

Works Cited

Endo, Shusaku. *A Life of Jesus*. Trans. Richard A. Schuchert, S.J. New York: Paulist, 1973.

—. *Silence*. Trans. William Johnston. New York: Taplinger, 1969.

—. *The Samurai*. trans. Van C. Gessel. 1980; New York: Kodansha and Harper and Row, 1982.

Gessel, Van C. "Voices in the Wilderness: Japanese Christian Authors." *Monumenta Nipponica* 37.4 (1982): 437–57.

Elison, George. *Deus Destroyed: The Image of Christianity in Early Modern Japan*. Cambridge: Harvard UP, 1973.

Elisonas, Jurgis. "Christianity and the Daimyo." In *The Cambridge History of Japan*. Vol. 4: Early Modern Japan. Ed. John Whitney Hall. Cambridge: Cambridge UP, 1991. 301–72.

Higgins, Jean. "The Inner Agon of Endo Shusaku." *Cross Currents*. 34 (1984–85): 414–26.

Nitobe, Inaze. *Bushido: The Soul of Japan*. New York: Putnam, 1905.

Said, Edward. *Orientalism*. New York: Pantheon, 1978.

13

Rigoberta Menchú
and the Conversion of Consciousness

David J. Leigh

The awkward but fascinating plot of the Guatemalan autobiography *I, Rigoberta Menchú* has puzzled readers since its appearance in English in 1983. Critics have discussed its use of secrecy to preserve the mystery of the native way of life (Sommer), its use of the testimonial genre and oral-to-written format to show its unique relationship to social movements in Central America (Beverley), and its cross-cultural situation in relation to its third-world origins and its first-world readers (Gunn). No one, however, has made sense out of the awkwardly didactic restructuring of descriptions and events by Menchú's Venezuelan translator, Elisabeth Burgos-Debray. A close analysis of the "plotting" of Menchú's story into thirty-four chapters suggests that three principles are at work beneath the structuring of this autobiography. First, the autobiography can be read as Menchú's encounter with three types of otherness—internal others within herself, external others in the dominant culture, and the "other" of death on the faces of suffering villagers, especially her dying brother, father, and mother. Second, these encounters with otherness lead to a conversion of consciousness, both within the autobiographer Menchú herself and within the minds of her readers. These conversions of consciousness are mediated by the subtext of a theology of liberation, which helps Menchú become aware of the divine suffering Other in the faces of her people, and of her own responsibility to work as a catechist and organizer in the altiplano of Guatemala. Finally, this conversion of consciousness (or "conscientization" as it was called by Paolo Freire) becomes the dynamic form that holds together the double plot of the autobiography. A close reading of the narrative events uncovers a first-stage plotting of Menchú's "cultural story" (Chapters 1–12), which is aimed at raising the consciousness of her readers, and a second-stage plotting of Menchú's "personal story" (Chapters 13–34), which reveals her gradual transformation of consciousness from that of passive traditionalist village girl to active resistance organizing woman.

Menchú's primary struggle in this story of her life is with several *internal* others—her parental models, her changing self-image, and her linguistic identity. The encounter with her parents provides an underlying motif of the autobiography, as it does for most twentieth-century autobiographies, but for Menchú this encounter becomes a struggle to integrate within herself, as Gandhi did, two quite different models of living provided by her father and her mother. From her father, an orphan who was "given away" by his mother to be a servant to a *ladino* employer, Menchú learns how to cope with life. As his favorite and most intelligent child, she imitates his early initiative, his steady work habits, his ability to resist injustice, and his political strategies (Ch. 26). Beneath these personal qualities, she constructs her character on the model of his love of native traditions together with his Catholic faith (81). From her mother, Menchú derives her love of nature and tradition, but also the need to challenge the limits of women's roles in the villages and tribes of northern Guatemala. Her mother teaches Menchú to express her feelings and not to avoid painful emotional scenes which her father and other men can not face publicly, especially the burial of the dead. More significantly, her mother teaches her the customs and values of her people—marriage preparation, family living, tribal solidarity, sowing and harvesting, predicting the weather, and the rules of gift-giving. However, her mother's own growth as a woman in social awareness is perhaps an even greater legacy to Rigoberta, for her mother shows her how to resist machismo within a marriage and a tribe. From these double parental models, Menchú internalizes an integrated sense of her identity, including, as both her parents taught her, "to be politicized through her work" (218), for her father was the main political leader in her village and her mother was the first woman in their area to join the struggle for liberation.

From this struggle to integrate these two models within her own self came the search for an adequate directional self-image, a model of self-identity which would sustain her as it has sustained many modern writers of spiritual and political autobiographies from Gandhi to Dorothy Day to Malcolm X to Nelson Mandela. After a childhood in which Menchú sees herself as a timid, fearful, and awkward girl, and then an adolescence in which she is told by the dominant *ladino* overseers that she is a dirty, stupid Indian, and an early adulthood in which she is told by middle-class leaders in the resistance movement that she is only a woman, Menchú, with the inspiration of her parents, eventually creates the self-image that she uses to open her autobiography. She takes on the dynamic identity of a witness for her people to the world:

> My name is Rigoberta Menchú. I am twenty three years old.
> This is my testimony. I didn't learn it from a book and I didn't
> learn it alone. I'd like to stress that it's not only *my* life, it's
> also the testimony of my people . . . My story is the story of all
> poor Guatemalans. My personal experience is the reality of a
> whole people. (1)

This imaging of herself as a witness for a people in a socio-religious
struggle from the 1970s to the 1980s embodies the people's coming to
awareness through Menchú's personal experience in her first twenty
years. Both Rigoberta and her native village in Quiche begin their journey into consciousness as passive childlike victims of an oligarchical
social system with power held by *ladino* landowners, government officials, and the Guatemalan army. As Menchú tells her story in the framework of tribal and personal testimony, she and her people transform
their self-image from that of passive traditionalists to active revolution-
aries. This image, of course, is present from the start in the title, words,
and narrative structure of the autobiography, but present as an image
created (with more than a little help from her editor) from her final
standpoint as a committed Catholic and native liberationist (Berkeley
96).

Finally, Menchú struggles with a linguistic "other" within herself.
Her desire to learn to speak and read Spanish, even against the wishes
of her more traditional father, is a recurring motif of her story, one that
drives her to a more complex level of social awareness. She uses the
new language not to substitute for her native tongue and identity but as
an enriching otherness that contributes to her usefulness in the liberation movement. Yet she discloses only a small amount of her inner
struggle to learn and use Spanish, the language of her people's oppressors but also the language which opens her to communicating her story
to the others of the first-world.

These three struggles by Menchú with internal "others" take place,
in fact, within the surrounding lifelong struggle of herself and her people
with an external other—that of the dominant *ladino* culture. Beyond
this encounter, of course, lies the powerful world cultures of the indus-
trialized east and west, engaged during this time in the cold war. This
encounter with the dominant *ladino* and world cultures presents Menchú
with first a personal crisis and later a literary challenge. The personal
crisis forces her to strive to maintain her identity and preserve her culture in the face of exploitation on the fincas, cultural discrimination in

the city, and both exploitation and oppression in the altiplano villages. As several critics have noted, Menchú cannot avoid negotiating with these cultural others. Thus, as we shall see, she must learn to distinguish among various persons and classes in the *ladino* culture; she must learn to use its language and ways of organizing resistance; and she must learn to use its Spanish language as a means of communication. In learning these things, she creates the very form of her autobiography. Within the autobiographical form, however, she is presented with a difficult problem of communicating her experience and social situation to the culturally "other" modern world. With the help of Burgos-Debray, Menchú mixes a form of idealized "cultural stories" within her realistic personal narrative. This mixture succeeds in raising the consciousness of her readers, but simultaneously undermines some of her credibility.

These encounters with internal personal otherness and external social otherness are assisted in part by Menchú's positive experience with what Emmanuel Levinas calls encounters with the face of the Other. For Levinas, full human ethical, and even religious, enlightenment is brought about by a compassionate meeting with another person in his or her suffering. This suffering personality is revealed most strikingly in direct encounters with the "face" of the other person. Unlike alienating encounters with internal or cultural otherness, this sort of encounter can be a moment of transformation. As we shall see, Menchú explicitly describes in great detail the crucial moments of her encounter with the disfigured faces of her brother (Ch. 24) and her mother (Ch. 27). These encounters, as both personal and representative of the faces of all the suffering others in Guatemala, confirms her final conversion to become a committed Christian resistance worker.

Contemporary conversion theory sheds light on the structure of Menchú's autobiography. If the autobiography is read as a document aimed at transforming the minds of its readers both by its narrative of the ideal cultural story (Ch. 1–12) and by its subsequent narrative of the realistic personal story of Rigoberta Menchú, then the process of conversion is central to this autobiography's method. According to Wayne E. Oates, conversion stories are expressed in three images—unification (of a divided self), turning (in a new direction), and surrender (in love to another, especially to God or some ideal). Menchú's story fuses all three of these images within its basic structural pattern of conversion of consciousness (Oates 149ff). Menchú unifies the family and cultural conflicts with her internal others; she turns from the old passive direction of fatalistic flight away from the dominating enemies, and she surrenders herself in total commitment to the community of her native peoples in whom she finds "the kingdom of God on earth" (Menchú 134). According to an expanded version of Walter Conn's model of conversion, the process of radical self-change has five dimensions. As conversion, these changes call for a leap from one level of human aware-ness to another, a leap that transforms the self and its framework of beliefs (Conn 27). Menchú exhibits the first dimension, affective con-version, when she begins in her early teenage years to move from self-absorption to concern for the feelings of others. She undergoes a sec-ond dimension, imaginative conversion, when she first imagines her-self as a witness for her people to the world, an image that eventually becomes the title of her story. She undergoes a third dimension, intel-lectual conversion, when she moves from simple direct awareness of the horrors of her people's suffering to a reflective awareness of the causes of this suffering. She experiences a fourth aspect of conversion, moral transformation, when she commits herself to work for the com-mon good of her village and the entire native peoples. Finally, she brings in a transcendent dimension, a religious conversion, when she learns through liberation theology to see the suffering of her people as also the suffering on the human face of the ultimate Other.

What makes Menchú unique, in fact, among modern spiritual autobi-ographers is her attempt (mediated by Burgos-Debray) to construct the plot of her life story in accord with the conscientization process of lib-eration theology. This mixture of social and theological movements that began in Latin America in the 1960s was distinguished, as Menchú's autobiography shows, by its ability to use concrete social situations of oppression (in this case, experiences of her people and their persecu-tion by the Guatemalan army and economy) as the context for religious reflection and growth. As summed up by one current theologian, lib-eration theology "is an attempt to interpret Christian doctrine in a way that is responsible to the universal problem of human suffering, which is especially manifest in the social oppression of today's world. . . . By uniting theology, ethics, and spirituality, it provides answers to fun-damental questions of why one chooses to be a Christian in the modern world" (Haight 276). For Menchú, who chooses to be such a Christian, the portrayal of the contrast between the ideal village life of her culture stories and the realistic pain of her personal stories provides an opening for theological reflection. In response to these conflicts, Menchú ap-plies theological and Biblical teachings to illuminate her situation and to motivate her readers. Since a central term and goal for liberation theology is conscientization (the development of awareness by oppressed people that they are unjustly treated but that they have the moral power and duty to transform their situation), it is no surprise to discover that Menchú's primary plot structure derives from liberation theology's pattern of consciousness-raising.

What is troubling, however, is that the patterns of liberation theology both mask and uncover the struggle within Menchú to find a way to integrate her religious conversion experience of the divine suffering Other (in Christ) with the human suffering others she wants to identify with. Liberation theological patterns mask the struggle insofar as Menchú lacks the creative literary power to convey her religious experience in any but conventional language from her catechetical role in the tribal life. However, despite this limitation, the patterns of liberation theology help her to incorporate a theology of consciousness-raising into the basic outline of her own personal story in Chapters 13–34. The very subtitle in Spanish of the autobiography ("the birth of my consciousness") reinforces the liberation theology patterns beneath the plot. What is theologically most significant is that Menchú, brought up in a traditional and radical Catholicism at the same time, came to realize that the divine Other had identified itself in Christ with the least of the brothers and sisters, precisely the human marginalized others whom Menchú identifies with. The plot of the personal story is primarily a narrative of such conscientization—the step by step realization by Menchú of her converted identity as a worker, a daughter, a native, a woman, a resistance worker, and a Christian believer in a liberating divine Other who is revealed in the faces of the suffering people around her. A closer analysis of the plotting of the autobiography will reveal this conversion pattern to be the main form of her story.

As we have indicated earlier, the overall plotting of this autobiography can be divided into two parts, each with a different narrative genre, purpose, and imagined audience. The first twelve chapters provide primarily a series of culture stories about the customs and values of the native Quiche peoples for whom Menchú declares that she speaks in her opening account as a witness in Chapter 1. In these first chapters, at the urging of her transcriber, Menchú describes the initiation ceremonies (Ch. 2), the animal identity (Ch. 3), the work patterns in the fincas (Ch. 4), the family life in the villages (Ch. 8), the agricultural religious ceremonies (Ch. 9–10), the courtship and marriage customs (Ch. 11), and the social and religious life of the villages (Ch. 12). The form of these culture stories is that of an anthropological ideal model, told in a direct descriptive style by a naive narrator, with the intended effect of winning sympathy from the reader for the values and traditions of the people portrayed. Even the occasional admission of the fatalism, excessive labor, machismo, and alcoholism among the people seems only to contrast with the idealized pictures of this anthropological model (48, 50).

When Menchú begins her personal story, it serves as a violent contrast to the idyllic world of the culture story in which she is raised. For her personal story—as an embodiment of liberation theology—is one of gradual coming to an awareness of the injustices done to her culture by the *ladinos* and a coming to a commitment to take on responsibility for resistance to these injustices. This conscientization process that makes up her personal narrative takes Menchú through her conversion process in five stages:

> • Conversion (affective) to direct awareness of problems within her childhood (Ch. 5–7)
> • Conversion (naive moral) to direct awareness of the unjust social situation and of her responsibility to change it (Ch. 8–9, 12–13)
> • Conversion (intellectual) to reflective awareness of the causes of these injustices (Ch. 14–16)
> • Conversion (complex moral) to reflective awareness of and commitment to social, gender, and theological distinctions (Ch. 17–23)
> • Conversion (imaginative and religious) to full commitment to personal and social transformation by seeing the human and divine Other in the faces of the suffering (Ch. 24–32)

Menchú's first account of the childhood seeds of her consciousness-raising occurs when at age seven she gets lost in the mountains. As she says, " . . . *t*hey lost me for seven hours. I was crying, shouting, but no one heard me. That was the first time I felt what it must be like to be an adult, I felt I had to be responsible, more like my brothers and sisters" (29). As she later acknowledges, her predicament of "being lost" was a symptom of the social "lostness" of her family in their poverty. Even when she is found again, she speaks primarily "of the anger I felt at the way we live" (29). This minor episode of an emotional change prepares the reader for the many small steps into consciousness that Menchú takes during the years leading up to the death of her parents. She also recalls that at age five, "my consciousness was born" from the affective experience of watching her mother work herself to exhaustion on the fincas (34). At age eight, Menchú reacts to her family's being fired for attending the funeral of their child by crying out, "From that moment, I was both angry with life and afraid of it . . . I remember it with enormous hatred. That hatred has stayed with me until today" (41). These instances from Chapters 5 to 7 show the early affective conversion to an emotional awareness of the problems in her life.

When Menchú reaches her tenth birthday, she is formally initiated into the customs and responsibilities of young adults in her village. It is at this point that she begins a moral conversion to a direct awareness of the injustice in her family's situation and of her responsibility to respond to it. As her father tells her, "From now on you must contribute to the common good" (49). When she becomes twelve, she beings to think, as she puts it, "like a responsible woman . . . I joined the communal work; things like harvesting the maize . . . I began taking over my mother's role too" (79). At this point, she also leaves behind her naive childhood faith to take on the task of spreading Catholic teaching as a catechist. As she sums up her inculturated Christianity, "By accepting the Catholic religion, we didn't accept a condition, or abandon our culture. It was more like another way of expressing ourselves . . . . We feel very Catholic because we believe in the Catholic religion but, at the same time, we feel very Indian, proud of our ancestors" (80–81). After she narrates at length her new religious duties, Menchú gives an account of her first direct consciousness of the evils in the plantation system. The catalyst for this moral conversion is the death from poisoning of her best friend, to which she responds, "I was afraid of life . . . . I was mad with grief" (88–89). It is at this point that she first confesses that she wants to learn Spanish, a skill that would help her learn more theology from the circuit-riding priests to help her as a catechist, and would give her greater skills to deal with the *ladinos*.

Menchú soon learns more than she anticipated. As she describes her work at age twelve as a housemaid in Guatemala City, she shows that she is awakening to the causes of her people's problems in the racial prejudices and exploitation of Indian peoples by the *ladinos*. In this vivid account of her humiliations and degradations as a maid for a rich family, her reflective conscientization expresses itself in pure narrative (Ch. 14). Then, in the following Chapter, Menchú recounts the event that is the final stage in awakening her and her village to the systemic injustices of the land reform and the need for united resistance—the mistreatment and imprisonment of her father. She recalls the earlier conflicts with the landowners which led to her father's twenty-two years of resistance. In particular, she gives a detailed description of the event in 1967 when the government threw her village out of their homes in their newly claimed and cultivated land in the altiplano. As she says, "Those few days confirmed my hatred for those people. I saw why we said that *ladinos* were thieves, criminals, and liars" (106). Admitting that at that date "we didn't have the political clarity to unite with others and protest about our land," Menchú describes her father's awakening to consciousness of the systemic nature of the injustices and the need to form a union, an action that leads to his imprisonment for fourteen months (111). After a second imprisonment in 1977, he is forced to work underground, and Rigoberta herself begins traveling with him. From these events, Menchú tells of the community conscientization: "We began thinking, with the help of other friends, other *campeneros*, that our enemies were not only the landowners who lived near us . . . We started thinking about the roots of the problem and came to the conclusion that everything stemmed from the ownership of the land. The land was not in our hands" (116). At this point, too, the village learns not only the systemic causes of their problems but also learns how to form an organization to resist the government, the Peasant Unity Committee (CUC). As Rigoberta travels around to other villages, she also is shocked to learn of the degraded status of Indians in the minds of even the poorest *ladinos*, who tell her, "Yes, we're poor but we're not Indians" (119). At this point, she admits that she is only partially transformed: "I still hadn't reached the rewarding stage of participating fully, as an Indian first, then as a woman, a peasant, a Christian, in the struggle of all my people" (120). She still has two more aspects of full conversion to undergo—reflective awareness of several crucial distinctions, and then full commitment based on religious and human response to others.

The complex moral distinctions do not come easily to this young unsophisticated village girl. She spends two chapters telling the story of the "painful change in herself and her village" as they decide, after studying their situation and the Bible, that they are justified in using force in self-defence (Ch. 17–18). Beneath her summary of the methods of reasoning within her "base community" (as liberation theology calls it) lay her faith in Christ as resurrected and present Liberator: "For me, as a Christian, there is on important thing. That is the life of Christ . . . there was no other way of defending himself or Christ would have used it against his oppressors, against his enemies. He even gave his life. But Christ did not die, because generations and generations have followed him" (132–33). While this testimony seems to overlook the power of nonviolent resistance which many find in Christ's sermon on the mount, the testimony provides Menchú with some justification for the use of force in defending the villages of the altiplano. She is forced, however, to place most of her rational arguments on examples of Judith, Moses, and David in the Hebrew scriptures. Her motivation in working out these distinctions is largely religious, for, as she says, "as Christians, we must create a Church of the poor . . . we feel it is the duty of Christians to create the kingdom of God on earth among our brothers" (133–34). But her consciousness raising does not stop at her new ability to make theological distinctions. She also becomes radicalized as a woman, especially after learning of the brutal butchering of her friend Patrona Chona at the hands of a lustful son of a landowner (Ch. 20). She becomes more sophisticated economically when she learns by following her father's example of the need to organize the villages (Ch. 21) and the need to protest against the individualistic plans of the government for isolated family plots (Ch. 22). These new distinctions lead her in 1979 to join the CUC and to learn several native languages in addition to Spanish so that she can become an effective community organizer. The travel in her organizing work also teaches her to make distinctions among the "enemy" *ladinos*: one friend "taught me to think more clearly about some of my ideas which were wrong, like saying all *ladinos* are bad" (165). As she concludes, "So I learned many things with the *ladinos*, but most of all to understand our problem and the fact that we had to solve it ourselves" (167). All of these distinctions are part of her complex moral conversion which also includes, as the praxis-based theology of liberation requires, a commitment to action and to learn from action.

Menchú saves the most dramatic stage of her conscientization process for Chapters 24–34. In these chapters, she gives a realistic account of the violent effects of class and cultural warfare by the government against her family, her people, and especially against native women. She describes in brutal detail the torture and death of her brother, and then the fiery death of her father during the occupation of the Spanish Embassy in Guatemala City in 1980. In describing the torture of her brother, she emphasizes the disfigurement of his face: "They took my brother away, bleeding from different places. When they'd done with him, he didn't look like a person any more. His whole face was disfigured with beating, from striking against the stones, the tree-trunks; my brother was completely destroyed . . . . And his face, he couldn't see any more, they'd even forced stones into his eyes, my brother's eyes" (173–74). This evidence of the suffering on the face of her brother is repeated in her description of her mother's rape and torture: "On the third day of torture, they cut off her ears. They cut her whole body bit by bit . . . . From the pain, from the torture all over her body, disfigured and starving, my mother began to lose consciousness . . . Then they started raping her again. She was disfigured by those same officers" (198–99). When Rigoberta and her family are brought in to view her last agony, they notice that "her face was so disfigured, cut and infected." After her mother dies, Menchú notes with horror that "the soldiers stood over her and urinated in her mouth" (199) This emphasis on the suffering on the faces of her brother and mother, in the light of Levinas' notion of the ethical imperative derived from confrontation with the face of the other, especially the suffering other, suggests that here Menchú has reached the fullness of her moral, imaginative, and religious conversion. For, according to the theology of liberation, she has learned to see the divine Other embodied in the suffering others in her family, especially in their faces as they are dying in disfigurement. This vision of the divine Other in the suffering human other leads Menchú not to withdraw in fear but to commit herself with confidence to reach out to these others in solidarity.

This final conversion to commitment in solidarity includes four important dimensions. First, she learns from the funeral of her father to break through all boundaries of class and race: "People at all levels— poor, middle class, professional—all risked their lives by going to the funeral of the *companeros* from the Spanish embassy" (186). Second, she learns from the treatment and life of her mother to carry on her struggle for a radical change in the position of women in Guatemala, not only in cultural matters such as the fiestas but even more importantly within the resistance movement itself, where she uses her personal authority to teach the macho leaders some respect for women (Ch. 30–31). She also believes that the needs of the people take precedence over her personal happiness, thus leading her to postpone any thought of marriage until after the revolution (225). Thirdly, she learns the need for solidarity among all the various groups working for revolution. As she says in her account of the results of the 1980 agricultural strike: "We came to the conclusion that we had to form a united front" (231). This solidarity is expressed in the 31st of January Popular Front which encompassed six organizations in 1981, including the one to which she belongs, the Vincente Menchú Revolutionary Christians, named after her father. Finally, Menchú learns to live out her religious commitment with sophistication and hope in the face of exile. While recognizing the differences within "the Church of the rich" and "the Church of the poor" (234), she is convinced of her vocation as a leader "practicing with the people the light of the Gospel" (246). As she says on the concluding page of her testimony in words that indicate the deeply religious dimen-

sion of her conscientization, "I know that no one can take my Christian
faith away from me . . . together we can build the people's Church, a
true Church . . . I chose this as my contribution to the people's cause . .
. . That is my cause" (246).

Works Cited

Beverley, John. "The Margin at the Center: On *Testimonio* (Testimonial Narra-
tive)," in *De/colonizing the Subject: The Politics of Gender in Women's
Autobiography.* Ed. Sidonia Smith and Julia Watson. Minneapolis: U.
Minnesota P, 1992. 91–114.

Conn, Walter. *Christian Conversion.* New York: Paulist, 1986.

—, ed. *Conversion: Perspectives on Personal and Social Transformation.* New
York: Alba House, 1978.

Gunn, Janet Varner. "A Window of Opportunity: An Ethics of Reading Third
World Autobiography." *College Literature* 19 (1992): 162–70.

Haight, Roger. *An Alternative Vision: An Interpretation of Liberation Theology.*
Ramsey, NJ: Paulist, 1985.

—. "Liberation Theology," in *The New Dictionary of Theology*, ed. Joseph
Komanchak, Mary Collins, and Dermot A. Lane. Wilmington, DE: Gla-
zier, 1987. 570–76.

Levinas, Emmanuel. *A Levinas Reader.* Oxford: Blackwell, 1989.

Menchú, Rigoberta. *I, Rigoberta Menchú: An Indian Woman in Guatemala*, ed.
and intro. by Elisabeth Burgos-Debray, tr. by Ann Wright. London: Verso:
1984.

Oates, Wayne E. "Conversion: Sacred and Secular," in *Conversion*, 149–68.

Sommer, Doris. "No Secrets: Rigoberta's Guarded Truth." *Women's Studies* 20
(1991): 51–72.

Stoll, David. "*I, Rigoberta Menchú* and Human Rights Reporting in Guatemala," a
presentation at the Western Humanities Institute Conference on 'Political Correctness' and Cultural Studies, at the University of California-
Berkeley, 20 Oct. 1990.

Index

194